# *Sense and Sensibility in Modern Poetry*

BY

WILLIAM VAN O'CONNOR

UNIVERSITY PAPERBACKS

BARNES & NOBLE · NEW YORK

*Publishers · Booksellers · Since 1873*

L. C. Catalogue Card Number: 63-15068
Reprinted by Barnes & Noble, Inc.,
by Special Arrangement with The University of Chicago Press
*Second printing, 1964*

*For*

MARJORIE HOPE NICOLSON

Printed in the United States of America

# *Preface*

SOME of the material in this book has appeared in articles.[1] Each of the articles has been reconsidered and reabsorbed into the general problem considered in this study. The problem was formulated in a manner and to an extent somewhat comparable to its final form when I became aware that those who concerned themselves with certain problems—with the attitudes of various generations toward faith in the literal truth of religious or political beliefs as opposed to myth, judgment as opposed to fancy, abstract, denotative expression as opposed to imagistic or symbolical expression, "scientific" or objective expression as opposed to subjective expression, etc.—were concerned with ramifications and consequences of the same phenomenon T. S. Eliot had touched on lightly in his now famous account of the "dissociation of sensibility." In analyzing the diction and idioms of poetry subsequent to the Jacobeans, Eliot noted many attempts to split language into an emotional component and into an intellectual component, to express objective, *genuine* thought in an abstract, nonmetaphorical language and to allow subjective, *poetic* thought only a subsidiary, supplementary function. The language of abstraction, in other words, tended to be a vehicle for thought in poetry, whereas the language of metaphor, when not merely serving a supplementary function, tended to be vague and misty. Consequently, Eliot said, poets often have been ruminative, on the one hand, or sentimental, on the other. The attempt to keep intellect and emotion at opposite poles

1. In *Poetry: A Magazine of Verse*, *Meanjin Papers* (Australia), *A Comment* (Australia), the *Sewanee Review*, the *Kenyon Review*, the *American Scholar*, the *University of Kansas City Review*, *College English*, the *Quarterly Review of Literature*, the *Journal of Aesthetics and Art Criticism*, and the *New Mexico Quarterly*.

has had the effect of causing poets to think and feel by starts and has caused them to lose the art of expressing strong emotion and keen insight at the same time.

Eliot, as subsequent observation has indicated, was seeing the matter in too limited a focus. He laid the blame for the changes in poetic idioms on Dryden and Milton, as though the language later poets used had been formed not by the society as a whole but by its great poets. Critics after Eliot, and indebted to him, have been able to see that the changes in language were a part of the consequences of the adaptation of a culture to the scientific viewpoint.

This attempt at adaptation tended, as Lewis Mumford says, to throw the weight of emphasis in intellectual matters outside man himself, into the objective world. Post-Renaissance man, therefore, he continues, has overemphasized the objective, the quantitative, and the measurable in opposition to the subjective, the qualitative, and the nonmeasurable. This cultural history and influence, he concludes, is behind modern man's emphasis on practical knowledge, his willingness to exchange faiths and constructed systems for hard, cold (and isolated) facts, and his preference for stark realism as well as his frank dislike for poetry.

That many artists have felt themselves isolated because of these popularly held views is readily understandable. And that artists individually and as members of movements have in reaction explored the depths of a highly subjective and personalized realm is equally understandable. The modern poet consequently has felt himself impelled to devise not only standards of value to whatever extent this is possible but interrelated bodies of symbols (myths) which will enable the reader not only to understand but to *experience* his attitudes and perceptions. Understandable, too, is the phenomenon of the twentieth century having given rise to at least two generations of poet-critics; the poet cannot function freely as a poet until he sees with some clarity his role in a society that has lost its supernatural sanctions for values and has tended to exclude the artist. In the first chapter of this study, "The Dissociation of Sensibility," I have tried to indicate the breadth of this critical problem and the work of contemporary critics who are aware of it. And in subsequent chapters I have attempted to treat its implications as they can be observed in the body of modern poetry.

Among the many who have assisted me through suggestions and general criticism, I am especially indebted to Professors R. L. Ramsay, Robert B. Heilman, Edwin S. Miller, Robert Penn Warren, Alan W. Brown, and William York Tindall. I am greatly indebted to Professors Marjorie Nicolson and Lionel Trilling, as well as to my wife, Mary Allen O'Connor.

I am also deeply grateful to the Rockefeller Foundation, whose grant assisted me in undertaking this study.

To the following publishers and poets I am indebted for permission to quote:

Brandt and Brandt: Edna St. Vincent Millay, "God's World" (copyright, 1913, by Edna St. Vincent Millay), *The Harp-Weaver* (copyright, 1922, by Edna St. Vincent Millay), and *A Few Figs from Thistles* (copyright, 1930, by Edna St. Vincent Millay).

Chatto and Windus: Roger Fry, translator, *Poems by Mallarmé*.

Dial Press: Randall Jarrell, "The Death of the Ball Turret Gunner."

Doubleday, Doran and Company: Paul Engle, *American Song* (copyright, 1933, 1934, by Doubleday and Co., Inc.).

Harcourt, Brace and Company: Robert Lowell, *Lord Weary's Castle;* Robert Penn Warren, *Selected Poems, 1923–1943;* T. S. Eliot, *The Family Reunion* and *Collected Poems, 1909–1935*.

Henry Holt and Company: Robert Frost, from "Two Tramps in Mud Time," *Collected Poems* (copyright, 1930, 1939, by Henry Holt and Company; copyright, 1936, by Robert Frost); Walter de la Mare, "Peeping Tom," *Collected Poems* (copyright, 1941, by Walter de la Mare); A. E. Housman, "Poem 27," *A Shropshire Lad* (copyright by Henry Holt and Company).

Houghton Mifflin: Archibald MacLeish, *Conquistador*.

International Publishers: Michael Gold and Max Bodenheim, *Proletarian Literature in the United States*.

Alfred A. Knopf, Inc.: Wallace Stevens, "Sunday Morning," "Theory,"

"Peter Quince at the Clavier," *Harmonium* (copyright, 1923, 1931, by Alfred A. Knopf, Inc.), and "Anything Is Beautiful if You Say It Is," *Parts of a World* (copyright, 1942, by Wallace Stevens); Elinor Wylie, "Let No Charitable Hope," *Collected Poems* (copyright, 1932, Alfred A. Knopf, Inc.); John Crowe Ransom, "Winter Remembered," "Janet Waking," "Her Eyes," "Parting without a Sequel," *Selected Poems* (copyright by Alfred A. Knopf, Inc., 1924, 1927, 1934, 1939, 1945).

Liveright Publishing Corporation: Hart Crane, *The Collected Poems of Hart Crane;* H. D., *The Collected Poems of H. D.*

The Macmillan Company: Marianne Moore, *What Are Years* and *Selected Poems;* Edgar Lee Masters, *Spoon River Anthology;* Sara Teasdale, *Rivers to the Sea;* W. B. Yeats, *Collected Poems.*

New Directions: W. C. Williams, "Queen Ann's Lace" and "The Descent of Winter"; Dylan Thomas, "Twenty-four Years."

*New Masses:* Alfred Hayes, "The Craneman."

Frank O'Connor: "Autumn."

Kenneth Patchen: for lines from several of his poems.

*Poetry:* Lloyd Frankenberg, "The Years of Enormous Addresses"; Ian Gordon, "For Us No More in Epic Encounter."

Random House: Stephen Spender, "The Funeral"; Louis MacNeice, "An Eclogue for Christmas"; W. H. Auden, "In Memory of W. B. Yeats" and "At the Grave of Henry James."

Reynal and Hitchcock: Karl Shapiro, from *Essay on Rime;* Josephine Miles, from *Local Measures.*

Charles Scribner's Sons: Allen Tate, *Selected Poems;* Conrad Aiken, *Prelude for Memnon;* Oscar Williams, *Selected Poems.*

Sidgwick and Jackson: W. J. Turner, "In Time like Glass."

Viking Press: Dorothy Parker, "Ballade of Great Weariness," "The Little Old Lady in Lavender Silk," and "Fair Weather," *The Portable Dorothy Parker.*

Oscar Williams: Robert Lowell, "The Capitalist Meditation," and Mark Van Doren, "Down World," *New Poems, 1943;* Oscar Williams, "On Meeting a Stranger in a Bookshop."

Yale University Press: Muriel Rukeyser, *Theory of Flight.*

UNIVERSITY OF MINNESOTA

W. V. O'C.

# *Preface to the Paperback Edition*

*Sense and Sensibility in Modern Poetry* was published shortly after World War II, when the modern critical movement was beginning to transform the study of English in colleges and universities. Therefore it probably carries some of the fervor that discussions of literature at that time usually generated. In the past few years we have been watching the end of modernism in various ways, and I have tried to outline and analyze this in a recent book *The New University Wits, and the end of modernism.* It is interesting to me to think of the two books in relation to each other. Clearly T. S. Eliot was right when he wrote about the literature *entre les deux guerres.* Modernism did produce a great literature; as it recedes in time it does not diminish in magnificence.

University of California, Davis

William Van O'Connor

# *Table of Contents*

CHAPTER ONE

# *Introduction: The Dissociation of Sensibility*

*It is science, ultimately, that makes our age different, for good or evil, from ages that have gone before.*—BERTRAND RUSSELL

A PART of the corpus of modern criticism is the attempt to explain the effects of scientism on post-Renaissance poetry. It is an investigation of certain theories and attitudes which as by-products of the scientific movement affected not only the actual writing of poetry but the respect in which poetry has been held. It is not an indiscriminate attack on science.[1]

The separation of rational thought, in so far as this is possible, from the mythic and the emotional was necessary apparently for the functioning of the scientific mind and the employment of the scientific method. Subsequently, it has become apparent that suspicion of the emotions and the restriction of their functioning have had dire effects. It has become apparent that the subjective world of desire, imagination, and myth is, in the complex economy of human nature, the world from which arise ideals, morality, and esthetic expression. To establish a dichotomy of the emotional and the intellectual, and to suspect the "subjective," fosters distortions of many kinds.

The source of the distortions has been variously attributed. One critic tends to find it in Johannes Kepler's invidious comparison of objective and subjective qualities, in the suggestion that truth is solely objective and verifiable.[2] Another tends to see the trouble arising from Descartes's division or disjunction of "mind" and "matter."[3] For poetry this meant the assumption of the existence and life of "ideas" separate and distinct from matter and therefore from symbol and metaphor. Yet another will find the source in Francis Bacon[4] or Thomas Hobbes,[5] each of whom encouraged "the monopoly of the scientific spirit over the mind." All were a part of an intellectual climate that was beginning to favor the intellect at the expense of the emotions.

This emphasis upon the intellectual constantly held to at the expense of a great many basic emotional needs has become pervasive in the entire thought and activities of the post-Renaissance world. The by-products, as it were, of the emphasis may be seen in contexts ostensibly social, moral, linguistic, or esthetic. In an examination of modern poetry we find certain preconceptions which seem to be the result of attempts to evaluate all experience in terms of attitudes and beliefs popularly held to be scientific. Among them is the assurance that *reality* has to do with physical, objective, measurable facts and that such ideals as love or mercy or the values in various moral systems, being the product of human imagination, are somehow unreal.

All post-Renaissance poetry as interpreted by certain contemporary critics, then, appears to have been influenced by the scientific emphasis. Neoclassicism de-emphasized the irrational and the mysterious and, in so doing, expressed a faith in the power of rationality. The Romantic Movement was the reaction. Nineteenth-century naturalism was a later "scientific" expression in that it encouraged literal realism and detailed description of objective situations. Symbolism was the reaction.[6]

The belief that fancy or imagination was the "irrational" faculty and judgment the rational faculty restricted the writing of poetry in various ways.[7] Following the Romantic Movement, however, emotional and highly subjective expressions were encouraged, as though in reaction from the former restrictions. Unfortunately, the belief that intellect is somehow opposed to emotion and to art persisted.[8] By and large, nineteenth-century poets accepted Hobbes's division between judgment and fancy. Consequently, the nineteenth century witnessed bodies of poetry from which a precise intellectuality was carefully excluded. There was a tendency toward sentimentality. There was an effort to call up emotions through the use of standardized symbols. And, beginning in France, there was an attempt to separate the "aura of feeling" around words from the "rational content" at their center.[9] Chief among T. S. Eliot's contributions to English poetic theory and practice, perhaps, has been his concern that intellect be restored to poetry.

Certain other seventeenth-century attempts to make knowledge "objective" affected the writing of poetry. There was a classification of experience into the dignified and the mean, the "poetic" and the "nonpoetic," the serious and the frivolous. Knowledge was to be held in stable categories. The division of intellect and emotion into separate categories led to an emphasis upon abstract, denotative, logical language.[10] Consequently, there was an avoidance of metaphor and ambiguity. The emotion which had to be generated, if there was to be poetry at all, frequently was aroused by wit, irony, and overstatement as well as by the employment of metrical forms. The point is that the poets were obliged to effect a compromise with categories of objective knowledge.

Behind this question of language was the question of the nature of the imagination and the freedom of the poet to express what his imagination created. Ultimately, the problem resolves itself into whether or not certain products of the imagination are to be accepted as genuine knowledge to the same extent, say, that the principles of science or the products of logical thought are.[11] The distrust of the imagination we inherit arises from our assurance that only what is measurable is really true.

Eliot has striven in his poetry to reunite thought and feeling—to transform an "observation into a state of mind," to achieve "a direct sensuous apprehension of thought into feeling."[12] There have been various poets, however, who preferred not to follow Eliot's lead. Some of these have been members of schools attempting various types of pure poetry.[13] It may be observed that most of these types favor the emotional at the expense of intellect. Conrad Aiken, for example, has attempted to employ "only the most delicately evocative aspects" of "emotions or things or sensations." He has aspired to write a poetry of hint, overtone, and suggestion. Both the Imagists and the Objectivists have striven to ignore or to be indifferent to idea. The emphasis has been upon the image or object in isolation. There seems to be implied the suspicion that the only genuine knowledge is the knowledge we have of objective fact. In so far as they suggest a distrust of the transforming power of the imagination and a fear of large systems of belief, they are obviously of our time.[14]

The tendency of modern poets, on the other hand, to write a highly imaginative, personalized poetry is in reaction against veristic forms of poetry, those in which a denotative, nonmetaphorical language was encouraged, as well as the acceptance of stable rules and attitudes.[15]

Further, many esthetic principles behind modern poetry can be related to the dichotomy of thought and sensibility. Poets have been concerned with a language of indirection—with concretion, wit, irony, tension—in which feeling and tone may be understood and experienced as something more than supplementary to abstract meaning. The emphases upon appropriate rhythms, metaphor, ambiguity, and dramatic statement are all means of making the emotional integral in the poetic statement. It is as though the modern poets were proving that ideas are not merely abstractions, meanings packaged and then handed back and forth, but that they may be made deeply meaningful only when they are expressed in a language that simultaneously involves the sensibilities and the intellect.

The dissociation of thought from sensibility is a theme running throughout Eliot's criticism. The significance of it dawned upon Eliot apparently when he was studying the differences between Elizabethan and later poetry. "In Chapman especially," he says in "The Metaphysical Poets," "there is a direct sensuous apprehension of thought into feeling which is exactly what we find in Donne." And in the same essay the perception and feeling of unified thought and sensibility he calls experiencing thought "as immediately as the odour of a rose."

Something, he asserts, "happened to the mind of England between the time of Donne or Lord Herbert of Cherbury and the time of Tennyson and Browning." Thereafter, however, he discusses the matter only in terms of literary influence: "In the seventeenth century a dissociation of sensibility set in, from which we have never recovered; and this dissociation, as is natural, was due to the influence of the two most powerful poets of the century, Milton and Dryden." This explanation might have seemed to be satisfactory in the case of Milton had his language of magnificence and grandeur been a strong and continuing influence. But Milton's language was not successfully imitated. The most basic influence did not originate with Dryden; it affected him. Under the influence of the scientific temper he attempted to separate the intellectual from the emotional, the abstract language of judgment from the fanciful language of images, and the serious from the mean. The attempted separation of thought from feeling meant alternative poetries of thought and feeling. "The sentimental age began early in the eighteenth century and continued. The poets revolted against the ratiocinative, the descriptive; they thought and felt by fits, unbalanced; they reflected." Eliot might have pointed out that the poets subsequent to the Jacobeans lived in an intellectual milieu—they did not cause it—in which thought and feeling were believed, popularly at least, to be opposed

That sensibility is integrally related to intelligence has significant implications. Setting thought and feeling in opposition to each other has led, writes Martin Lebowitz, to the virtual "separation of the cognitive from the moral and aesthetic," and the separation of the "practical or productive activities not merely from their fruits but from enjoyment and human (which is ideal) significance."

The cause of the isolation of modern poets as well as aspects of their poetry explicable in terms of this phenomenon can also be traced to the dissociation of sensibility.[16] The emphasis upon the practical and productive and the suspicion of all things not immediately useful, results of the dissociation, isolated the artist.

Modern poetry, then, can to some extent at least be explained and characterized as a part of the history of the post-Renaissance mind. Whitehead reminds us that the modern mind really begins with the scientific movements of the seventeenth century. The problem of myth and belief in poetry, which is of central importance, can be understood adequately only in terms of our inherited notions about what is *real* or *true* and in terms of our attitude toward the functions and products of the imagination. Again, the language of modern poetry is to some degree the result of a conscious effort to break free from certain restrictions imposed in the name of science. Lastly, the aspects of modern poetry related to the isolation of the poet are, if we may repeat, referable to the attempted split of thought from sensibility. It should be understandable, therefore, that a number of contemporary critics have been concerned to decry the effects, upon the modern mind, of what they call "scientism," and that many aspects of modern poetry can be examined in terms of this phenomenon.

CHAPTER TWO

# *The Employment of Myths*

*A fact truly and absolutely stated acquires a mythological or universal significance.*—HENRY DAVID THOREAU

THE isolated fact that cannot be related to a large or universal significance is merely observed, not perceived; or, we might say, when it is seen in relation to a narrowly conceived myth, it has no transcendental reference or applicability. It is not accidental, then, that our age has been preoccupied with the collecting and sorting of historical facts; with, in fiction, describing in realistic detail; and with, in poetry, discovering or borrowing a controlling pattern of belief. The phenomenon of specialized meanings—ideologies, narrow religious persuasions, economics, sociology, and art—precludes universal references.

Certain characteristics of modern poetry may be explained in terms of—or at least be seen as relevant to—the confusion of values and the multiple forms of belief which have developed in the post-Renaissance world. The various forms of naturalism, which are derived from the assumption that one is always nearer to the truth in remaining close to the demonstrable and measurable, are chief among the tenets held by our world. Since we are now hard put to find sanctions for forms of idealism, individual poets must rely upon whatever perspectives they can work out for themselves. It follows, again, that poets are frequently concerned with values, with analytical examination of intellectual themes—with examining the context of the culture in which they live. Only extremely able poets can present such concerns in a language that evokes strong feelings at the same time that it objectifies insights. And since we do not have any central myth, most poets feel obliged to restrict themselves to short lyrics, to themes that can be treated, as it were, tangentially.

There is a fairly large body of poetry in which the consequences of our living in a thoroughly secularized and would-be mythless society are examined. Lloyd Frankenberg in "The Years of Enormous Addresses," for example, refers, somewhat obliquely, to a world in which personal relationships are subject to suprapersonal forces. The instruments of mechanization, made to serve large designs, are often at odds with individual human purposes.

> In the years of enormous addresses
> everyone's in care of the postmaster
> farther and farther apart
> in the smallest of possible worlds.
>
> Lovers' meetings end in journeys;
> any fool knows that.
> We travel a thousand miles an hour
> away from each other.
>
> Letters are all that link us.
> Our lives are franked and cancelled
> and love is a postscript
> blue pencilled.

The "pressure of reality," or of *facts*, in opposition to the pressure of idealism is even more apparent in our incapacity for heroic action. In our world the individual is peculiarly alone. The physical world is apart from man—since he feels nothing human in nature, he has no sense of "continuity with the environing world." And in the absence of myth he is alienated from his fellows. In vital circumstances, such as this presented in Ian Gordon's "For Us No More in Epic Encounter," the lack of radical significance in our acts is expressed.

For us no more in epic encounter
The physical joy of the Iliad
The faith of the Paradiso
(Steel structure of Thomas Aquinas)
Now no more Aegean or Mediterranean
Blind Maeonides and the exiled Florentine
Moving assured in worlds they could understand:
Rather for us the Virgilian indecision
The *lacrimae rerum* and the question unanswered.

Our bleak promontory the mists encircle;
We who are heroes
Not by choice but mere chronology
Lug the machine gun to the dismal beach
And await the onset of a heroic age.

Obsequiousness in the face of facts means passivity, loss of imagination, and, ultimately, the loss of those qualities of mind and spirit that allow of our moving from symbol to vision. Having destroyed one vision, that of Christianity in its period of major expression, the modern mind shies from all visions. Demonstrably, as Dreiser and O'Neill in the novel and play and Kenneth Fearing and Alfred Hayes in poetry have shown, man viewed from close up frequently is a pitiful creature. That he is acted upon, frustrated, and weak are undeniable facts. But he has another side. His imagination and determination elevate him, spiritualize him. The former facts seem more readily demonstrable, but their demonstrability in no way makes them the more significant facts. To focus on stupidity, frustration, and weakness alone is, as Yeats says, to withdraw "into the quicksilver at the back of the mirror. No great event becomes luminous . . . it is no longer possible to write *The Persians, Agincourt, Chevy Chase:* some blunderer has driven his car to the wrong side of the road." The naturalists put their faith in "objectivity."

Recognition of the discrepancy between our ordinary acceptances, like that of the love myth, and the objectively verifiable, has caused poems like *The Waste Land* and commentaries like Joseph

Wood Krutch's *The Modern Temper*. In his "Love—or the Life and Death of a Value" Krutch observed that his contemporaries who paused to question the values they had inherited from the Victorian world recognized that love is "not a fact in nature . . . but rather a creation of the human imagination." It did not occur to him that the basic orientation of a scientific-minded world, its presuppositions, had caused such functioning of the imagination to be considered valueless. The fact that love, in its varied qualities, is experienced is not, according to this orientation, enough to make it real or give it validity. Love when analyzed according to reductive principles is seen as an "illusion." Krutch was not merely indulging himself in an armchair pessimistic philosophy. The same temper of mind, born of the same presuppositions, can be seen to have influenced, though not always negatively, such figures as D. H. Lawrence, Joyce, and Eliot. In "The Fire Sermon" Eliot contrasts the love myth as it was stated by Spenser in the *Prothalamion* with such ignoble and sordid sexual relations as those of the "young man carbuncular."

In a recent poem Wallace Stevens asks, "What should we be without the sexual myth?" In *Brave New World* Huxley affords an answer by establishing polar opposites between the love myth of *Romeo and Juliet* and the sex-release doctrine of a "perfectly conditioned society." The believers in this doctrine cannot understand why either Romeo or Juliet should so grieve at the loss of each other as to will his or her own death. Accepting as most reasonable their own attitude toward the delimited fact of sex, Huxley's characters could not possibly feel a need for mythologizing love. Centering their attention almost solely on the fact of sex, they could not conceive of a reality in which the imagination, by subsuming the fact, functioned to give quality to experience by calling upon a depth of emotion and creating a profundity of spirit. We have not, as a people, certainly, devolved to the completely mythless existence of the characters Huxley has imagined. It remains that such an existence could not have been imagined by an Elizabethan. In so far as we have lost a part of the capacity for mythmaking, we have to a similar degree lost our capacity to write a poetry sustained by a resilience of spirit.

The problem of perspective in our poetry can be illustrated in an anecdote told by Yeats. "I showed Lady Gregory," Yeats wrote, "a few weeks before her death a book by Day Lewis. 'I prefer,' she said, 'those poems translated by Frank O'Connor because they come out of original sin.' " Hers is a significant insight. Original sin is a far more profound consideration, holding permanent illumination, than a surface kind of social criticism. Social criticism grounded in an awareness and feeling for original sin could partake of this profundity. The point here is that Day Lewis has not grounded his poems in this or any other awareness that partakes of a vision, whereas O'Connor has, as in his poem "Autumn."

Woman full of wile
Take your hands away
Nothing tempts me now,
Sick for love you pray?

See this hair how grey,
See this flesh how weak,
See this blood gone cold—
Tell me what you seek.

Think me not perverse.
Never bow your head;
Let love last as now,
Slender witch instead.

Take your mouth from mine,
Kissing's better still;
Flesh from flesh must part
Lest of warmth come will.

Your twined branching hair,
Your grey eye dew-bright,
Your rich rounded breast
Turn to lust this sight.

All but fill the bed
Now that grey hairs fall,
Woman full of wile
I would give you all.

A wonderfully rich parable, as this is, would have had the same meaning for David and the Irish bards that it has for us. Day Lewis' "Come Live with Me"—

Come live with me and be my love
And we will all the pleasures prove
Of peace and plenty, bed and board
That chance employment may afford—

on the other hand, is, with its economic emphasis, peeled from the surface of our own time. By emphasizing a social criticism, the more basic human concern, love, is slighted and made to seem largely dependent upon economics. (There are those, of course, who say it is so dependent.) The poet is looking through the wrong end of the telescope.

The sense of evil, however, often with a mien of terrible urgency, has begun slowly to pervade modern literature. And the emphasis put upon it has, in turn, become a problem of serious critical import.[1] There is a sense of doom, threatening if not inevitable, that with increasing awareness we feel to be outside the neatly constructed system of rationality in which, since the seventeenth century, men have generally felt themselves to be living and to be making more secure. Scientific achievements gave to many a false sense of security.

When T. E. Hulme and Eliot and their followers first questioned the doctrine that "man is by nature wonderful," and composed of "unlimited powers" which would appear once the "external obstacles and fetters" had been removed, the quarrel seemed to many to be merely academic. Those with faith in the brave new world saw in these poets and critics the denial of "the possibility of utopias, the inevitability of progress, the liberal optimism, which had been the feature—often the main feature—of Western thought for centuries." In dismissing them as "traditionalists" or "medievalists" and in ridiculing their belief in original sin, their critics did not pause to examine the evidence other moderns had produced. The anthropologists had shown how many "primitive" folkways we are governed by; at the same time, Freud and his followers had indicated the extent to which we are governed by irrational pulls. And the various political mythologies suggested that our destinies were not merely awaiting a scientific control. Only the very recent public knowledge of the terrors implicit in "control" of the atom has forced the recognition of the radical imperfectibility of man. It follows that a new vision of the world is forming. "By attending," Louise Bogan writes, "with intense and detached interest to what the imagination (at all levels) presents to us, we may hope to catch at times a hint concerning the myth that is forming at the heart of our world." Whether it will be a tragic vision will depend upon our capacity for conceiving man as noble. It is apparent, with our literature as evidence, that the shapes of evil will form an important part of the new pattern.

Within any "age of reason," Miss Bogan goes on, there will be a counterdevelopment of the irrational. As evidence she points to the eighteenth-century development of John Wesley's Methodism, the most "frenzied" of testifying sects, and to the "graveyard poets" and the Gothic romances. The Romantic Movement was, William Troy says, the eager readmission of myth into Western consciousness. Since, however, the popular faith in the power of science, with the related concepts of scientific government and of man's capacity for personal adjustment to sheer rationality, has continued to develop, we may question how eagerly myth was readmitted. An unquestioned belief in the idea of progress would hardly have matured in a society believing that its darker, irrational, or nether side was controverting its rational purposes. Control, a product of rationality, itself has developed demons. In Franz

Kafka's *The Trial* we have the modern hero, a member of the state which so controls, so orders life, that "everything 'means something'; we share the obsessive suspicions of the insane; everything whispers, cunningly cajoles and promises hollowly; accuses and waits." Nationality spins foolproof ideologies—which war on each other.

Modern poets had educed a vision of evil some years before the ideal of absolute rationality had been exploded. They have helped us recover, in the face of the scientific emphasis, a fuller awareness of the complexity of human nature. They have not furnished us a myth, but they have helped to restore a realization of the way evil intertwines with goodness, and rationality with irrationality, realizations necessary to the creation of any myth arising to serve the needs of the whole man.

The same poets and critics who have helped to recover the vision of evil have pointed to another need, the need for ritual, which was denied both by the more intense Christian reformers and by those who have had a vision of man's life being controlled by the white light of unaided reason. In the first of Allen Tate's "Sonnets at Christmas" we are reminded of the inability of modern man to participate in ritual. He has not the belief to justify the ritual, and he is suspicious of ritual because it is associated with superstitions.

The justification for regarding the ritualistic function of poetry as legitimate can be seen in the implications of one of Santayana's commentaries. Poetry, he says, is "arrested in its development if it remains an unmeaning play of fancy without relevance to the ideals and purposes of life." The "play of fancy" and the delight in sensuous detail and euphonious sound are pleasant in themselves, yet they are given a greater importance in being related to a body of ideals, in serving, as Santayana puts it, the "ultimate demands of the soul." Santayana holds that religion and poetry, in the sense indicated, are "identical in essence" but differ in the way they relate to "practical affairs. Poetry is called religion when it intervenes in life, and religion, when it supervenes upon life, is seen to be nothing but poetry." Religion intervenes in the sense that it offers precepts, a code of behavior, for the guidance of believers; poetry, if written in terms of ideals and attitudes which are encompassed by religion, offers not precepts but a dramatic presentation of values. The precepts are stated barely and directly. In poetry the precepts may be seen to function in a complex, in relation to a situation that is more than moral statement

Sidney and Spenser were among the Elizabethans who, as W. R. Renwick reminds us, "regarded poetry as a means to persuade men to righteousness." And they looked upon the refinement of the native language in a similar fashion. The improvement of the language, as Richard Mulcaster, Spenser's schoolmaster, saw it, was a duty not only of the poet but of all people. In accepting moral teaching and the refinement of language as duties, they viewed poetry as the creation of forms which served ritualistic purposes.

In *A Midsummer Night's Dream* Shakespeare is concerned, perhaps unwittingly, with married love as ritual. The church prohibits sexual love, of course, outside marriage. Yet it is apparent that Shakespeare is not, in a didactic fashion, attempting to justify this restriction of love. He accepts marriage as a part of his world. He accepts it further as a state in which love may reach ideal forms and expression. It is, for him, a secular ideal—which relates to Christian precept only because poetry and religion have to some extent a subject matter in common.

In *Romeo and Juliet* Mercutio is a kind of devil's advocate. He finds Romeo's vision of love a little naïve. Romeo sees love in more idealized terms: as pure, undying, and somehow ethereal. Mercutio, like the Nurse, is a realist. He makes bawdy jokes about the physical aspects of love. Even so, he accepts romantic love as an ideal. And the audience could accept it, as well, after seeing that the voice of the opposition was not strong enough to destroy the "initial conception" of the worth of "human love" which is the strength of the play. *A Midsummer Night's Dream*, we might say, is a naïve statement of the ideal of married love. Attitudes which might oppose such a concept are not given a hearing. In *Antony and Cleopatra* they are heard. The love that dominates the play is extramarital, illegal. Yet, when Cleopatra is dying, she refers to Antony more than a little wistfully as her husband.

Husband, I come!
Now to that name my courage prove my title!

She does not blink the fact that their love, however great, was illegitimate. The naturalistic emphasis is stronger than in the earlier play, but not so strong that the ideal of married love is denied. In our time, however, the function of literature as ritual undoubtedly is infrequent because the beliefs and attitudes necessary to it must be fairly stable and widely held.

A fairly long study might be made of the usages Eliot has made of ritual in his poetry. A ready indication of its ironic function appears in "The Hollow Men," where the ending of the Lord's Prayer—"For Thine is the kingdom and the power and the glory, forever and ever"—is broken into meaningless fragments,

For Thine is
Life is
For Thine is the

. . . *This is the way the world ends*
*Not with a bang but a whimper.*

Juxtaposed against "*Here we go round the prickly pear*" and used as a refrain to his comments on "empty men," the suggestion of the prayer evokes the entire system of Christian belief. The fact that it can be used in this way even now should underscore our recognition of the potential vitality of ritual, both secular and religious, to nourish our esthetic and spiritual selves.

In his *Speculations* T. E. Hulme pointed to the need we have for simple ritualistic acts. "Sentiment cannot easily retire into itself in pure thought; it cannot live and feed on itself for very long." We are inevitably drawn to some "form of ritual for the expression and outflow of the sentiment"; otherwise our thoughts wander or are displaced by other thoughts. "A man cannot deliberately make up his mind to think of the goodness of God for an hour, but he can perform some ritual act of admiration whether it be the offering of a sacrifice or merely saying amen to a set prayer. Ritual tends to be constant, even that seeming exception the impromptu prayers of the Non-conformist minister are merely the stringing together in accidental order of set and well-known phrases and tags." We need certain patterns of action which signify the way we look at things, the respect in which we hold them, and which allow us to manifest our feelings without first having to organize and work through a complex of ideas and feelings. Obviously, however, the society must possess its belief, its myth, before its ritualistic expressions can arise.

When an age is gone, there is little to be gained in trying to breathe new life into it. Our need is not the forms of ritual that served the medieval world. The specific difficulty we labor against is a distrust of ritual as such, failing to perceive that whatever form of belief arises will require the "rehearsed attitude"—which is ritual—to sustain it and make it meaningful.

W. H. Auden in his "Epithalamion," celebrating the marriage of Giuseppe Borgese and Elizabeth Mann, treats married love as a symbol of "human unity." His poem is not ritualistic in the way that Spenser's *Epithalamion* or Shakespeare's *A Midsummer Night's Dream* were. They expressed a society's faith in the power of love; Auden expresses a hope that the isolated fragments of his world can be thereby unified, "reconciled by love."

The successful use of large and pervasive myths by modern writers has been achieved only by indirection. "In order to get a foothold on religious tradition," Philip Blair Rice has said, Thomas Mann "has had to go behind, not only institutional religion, but even Christianity itself." In the Joseph stories he writes obliquely "about our own time, as well as the second millennium B.C." In *The Waste Land* Eliot affords an equally easy example. Isolated facts and phenomena cannot explain themselves. In "The Fire Sermon" there are these lines:

> I can connect
> Nothing with nothing.

When Eliot, shortly after the publication of *The Waste Land*, undertook to explain *Ulysses*, he stated the crux of the modern problem: "In using the myth, in manipulating a continuous parallel between contemporaneity and antiquity, Mr. Joyce is pursuing a method which others must pursue after him. . . . It is simply a way of controlling, or ordering, of giving a shape and a significance to the immense panorama of futility and anarchy which is contemporary history." John Peale Bishop, too, brought to poetry a primary concern with the collapse of public, and the consequent difficulty in maintaining private, values. In the decorum and concern with form of classical Rome, he found values to contrast with the confusion of his own postwar world. And in the decline of the Empire—"the barbarians are back in the passes"—he saw a disintegration to "parallel" that of his own time. The *Cantos* of Pound, on the other hand, seem to have no center.[2] The organization is not mythic because, although there is the suggestion of the strangeness of man's history, there is, despite the manipulation of certain parallels between several societies, little that resembles a body of belief within which a society could find its orientation. The confusion of belief and the consequent effects upon poets committed to long poems is peculiarly a modern problem. Some few aspects of the problem can be seen in contrasting Eliot's method with that of Hart Crane and in glancing at the efforts of those American poets who have attempted to create a myth after the fashion of Whitman.

## 2

Certain critics of *The Bridge*, the most ambitious attempt to grasp America mythically, agree that despite the greatness of his talent Hart Crane failed of his intention. Key sentences from each of three critics indicate a uniformity of opinion regarding his failure.[3] Yvor Winters believes Crane was unable to formulate the rational center of his poem:

> Crane repeatedly refers to an idea which he cannot define and which probably never had even potential existence.

Allen Tate finds in the poem further evidence that the modern mind suffers from cross-purposes it cannot reconcile:

> His world had no center, and the compensatory action that he took is responsible for the fragmentary quality of his most ambitious work.

Howard Moss states the failure in still another, yet similar, way:

> We know he failed because there is still no American myth; he left his material where he found it, in the disparate sections of American history.

Eliot's *The Waste Land* reveals the uncertainty underlying modern man's affectation of understanding his relation to the universe. The "understanding" is soulless and has led to the acceptance of doctrines which release the individual from seeking after nobility, to undermining love and to the easy rationalization of lust, and to the denial of selfhood and its regeneration through penitence, abstinence, and courageous acceptance of suffering. Eliot's attitudes, presented briefly and abstractly, run counter to the "liberal" notions which have developed in the wake of a fast-waning supernaturalism. Presented in essay form, they would be met by ridicule and dismissed as naïve. The great mysteries, however, despite our self-assurances that we have freed ourselves from superstitious fetters, are still those of the meaning of sentient existence, of birth and death, and of the way of endowing our lives with the greatest meaning and significance. Put in another way, Eliot's belief in the need for personal regeneration could not be effectively stated solely in terms of the society he was describing as a wasteland. The society would dismiss his doctrine as a form of boy-scoutism or ethical culture. He could give it no contemporary sanction.

Fortunately, Eliot was able through his discovery of the recurrence of the myth of desolation and rebirth to give his poem primitive force, to find a kind of sanction for his doctrine—which the Thunder states as "Give, Sympathise, Control"—in myths which found expression in the religions and cults of all older cultures. His "specific clue to the dramatic shaping of his material" was in the frequently recurring story of a land ravished by war or weakened by sickness and old age, wherein the " 'task of the hero is that of restoration,' not by pursuing advantages for himself, but by giving himself to the quest of seeking the health and salvation of the land." Thus wastelands, as that of the modern world, are shown to be an old, old story. Eliot's selection of detail—those living automa lives, finding no joy in love, only frustration in their easy living, and having no understanding of traditional values—makes the desolation unmistakable. Those in the other wastelands, however, had a supernatural sanction to justify their personal seeking after salvation through self-sacrifice. The modern has only a "parallel," an "analogy" in the death and rebirth of nature, to urge him on. Our culture affords us no strong belief in the need for spiritual regeneration. The pull of our culture seems in the opposite direction. For this reason the myth is Eliot's; it is now a literary rather than a cultural myth.

Like Joyce, Eliot chose the one method available to him "of controlling, of ordering, of giving a shape and significance to the immense panorama of futility and anarchy which is contemporary history." The modern most opposed to Eliot's belief is forced, almost, to pay attention, to see the modern world in focus against other centuries of human experience. Eliot's case, as it were, demands at least respectful attention. Further, his symbols support the myth—each object, situation, or chain of events relates to the theme of death or desolation and rebirth. The central symbol of the wasteland is the true center of the poem, as Crane's Bridge is not. The parts of Eliot's poem are integrated, illuminating the central conception, and sustained by the symbol he employs.

Crane's theme—which seems to be, in so far as it is consistent, that the age of the machine has given us a new freedom and that the energies of America, which have become identified with the machine in terrifying ways, will be released in some transcendentally brilliant future—finds readier acceptance than Eliot's. In fact, Crane conceived *The Bridge* as a kind of answer to Eliot's "pessimism." Yet, as Tate has observed, Crane's inability to find a moral focus or to treat the values implied in his theme, or subject, by minutely examining them in relation to an organizing symbol (provided that he had been as fortunate as Eliot in finding one) is proof of Eliot's major contention: that there has been a "decay of the individual consciousness and its fixed relation to the world." The confusions in the structure of *The Bridge* are ultimately derived from Crane's inability to examine his world in terms of a defined set of values and to accept the consequences. The power of the poem is not in the whole but in moments when his demonic sensibility attempted to transcend his incapacity to perceive his theme in a clear and orderly way.

Ultimately, Eliot's poem, because it turns upon a faith in spiritual rebirth, is not despairing. In "Quaker Hill" and "The Tunnel" Crane, occasionally using a phraseology very similar to Eliot's, refracts the vulgarity of the new money-valued society, and the devitalized people who are the victims of a sordid city existence, of a society whose chief value is the multiplying of sensations. He created a demonic city very similar to Eliot's unreal London. Yet he tried to see in the airplane, a part of the mechanical order, an escape from the "Tunnel," the airplane flying toward some great, but undefined, truth. All the evidence Crane presents substantiates the opposition of the person to the age of the machine—yet the theme of his poem demands that the machine be our salvation, the symbol of the new millennium. Thus at crucial points in *The Bridge* Crane falls back upon, or into, ambiguous phrasing. In "The Fire Sermon" Eliot catches up his theme, that lust, the symbol of which is fire, is self-consuming, in the phrases,

> O Lord Thou pluckest me out
> O Lord Thou pluckest
> burning.

Only the Lord, that is, can save those who are losing themselves in lives given to their senses. What, Crane seems to have asked himself, is to save those in his demonic city? and to have answered that they could be saved only by some fiery ideal. But the vagueness of his answer requires some form of expression suggesting at least the mien of a specific ideal. Thus his

> Kiss of our agony Thou gatherest
> O Hand of Fire
> O Hand of Fire
> gatherest.

The form "Thou" is ambiguous because Crane does not mean the Christian Deity, and whatever specific ideal he might have had in mind is not, unlike Eliot's "Lord," understandable in terms of a body of values. The closest Crane comes to stating the central conception of his poem is in Part IV, "Cape Hatteras."

Walt Whitman, the subject of this section, is made to bear the weight of whatever positive assertions Crane can discover. That the assertions are few and vaporous is implied in Crane's felt need to identify Whitman with the *Panis Angelicus*. Whitman's vision, a vaguely conceived democratic future, offers little in the way of objective fact or clear perceptions against which Crane's sensibility might play. Consequently, he pretends that there are *particulars*, justifying his bursts of imagery and apostrophes to the future—

And now, as launched in abysmal cupolas of space,
Toward endless terminals, Easters of speeding light—
Vast engines outward veering with seraphic grace
On clarion cylinders pass out of sight
To course that span of consciousness thou'st named
The Open Road—thy vision is reclaimed!
What heritage thou'st signalled to our hands!

And, finally, as though anticipating the cliché endings of grade B movies, he sees himself standing below "the rainbow's arch," hand in hand with Whitman. This maudlin end, Karl Shapiro has written in his "The Discarded Poem," is "the defeated cry of a demonic poet who has lost his way." Crane belonged with Poe, Baudelaire, and Rimbaud—with those who could perceive the configuration of evil intertwined through all existence. Crane was caught up by the shallow optimism, a part of the Whitman vogue which, for a number of reasons, carried many of his generation downstream.

The defect of *The Bridge* is not only, as one of his critics has it, in the formulation of the symbols; the parts do not live within the life of the major symbol—the bridge itself—because the impulse or concentration behind the poem is never clear. This being so, no symbol, however dynamic or widely available its implications in relation to his theme, would have saved the poem.

We may ask whether the bridge, the metaphorical strength of which, obviously, is its power to unite one part with another, is as powerful a symbol as Crane thought. The bridge, over and above its metaphor value, does have ready associations for an industrialized world. But a more basic consideration is this: Can any amount of arbitrary spanning or bridging on the part of the poet—Crane bridges the agrarian and industrial worlds; the Tunnel and the final vision of hopefulness—create a unity in the minds of a society that normally sees the parts in isolation or in opposition? It would seem that the bridge symbol, which would have been remarkably appropriate to the medieval world, is an ironic one for ours.

Again, we may note a comment D. H. Lawrence made in discussing the way in which the myths and symbols of more "primitive" societies remain in the mind of a later society:

> The power of the symbol is to arouse the deep emotional self, and the dynamic self, beyond comprehension. Many edges of accumulated experience still throb within a symbol. And we throb in response. It takes centuries to create a really significant symbol: even the symbol of the Cross, or the horse-shoe, or the horns. No man can invent symbols. He can invent an emblem, made up of images; or metaphors: or images: but not symbols.

We cannot, that is, will ourselves a significant myth. We can, on the other hand, investigate, as Eliot and Thomas Mann have done, whatever implications are available to us in the symbols that remain as the partial residue from a culture whose informing beliefs are no longer universally held. Yeats recognized the same power in the inherited symbol. After long experimenting with certain cabalistic symbols, he said, in effect, that he could create some effective symbols but that those which really matter to men of genius and to a culture are not chosen, they are given; and "the unity of a culture comes from a given unity of image—the figure of Apollo or of Christ." The bridge was no more amenable to Crane's purpose than the dynamo was, in contrast to the Virgin, for Henry Adams.

## 3

Crane's effort to capture America mythically was a natural impulse. Instinctively he was a mythic poet, and, if his culture had afforded him a large and unifying belief, he would have undoubtedly produced a poem worthy of his subject. The only theme which has seemed, in an age more political than religious, to promise a subject of mythic proportions is that of America itself. The poetic expression of it originated with Whitman, but the years of its appropriation by other poets have been relatively recent. Several reasons for the Whitman phenomenon suggest themselves. The most obvious one is that here was a poetic statement purporting to be *the* statement of American life and ideals. Certain poets and critics in the twenties objected to the Whitman vogue, stating that there is no idea of what America is held in common by all poets; but only recently have we had statements pointing to the absurdity of making Whitman out to be *the* American poet and holding up his vision of America as being or approximating the myth which is the organizing or controlling ideal of American life.[4]

In the twenties, however, Whitman's vision was appropriated by a number of "new" poets. Those wanting to hymn America easily fell into Whitman's idiom. Those shy of artistic forms because they were associated with the effete could appear as virile rhymers, and his loose meters easily became a part of the free-verse furor. Further, the left-wing movements, needing a poet of the common man, one creating images similar to those of the liberated worker in the left-wing murals, found their poet of the future society in Whitman. Lastly, there are in Whitman, particularly in his early work, Americans who are alive. They are his contemporaries, mostly workmen, in Manhattan and Brooklyn. There is much, that is, in his earlier work to justify his reputation. But Whitman and his followers—like Robinson Jeffers, Vachel Lindsay, Edgar Lee Masters, Carl Sandburg, Stephen Vincent Benét and William Rose Benét, and later Paul Engle, August Derleth, Muriel Rukeyser, Ben Maddow, and Alfred Hayes, all poets influenced to some extent by his idiom and vision—are not in the line of American writers who have deepened our knowledge of human motivation or action. They are, in so far as they are followers of Whitman, away from the tradition which runs from Hawthorne and Melville through James and Eliot. These latter are more truly mythic writers, since they are able to go deeply into the human mind and to touch those symbols that most suggest the mystery of man's existence. Crane was the only great poet to follow Whitman—and he was, when following the bent of his gift, more at home with Melville.

It is not surprising, of course, that a myth such as Whitman's has won adherents. The myth has afforded a literary "form" associated with the celebration of America. A part of its appeal presumably—and certainly a chief cause of the badness of much of the poetry inspired by it—is that it is vaguely conceived. One can agree almost literally with Yvor Winters' criticism of Whitman's doctrine: "It vanishes if pursued by definition."

Much of the fascination of Sandburg's *The People, Yes* arises from its being mostly a transcription of the sense of lostness many Americans suffer. In this, as in his earlier work, there are extended apostrophes to mechanical power, to energy and strength—but the refrain, which is a statement of the theme, is the pathetic questioning,

Where to? what next?

Reading this in conjunction with "Years of the Modern," we can see that Whitman's vision of "incredible rush and heat" and "ecstatic fever of dreams" has to a degree been fulfilled. The movement, the breaking-through of frontiers and the interlinking of countries Whitman foresaw, has come to pass. But the activity, the unceasing movement and change, is not in itself satisfying. "Where to? what next?"

Vitality, like freedom, that is not disciplined, brought under human as well as mechanical control, is not enough. Sandburg has asked the last question. The formless poetry of the Whitman-Sandburg tradition has mirrored the development of a country whose history has been, in large part, the roar of activity as the vacuum between two borders was being filled. A passage from Van Wyck Brooks's *America's Coming of Age* presented the historical development of Whitman's vision.

America is like a vast Sargasso Sea—a prodigious welter of the conscious life, swept by ground-swells of half conscious emotion. All manner of living things are drifting in it, phosphorescent, gayly colored, gathering knots and clotted masses, gelatinous, unformed, flimsy, tangled, rising and falling, floating and merging, here an immense belly, there a rudimentary brain (the gross devouring the fine)—everywhere an unchecked, uncharted, unorganized vitality like that of the first chaos.

The white light, the vague ideal of loving the common man, has not been by itself enough to give structure and form, to bring the vision near actuality. It has lost its Christian sanction, but it has attained no other. The passage above, if we may borrow two technical terms from critical discussions of the metaphor, might be considered the *vehicle*, or image, of the vaguely conceived *tenor*, or statement, the poets of the land seem to have been making, with far more optimism and with no sense of the gross devouring the fine.

There seems, further, a proclivity among these poets toward letting the poetry write itself. An investigation of the use of American names, for example, would indicate the remarkable frequency with which the word "America," like a talisman, is used as well as how frequently there occur the names of rivers, the Monongahela, the Wabash, the Mississippi, and the Ohio, and the names of towns, Sioux City, Salem, Painted Post, and Cheyenne. These poets hold language to expository and descriptive functions, merely ordering and transcribing American speech. The language generally is no richer from their having used it.

The depression burst of "America! America!" writing further illustrates the documentary nature of this kind of poetry. The camera and the W.P.A.-sponsored guidebooks to the states are appropriate symbols of the nature of the inquiry of most of these poets into America. The surface of America was presented—the jalopies on the road, the men working in orchards for a dollar a day, the migrants in camps or searching for a place to stay, the bread lines. This passage from Paul Engle sounds the characteristic note:

The Southern folk
Left the gay dances, the vineyards mellowed with
sunlight
On the terraced hills and as Wop and Dago joined
Polack and Bohunk in the towns of steel

Where the great fires burned their guts out—
Bethlehem
(*O mockery of the little Christ-found village*),
Gary, Youngstown, the hard, trip-hammer-beaten
names.

A little later we suffered a growing consciousness of Hitler. Many expatriates were heading back. A new nationalism was necessary, and MacLeish, echoing lines from Donne, could then write:

O my America—my new-found land . . .
How blest am I in discovering thee!

The new affirmation was under way. America was to be rediscovered—and acclaimed. Biographers wrote about the American schoolbook heroes, folklorists were busy refurbishing ballads and legends, anthologists were editing anything that praised freedom and liberty, and novelists documented America for Book-of-the-Month Club readers. A lovely haze was settling over America's past.

In what purported to be criticism, an attack was directed against the writers who had dominated literature between the two wars. In answering one attack, T. S. Eliot wrote that Van Wyck Brooks "might have been interested in not merely denouncing modern art, but in inquiring *why* it is what it is." Such an inquiry might have indicated not only the sickness of the society, world-wide, that infected literature but the futility of successive cycles of negation and affirmation. The critical evangelism that is pleased to give unqualified approbation to a "synthetic myth" of America is misdirected and dangerous. It delays the wide acceptance of an American poetry written within the necessarily prescribed view of the individual artist and deludes its audience by creating a spurious vision as a symbol of an America which in her constant evolution is in greater need of insights than of unqualified affirmation.

The Whitman-Sandburg tradition has been exploited. Because

the exploitation is an established mode of writing, America is foregoing many of the insights that poets may derive from facing and reconciling political, ethical, and personal elements as these are framed within their poems. Such exploitation serves a hypnotic purpose. The historico-myth equivalent of America—as vague and sprawling as our development in the West—is transcribed. The materials, the heroes, and the poorly defined concepts, which have been presented before in this poetry, are easily re-worked. The themes are predetermined: the railway tracks over thousands of miles of farm lands and unending plains, memories of folk legends and frontier heroes, the great cities and the lovable people. This poetry renews a third-generation vision of America as a touchstone of political, social, and moral wisdom. These poets are in a sense no longer artists—they know in advance the "America" they will present. They have failed to recognize that "such is the nature of the poetic imagination that the more fully it creates the more closely it approaches truth, ceaselessly resolving, recording and forming anew the emotional forces that affect human beings."

It is pertinent to note that one of the first God-bless-America books to be issued during World War II was Struthers Burt's *War Songs*, the individual pieces in which are, at least in theme and general form, indistinguishable from earlier work by Sandburg, Stephen Vincent Benét, Archibald MacLeish (half of whose work follows the direction of Eliot), Paul Engle, and the dozens with lesser names. Muriel Rukeyser, too, found it expedient to use the idiom of this tradition for her "Wake Island."

Karl Shapiro in his *Essay on Rime* endeavors to explain something of the phenomenon whereby the whole "geography" of America is revealed in this kind of poetry. Intending apparently to justify and prove our transcendental unity, these poets

> Recite the whole geography and construct
> A gigantic stage perennially set
> For some Siegfried who never comes.

Shapiro, in effect, is saying that we have, at least as yet, no unity of spirit, belief, and purpose that would justify these attempts at American epics. It would follow that this tradition of poetic writing should not be held up by literary historians, as it seems in danger of being, as the poetry most distinctively American. It is reflective of American development—but it hardly indicates the development of the individual poet's mind as this is shaped in America and, in turn, helps to give definition to America. Shapiro says also that the failures of these poets of "the official muse" stem from their not having seen that Whitman's oratory on democracy and geography is personal, "particular to his character." The permanent value is in Whitman's "Song of Myself."

It is not sufficient for the poet to adulate a continent. The poet as an artist must so envelop and absorb the raw materials of his art that they arise from his mind transmuted, different in character, with the form they have taken dictated by the nature of the mind that has given them their new character. Even Whitman, who first saw the democratic vista in poetry, was incapable of "processing" all "the raw untreated data" with which *Leaves of Grass* is strewn. And his America was far less complex than ours, of which the contemporary "westering" poets write. The poets who are concerned to write an individual idiom and to discover their own vision are more likely to be regionalists, members of a school, expatriates, or experimentalists: All these latter would recognize the insuperable difficulties in bringing, other than as stillborn, the whole of America to birth in anything resembling epic form. Most of them, too, would probably agree with Philip Wheelwright that no myth is produced by fiat, as well as with Tate that the poets "unaided and isolated from the people" cannot create a significant myth.

# CHAPTER THREE

## *The Break with Verism*

> *The chief characteristic of modern art—of art, that is, left to follow its own inspiration free from academic patronage—is power of expression.*—Eugene Veron

A really adequate definition of verism would undoubtedly require a large-scale philosophical study. Yet, even though such a term possibly cannot be given any absolute definition, some few generalizations may be helpful in indicating its nature and the kind of esthetic with which it is likely to be associated. Verism, which suggests its kinship with verisimilitude and naturalism, is an emphasis that inclines one toward the objectivity usually associated with science, as opposed to the subjectivity usually associated with art. It is an attempt to embody actuality, with a minimum of distortion by the artist, in an artistic medium.

Verism, which derives from the scientific point of view, implies that reality is only understandable in terms of abstract categories. The language which serves verism is necessarily logical, denotative, and abstract—which is not, certainly, the sole language of poetry. Verism, too, outlaws myth and purely subjective forms of symbolizing experience—neither of which the poet can forgo. The categories which the poet makes as a mythologizer necessarily conflict with the categories of science. The poet who functions as a verist chooses to observe the predetermined categories of science.

The veristic emphasis, which depends upon abstractions drawn from the objective world, tends to ignore the subjective, which, according to most moderns, is the realm of values. It also ignores the need we have to dramatize (mythologize) our knowledge. The abstract categories of values could hardly be qualified or enlarged by a medium which was narrowly in their service. Poets and critics participating in the modern poetic revolution tried to break with inherited values. An aspect of their revolt is their attempt to keep their medium from expressing values at all.

George Santayana in his "Penitential Art" has characterized the modern period of art as "lenten"—that is, art is trying to recapture its innocence, its former purity. He means, simply enough, that reproductive, discursive, and didactic art, the forms of verism, were the temptations to which post-Renaissance art succumbed. The suppression of understanding in most forms of abstract art and the withdrawal from any practical purposes imply an effort to purify the "medium" itself. Art had been attempting to compete with science both by seizing upon permanent categories of abstract knowledge and by depicting natural objects. Now it is repentant.

> Vain, vain it says to itself, was the attempt to depict or beautify external objects. . . . Nature has the urgency of life, which art cannot rival. . . . What is that to the spirit? Let it confess its own impotence in that field, and abandon all attempts to observe or preserve what are called *things:* let it devote itself instead . . . to purifying its sensibility, which is after all what nature plays upon when she seems to us beautiful. Perhaps in that way spirit may abstract the gold of beauty and cast the dross away—all that allow of preoccupation with material forms and external events and moral sentiments. . . . It was an evil obsession with alien things that dragged sensibility into a slavery to things which stifled and degraded it: *salvation lies in emancipating the medium.*

Art had tried to be practical, to serve the society as applied science served it. Poetry, as many moderns viewed it, had been put to use to prettify the sentiments of the society, its morals, and its doctrines. Modern art was the reaction.

Contemporary art historians furnished an easy justification for the break with naturalistic forms simply by pointing out that most of the great art of the world—"Gothic, baroque, primitive, and

Asiatic"—has been unrealistic; or, as Melvin Rader adds, that the "realism" of art is "spiritual." The reasons for dismissing the theory of verism are undoubtedly complicated and intricately interwoven. Most artists are clear nonetheless on the point that their job is not reproduction. "A copy of the universe," Rebecca West has said, "is not what is required of art; one of the damned thing is ample." If reproduction is not required, then symbolic representation is. (Some forms of verism, of course, continue in modern art and literature, just as a certain amount of symbolism functioned in the most studiedly imitative art.) And such representation requires the expression of the artist's personal insights. To some extent, through his indication of preferences, his selection, and his emphases, the values of the artist are expressed. The interpretation of the nature of the values expressed, what they signify and in what way they relate to an extrinsic scale of social or moral values, is a delicate problem for esthetics and criticism. To restrict the meaning of "values" to the "qualities" the work of art generates, to narrow its meaning down to problems of technique alone, is to hurry the process of dehumanization which is an aspect of modern art forms. To put an artistic medium into the service of narrowly conceived moral or propagandist views is, on the other hand, to deny the artist those insights he might express as a free agent.

## *2*

The scientific emphasis, which began with the setting-up of a subject-object dichotomy of man and the external world, worked in so far as art was concerned in this way: The objects in the external world were not to be distorted by being passed through man's imagination. Their true nature could be maintained by reproducing them as faithfully as possible. In painting this meant a strict verism, while in poetry it meant a close adherence to discursive language, an avoidance of the metaphorical or symbolic except as they could be used decoratively. Because the language of science—the elements, for example, used in mathematical formulas—could be used successfully in advancing a knowledge of the physical sciences, it was assumed that the language of prose, and poetry, if similarly subjected to the control of denotative meanings, would best advance a knowledge of human affairs. To some extent, certainly, the assumption is justified. But a single-minded faith in a denotative language implies an ignorance of the part played by the sensibility and imagination in human understanding.

The assumption that a mathematic language or a denotative language, used for strictly discursive or logical purposes, is the only sure way of arriving at truth is unfortunate. A word whose denotation is definite is, like a veristic painting, a kind of symbol in that it stands for its object; it effects, as it were, a transition from the objective world of things (and of *ideas*) to the mind with a minimum of distortion. But as human beings we are interested in further aspects of the object—its special *qualities*, its *significance*. We are also interested in how we *feel* about it. A denotative meaning, like an exact reproduction of the object, does not necessarily suggest either its special qualities or its significance. The artist, when he is not trying to achieve a literal representation, which is the function of science and of certain forms of prose, employs various techniques, depending upon his medium, to catch, as Santayana puts it, "the *spirit* of the thing." He isolates details, understates, caricatures, makes comparisons or establishes contrasts, and uses whatever devices for arousing feeling he finds appropriate.

Such overemphasis or distortion, correctable for scientific purposes, is a kind of dramatization which enables us to experience, to see and feel, relationships in a new way. "The more," Santayana says, "we transform things in seeing them, the more we seem to spiritualize them and turn them into forms of our own sensibility, regarding the living image in us as the dramatic essence of the object." In the exact orderings of rational thought, objects or ideas are placed in neat categories. The mythic part of the poet's mind urges him to leap the categories, to conjoin objects or ideas regardless of their "proper" spheres. Just as the prescientific or mythic mind can classify a butterfly as a bird because both fly, so can the poet, finding a common point of similarity, bring two objects or situations together, thereby illuminating both and the spheres in which they ordinarily are seen to inhere.

Examination of the external world affords categories of information permanently applicable to scientific problems. The knowledge of the truth of the world, however, is twofold, subjective as well as objective. If the emphasis held by certain seventeenth-, eighteenth-, and nineteenth-century figures were rightly on the objective world, if the truths of reality were to be found thereby, then it was the duty of the artist to be a verist—to represent the world with a minimum of subjective distortion. (We know from the subjectivist movements in philosophy and poetry that this emphasis was not universally held.) In his discussion of "Implied Desiderata in Works of Art," in their accordance with "Nature," Professor A. O. Lovejoy shows that Nature, for the most part, was an *objective* norm, a way of keeping the individual imagination in check.[1] Inevitably the desiderata were "literal realism," "depiction of general types," "adherence to rules and precedents," etc.—all forms implying the poet should observe the neat rules and categories assumed to have been furnished by Nature. The poet would therefore be *informative*, *descriptive*, *expository*. If, too, the facts and principles of the objective world were verifiable and stable, then presumably moral, political, and esthetic (subjective) principles were verifiable and stable. It hardly would have occurred to any of these societies that their principles and their mores were locally agreed upon myths. The poets who versified the beliefs of the mores were also veristic poets, *expository* and *didactic*. The modern artist rediscovered the subjective world, with its constant movement, dark labyrinths, and instability. The degree of subjectivism in modern art—symbolism, impressionism, surrealism, etc.—is understandable as reaction against the excesses of societies which found in verism the mirror that reflected truth.

Nor is it surprising that, in examining the structure of English poetry in various periods, F. W. Bateson should find that, prior to the subjective moderns, Dryden was the last poet to *approach* the ideal of writing a poetry "coextensive with the language in which it is written."[2] The diction and the structure of poetry, as interpreted by Bateson, appear variously as reactions against or compromises with prose. Sometimes the structure of poetry was loosened by unnecessary "explanations," sometimes the ideal of denotation made the poetry thin and prosaic, and sometimes, because poetry was expected to deal with feelings alone, not thought, the vague connotations effected a diffuse emotionalism that was all heart and no head. The genuine poets, whatever their successes, had to work in the face of such tendencies. The tendencies had as their common denominator the belief that the categories presented by science alone were trustworthy. It was a faith in the reality of the objective as opposed to the subjective world. And its language was prose.

Certain students have recognized that language "exhibits two entirely different modes of thought. Yet in both the mind is powerful and creative. It expresses itself in different forms, one of which is discursive logic, the other creative imagination."[3] The former, of course, is used in the service of practical and scientific knowledge; the latter, once in the service of unquestioned myth, in the service of art expressions.

Ernst Cassirer's thesis, in part, is that myth and language are the products of man's inherent capacity for creating metaphors and symbols. Language—unlike myth, which, in his definition, always remains within "the magic circle of its figurative ideas"—breaks loose, finally achieving the level of "logical thought." "Reason," Mrs. Langer comments, "is not man's primitive endowment, but his achievement. The seeds of it—fertile, yet long dormant—lie in language; logic springs from language when that greatest of symbolic modes is mature (as it is by the time we meet it in history or ethnology)." Discursive thought and language, given enormous impetus by the scientific movement, serve different ends from "mythic" thought and language. Mythic thought and language create an imaginative symbolism whereby understanding is suffused with emotion and belief is sustained.[4]

Discursive thought begins with a "single perception" which is examined in terms of progressively considered relationships. But the single perception, fact, species, or genus is not lost in the totality. It fits in with the whole without sacrificing its identity. The process always is one of supplementation and extension. Mythic thought functions quite differently, toward compression and intension. All significance is, as it were, "distilled into a single point." (This is not to say, of course, that individual mythic figures or representations may not be subsumed into a larger myth.) Over discursive thought light seems to be evenly diffused; over mythic thought it seems concentrated at points. The conceptions embodied in mythic language "must be taken not in extension, but in intension; not quantitatively, but qualitatively." Individual differences lose their character in the whole. In all myth, Cassirer adds, "the principle of *pars pro toto*" operates.

The problem presents itself, then, as the relationship of myth and language to poetry. The mythic projections of the poet make the world *live*, give vitality and significance to the objects and situations the imagination plays with. In his study of William Blake, Mark Schorer quotes a passage from Carl Jung which suggests the problem of the poet in a scientific-minded world. "In my picture of the world there is a vast outer realm and an equally vast inner realm; between these two stands man, facing now one and now the other, and according to his mood or disposition, taking the one for the absolute truth by denying or sacrificing the other." Once the subjective world became suspect, as a well of the irrational, the cultural emphasis was all but exclusively focused against the objective world. "Employing the myth [or paramyth] of contemporary science," Schorer says, "eighteenth century poetry more and more took to itself the *functions* of science, which are exposition and description." Myth, that is, did not die when exposed to rationalistic thought—it became rationalistic. The difficulty was not in the absence of myth but in the quality of the myth. The belief that reality was to be found in an abstract understanding of the universe served poetry badly, for, as Cassirer and others have noted, concepts far separated from physical symbols seem divorced from reality. The belief, as Jung might put it, is the result of an overconcentration on "the outer realm" and failure to remember that what we *experience* through physical symbols, what is dramatized for us, we understand best. The denotative uses of language, on the other hand, were those that were believed best suited to designate the abstract nature of reality.

As logic developed, words were more and more reduced to "conceptual signs." Language became a vehicle for exacting differentiations and categorizing—but "at the price of foregoing the wealth and fullness of immediate experience. In the end, what is left of the concrete sense and feeling content it once possessed is little more than a bare skeleton." Language no longer creates mythical figures, peopling the world with gods and demons. Rationally ordered language, serving the scientific emphasis, has lost much of its concreteness, and therefore much of its power to project symbols capable of calling forth strong feeling or of suggesting insights and significances. Myth, however, did not die with the rise of discursive language. In fact, many rigid systems of belief are buttressed by the more abstract language. Ironically, the "mythic" images of the poet are sometimes used to startle us into an awareness of the limitations of too rigid systems. Unfortunately, however, poets have sometimes neglected their mythmaking power, have compromised with their role as poets to serve a set point of view of a religious or political group.

Robert Browning, for example, frequently versified many of the stereotypes of the Victorian mores. And often he used anecdotes to which he attached the little social or moralistic dicta of his society. Many of these stereotypes are packed into one stanza of "Rabbi Ben Ezra":

> Grow old along with me!
> The best is yet to be,
> The last of life, for which the first was made.
> Our times are in his hand
> Who saith, "A whole I planned;
> Youth shows but half. Trust God; see all,
>     nor be afraid!"

There is an unqualified optimism, unquestioned faith in Providence, and an admonishment to courage. Browning rarely used those techniques of his medium, the instrument of paradox, for example, which enable the poet to see an idea from various sides and to see it in other than simple terms. Browning presented what seemed to him the "actuality" envisioned by his society. He is the poet of a coherent social system with categories of quite rigid attitudes and beliefs. He did not use his medium, as a more critical-minded poet in a similarly coherent system might, to cut across the categories or to exaggerate or understate its aspects that his readers might feel the quality and temper of the Victorian mind. He is a veristic poet in that he reflects, rather than interprets, his mores. He never got behind the mirror.

The Victorian, for example, was unwilling to acknowledge that the beautiful and the ugly were not absolute categories. Or, if he recognized that they were not absolutes, he was hardly free to incorporate his knowledge into his poetry. Rupert Brooke, among the Georgians, could say: "There are common and sordid things—situations and details—that may suddenly bring all tragedy, or at least the brutality of actual emotions, to you. I rather grasp relievedly at them after I have beaten vain hands in the rosy mists of poets' experiences." Poetry, serving the accepted beliefs of the society, was for "beautiful" things alone. A modern poet is free to accept the evidence of his senses. Thus Wallace Stevens, in "Anything Is Beautiful If You Say It Is," can give evidence of the element of the beautiful or of the moving in those objects ordinárily categorized as ugly—

> The very will of the nerves
> The crack across the pane,
> The dirt along the sill.

Stevens, viewing the dirt on the window sill or the crack in the pane, was free to symbolize them as he would. His medium was not restricted to a veristic purpose, to reflecting "actuality" as defined according to any rigid system of belief and attitudes.

Denotative language employs a static kind of symbol, which attempts to mirror rather than to interpret what it symbolizes. Denotative symbols are employed not for their own sake but to achieve clear statements. Thus there is the ideal of certain kinds of prose writers to express themselves so clearly that the reader is not conscious of the medium. Such writers, in effect, attempt to present *pure* idea. Connotative and imagistic symbols, on the other hand, serve to forward the idea being developed at the same time that they draw attention to themselves. The connotative symbol leads one to examine alternative meanings, while the imagistic symbol draws attention to its concrete self as well as to the idea it represents. Denotative symbols make for pure statement; the latter two for dramatized statement.[5]

Several lines from Hamlet's speech to Horatio, asking him to watch for signs of Claudius' guilt, may serve as an example of a use of the medium to *dramatize* an idea.

> I prithee, when thou seest that act *a-foot.*
> Even with the very *comment of thy soul*,
> Observe my uncle: if his *occulted* guilt
> Do not itself *unkennel* in one speech. . . .

Each of the italicized terms intensifies the explicit meaning. First, there is the signal, the "act a-foot," an image that emphasizes the beginning and movement of a crucial period, during which uncommon concentration is to be employed. Claudius' very guilt will be dramatized. The effectiveness of "comment of thy soul" inheres in its drawing upon the emotion derived from all the unnamed associations with the word "soul" that were resident in the minds of a people, unlike us, whose long heritage of civilization was vitally alive in focus about this word. The term "occulted" was likewise charged for an audience that kept warm their notions that preternatural powers and human action were inextricably linked. The term "unkennel" underscores the creeping nature of Claudius' guilt and calls up the numberless associations that usually hover in the Anglo-Saxon mind in connection with such words as "dog" and "bitch." It is an indirect statement of Hamlet's contempt.

By way of contrast we may look at several lines from John Pomfret's "The Choice," a poem, according to Dr. Johnson, which eighteenth-century readers "oftener perused" than any other "in our language."

> If Heav'n the grateful liberty would give,
> That I might choose my method how to live;
> And all those hours propitious fate should lend,
> In blissful ease and satisfaction spend;
> Near some fair town I'd have a private seat,
> Built uniform, not little, nor too great;
> Better, if on a rising ground it stood;
> On this side fields, on that a neighb'ring wood.

The statement is explicit, and the meaning is quite as clear as Hamlet's. There are no words like "unkennel" or "occulted," however, to dramatize the meaning. No single word is surprising in the context; none draws upon emotions associated with situations foreign to the one being discussed or is startling enough to draw attention to itself. The lines are veristic. They state, in a polite idiom, an eighteenth-century ideal. They neither qualify nor intensify. The language is denotative, each word adding to the simple meaning. It is a poetry opposed or indifferent to the imaginative metaphor.

The break with verism achieved by modern poets recovered for them the power to dramatize, to mythologize more fully. The recovery is evident in the following lines from Dylan Thomas:

> Twenty-four years remind the tears of my eyes.
> (Bury the dead for fear that they walk to the
> grave in labour.)
> In the groin of the natural doorway I crouched
> like a tailor
> Sewing a shroud for a journey
> By the light of the meat-eating sun.

The artist who attempts to dramatize his understanding is likely to be more individualistic in his thinking than one employing denotative symbols because they tend to occur in common locutions. Unless the writer using denotative symbols has a strongly philosophical mind, he is likely to fall into cliché thinking simply because language presents him with stereotypes.

The poet accepting stereotypes, to any considerable extent, may be seen to ally himself with one or more kinds of veristic writing. He may be anecdotal because the anecdote is a kind of transcript, only slightly processed for effective telling, from his experience. It is factual. He may be imitative of other writers whose style, substance, manner, and attitudes have won approval. Or he may versify, usually in a largely discursive idiom, the attitudes acceptable to the mores or acceptable to a particular group. In this instance he will be didactic or propagandistic—that is, his understanding and his insights will not arise from his dramatization of ideas.

Very slowly philosophers as well as artists have come to the recognition that facts of themselves are neutral or lifeless and therefore meaningless and to the further recognition that limited systems of abstractions are in effect antirational. Philosophy, or that part of it which is willing to recognize the dead ends to which certain methods lead, has admitted that the tendency to emphasize things and the objective in terms of rigorously exclusive systems of abstractions has led to the ignoring of values.

The critics, other than certain Marxists who would use literature solely for propaganda purposes, most concerned with values in poetry are, perhaps, Yvor Winters, who attempts to show how the poet's moral attitudes inform his work, and I. A. Richards, who has attempted to evolve a broad theory of value and to explain how poetry serves values. Richards states his position most explicitly:

> To set up as a critic is to set up as a judge of values. . . . For the arts are inevitably and quite apart from any intentions of the artist an appraisal of existence. Matthew Arnold when he said that poetry is a criticism of life was saying something so obvious that it is constantly overlooked. The artist is concerned with the record and perpetuation of the experiences which seem to him most worth having.

There are, on the other hand, many who in reacting against the veristic art of the nineteenth century turned to so strong an emphasis upon the formal, stylistic elements of art that they deny it has much, if any, relationship to values. They see it as merely a means of inducing an "esthetic emotion." The existence of an "esthetic emotion," having nothing whatsoever to do with other human concerns, philosophical, ethical, religious, or social, was most easily rationalized by pointing to the new emphasis upon abstract painting. Such a consideration was a part of the revolution in esthetics and inevitably encouraged poets to seek something that might be called *pure* form.

Hugo Münsterberg's "isolation" theory of art appears to be an effort to sever art from any practical purposes. He emphasizes this distinction between art and science. The purpose of the scientist is to establish relationships, to show the connections between things, to build always toward "the complete system," the scientific description of the universe. The purpose of the artist is to isolate the object, to cut it off from the rest of experience. "The purpose for which we looked out in scientific knowledge was practical mastery of the world for the outer achievement; we had to know what causes were connected with what effects. No other kind of truth can help for this end; what can be the use of sinking with our mind into an isolated object." The art object, he adds, is merely to be enjoyed, like a sunset. Münsterberg's emphasis is undoubtedly a good one. No one should look to a poem or drama for a direct guide to practical affairs or for strictly factual information. And concentration on an object is possible only if it is seen in relative isolation. But the poem, unlike the sunset, may have a rational content, may imply a point of view, exhibit an attitude. The point of view or attitude quite possibly is completely justified only in the specific context and is not to be taken as a universally valid judgment. It remains in the reader's mind, however, as "information," as a "judgment," as an "attitude." Certainly a poem like *The Waste Land* is a kind of critique upon the modern society. The reading of the poem cannot be isolated. Münsterberg's thesis, it would seem, is valid in so far as the art object is isolated in a way that the object being examined for scientific purposes is not. It is not isolated in the sense that it has no relationship to judgments or values. The poem, as Whitehead might put it, leaves behind a lasting realization, which is a form of knowledge. In attempting to wrest the media of art from the verists, some have come to believe that art experiences can be isolated from all other human experiences.

This emphasis has also been given an exaggerated statement by Clive Bell in his discussions of "significant form." He relates the term, however, only to the visual arts. The import of "significant" is never made clear, but the gist of his thesis is understandable. Genuine art affords an "esthetic emotion" to those who can grasp "significant form." Art, he says, is quite "unrelated to the significance of life," to any of its sentimentalities. "The representative element in a work of art may or may not be harmful; always it is irrelevant. For, to appreciate a work of art we need bring with us nothing from life, no knowledge of its ideas and affairs, no familiarity with its emotions. Art transports us from the world of man's activities to a world of esthetic exaltation." Oddly, when Bell turned to a discussion of literary form, he completely reversed his emphasis.[6] In the work of nineteenth-century figures he mentions he finds "wit, pathos, drama, criticism, didacticism even" to be the "essence of literature." He concludes, strangely, that form is *the* consideration in painting but a negligible concern in literature. But Roger Fry, whose general position was very close, and antecedent, to Bell's, did not exclude literature from his theory of the importance of form. Fry found that the associations we have with "all sorts of objects, persons, and ideas," about which our feelings cling, are so strong that they lead us away from "formal design," which alone is capable of inducing esthetic emotion.

Rhys Carpenter, who accepts, like Bell and Fry, the notion of an "art emotion," sees the matter in a quite different way. He gives equal importance in painting to formal lines and to representational lines. From their fusion "arises a new thing which I call the esthetic or art emotion." He does not attempt somehow to isolate form from the substances from which it is made. "The forms of art, considered in and for themselves, are nearly always trivial and irrelevant." They are to be judged, however, not for what they are but for what they can do. The metrical beat in poetry or the jingle of rhymes is trivial by itself. Employed in poetic lines, either enables the poet to present his object, situation, or insight with appropriate intensity. What the poet is trying to say is as important to the completed poem as the representational line is to the finished painting. Neither will have intensity of itself. Form, that is, serves a purpose. It should not be held an end in itself. In fact, in using the term "form" in this context, we mean simply those techniques of the medium of poetry which make its effects possible.

In stressing the *formal* elements, in recovering the medium, poets and critics since the Symbolists have sometimes tried to isolate art values from human values generally. The break with verism, in other words, has been an effort to purify the medium. In the process the qualities peculiar to the medium have often been overstressed. The Victorians had inclined toward a poetry of explicit statement, employing the medium as sugar coating, while some of the moderns, trying to be virtuosos only, have attempted to extinguish meaning, treating it as a form of impurity. Thus occasional statements have been made which suggest an overemphasis and, when not examined in the light both of qualifying statements and of poetic practice, invite ridicule. They suggest a determination to limit the value of poetry to "esthetic values."

Fry celebrated Stéphane Mallarmé as "the first pure poet." He meant by this that Mallarmé tried to write in such a way as to evoke "esthetic emotion" and to avoid "echoes of the emotions which are aroused by actual life." One of the techniques primary to poetry, of course, is the use of words in such a way as to attain a "maximum of evocative energy," a complex of associations and feelings. This is peculiar to poetry and away from the prose ideal of simple description, narration, or exposition. The latter ideal is concerned with the representation of things in actual life. Rhys Carpenter, we may assume, would say that the two emphases should be joined to create best an art emotion—that poetic language is both *rational* and *evocative*, that the esthetic emotion generated in poetry is dependent upon an esthetic organization of idea and experience (equivalents of the representational in pictorial art). Mallarmé chose to emphasize only the evocative. "Narrer, enseigner, même décrire, cela va. ..." The veristic elements—narration, teaching, even describing—must be played down. Yvor Winters has examined the implications of this position in his *Primitivism and Decadence*. Mallarmé, he says, believed that "words have an obvious (that is, rational) meaning, and a fringe of feeling, which he chooses to call essential." Winters comments that

> if only one kind of content is essential, we are naturally inclined to try to eliminate the other, and we have in this confusion, which reappears spon-

taneously, and without any discernible indebtedness to him, in each successive generation of post-romantic poets, the real basis for post-romantic obscurantism. The sound idea that a poem is more than its rational content is thus perverted and distorted.

Such attempts to divorce esthetic values from more general human values are seen before and after Mallarmé. Théophile Gautier said: "There is nothing really beautiful except what is of no possible use. Everything that is useful is ugly." Rémy de Gourmont stated that style is everything, the subject very little, a remark that apparently inspired Hulme's epigrammatic "literature is the sudden arrangement of commonplaces." If Gourmont had held closely to the implications of his remark, he would have had to conclude that the insights afforded by poets are of equal importance—the way they are stated is everything. The emphasis common to these various statements is caught in little in the frequently quoted remark of Villiers de L'Isle-Adam's Count Axel: "Live? Our servants will do that for us." Even Eliot, at one place, joins in this kind of emphasis. "The chief use of the 'meaning' of a poem, in the ordinary sense, may be (for here again I am speaking of some kinds of poety and not all) to satisfy one habit of the reader, to keep his mind diverted and quiet, while the poem does its work upon him: much as the imaginary burglar is always provided with a bit of nice meat for the house dog." Eliot, of course, qualifies this statement, and an examination of his poetry indicates a primary concern with the problem of values generally, not merely with esthetic values. And in another essay he says: "Swinburne's form is uninteresting because he is literally saying next to nothing." One may conclude that exaggerated statements about form are sometimes made to emphasize the importance of the medium itself, to remind poets and their audience that the poet should not be merely a verist.

Richards points out that these various "isolation" theories of art have held sway for only a relatively short time. "Until Whistler came to start the critical movements of the last half century, few poets, artists or critics had ever doubted that the value of art experiences was to be judged as other values are." He explains the changed view further as due to the influence of German esthetics upon the English mind. These are ways of explaining the phenomenon, but both explanations may be considered as aspects of the break with verism. Artists—with Whistler, rather late, among them—wanted to purify their media. And the estheticians, observing the changing attitude, furnished the theory to rationalize it. The phenomenon is best explained perhaps as an overviolent reaction to certain nineteenth-century artists who too sedulously served the theories of verism.

Artists who seriously question the nature of their medium usually recognize that intimate acquaintance with individuality leads to skepticism about broad rules. It is for this reason, for example, that character as presented by the best dramatists and fiction writers is often very complex and that the many forms of irony play an important part in much of the best poetry. And for this reason, conversely, the poet or artist who holds close to his medium is hated or distrusted by the moralist, the rabid proletarian, and the philistine, none of whom is willing to examine the aspects of the individual case beyond that point where it conflicts with his rigid principles. The poet, attempting to understand and to present the full materiality, the implied contingencies and significance, of his subject is likely to be both more detached and capable of readier sympathies than one who examines it as the poet either of his mores or of his group. No poet, certainly, is purely a creator, just as no genuine poet in any period has been simply a verist. It would seem, however, that the temptation to verism is slightest in periods when the medium is looked upon as emancipated, not narrowly in the service of a mores or a group. The poet who inclines very strongly toward any of the forms of verism necessarily denies himself profundities of subjective experience. And, as has been said in *Ulysses*, the worth of art is dependent upon the depth of life from which it springs.

CHAPTER FOUR

# *The Compromise with Prose*

*In the writing of verse one can only deal with actuality.*—T. S. Eliot

The directions and purposes of modern poetry may be characterized as a break with verism, as an attempt to restore the personal imagination to an important and respected role. Any poetry, however, must take its character, to some extent, from the language and intellectual climate in which it is written. Modern poetry gives evidence that ours is a "scientific" milieu and that our language has been partially formed in the service of science. The chief evidence perhaps lies in the influence of the prose idiom upon poetry. A valuable consequence has been the enlargement and invigoration of the subject matter and a toughening of the idiom of poetry. An unfortunate consequence has been the dissolution, at the hands of some poets, of poetic forms.

To understand something of this history, and for easy textual reference, we may set a passage from Tennyson next to a somewhat comparable passage from Auden:

> In the spring a fuller crimson comes upon the robin's
>   breast;
> In the spring the wanton lapwing gets himself another
>   crest. . . .

And Auden:

> He disappeared in the dead of winter:
> The brooks were frozen, the airports almost deserted,
> And snow disfigured the public statues: . . .

There are two obvious differences between the passages: Tennyson has employed a romantic nature vocabulary, whereas Auden has employed not only a romantic nature vocabulary but contemporary "antipoetic" terms as well. Tennyson has employed a regular metric whereas the music of Auden's lines is achieved despite the flux of prose set over a regular metric. The antipoetic seems closer to the world of prose. Prose and poetry, it would seem, are in some ways closer as genres than they were in the nineteenth century.

Novelists like Virginia Woolf and William Faulkner exhibit a poetic cast of mind and a poetic coloring in their work. Long sections of James Joyce's work can be read as poetry. Poets of various skills, like Pound, Jeffers, and Sandburg, exhibit a prose manner in their verse. A full-scale examination of post-Renaissance cultural history would be necessary, no doubt, to explain the various reasons for these developments. A lessened, or at least a changed, sense of music, for example, may be one explanation of the prose quality of modern poetry.

Edmund Wilson, considering the influence of prose in poetry, makes this observation:

> In the Elizabethan age, the English were extremely musical: the lyrics of Campion could hardly have been composed apart from their musical settings; and Shakespeare's evocation of things seen is always compelling and brilliant; but the objects are more or less liquefied by music, a little like things seen under water. The main stream of English poetry continues to keep fairly close to music through Milton, and even through the less "poetic" Dryden. What has really happened with Pope is that the musical background has ceased to figure and that the ocular sense has grown sharp again. After this, the only music is in lyrics—that is, songs—and it becomes more and more of a trick to be able to write them so that they will seem to be authentic—so that they will sound like something sung.[1]

Wilson's statement does not take adequately into account the music in the songs of Blake and in the long poems of nineteenth-century figures like Tennyson, Swinburne, and Morris. In fact, the problem he raises undoubtedly is extremely complex, to be explained only by close examination of changing cultural patterns.

Alexander Blok, the Russian poet, in an essay on the decline of humanism gave a broad definition to the term "spirit of music." It signifies, he said, the life-impulse that urges one to seek harmony, to recapture a primal kinship with the rhythms of the seasons, of the sea, and of the flight of birds. It signifies a balance of interests and a form of belief which make a large harmony possible. In the early development of new cultures, he said, the ideals and beliefs encourage people to experience the "music" in their daily lives, in their multiple interests, and to express it not only in their human relationships but in their art. Turning to a discussion of the post-Renaissance world, he said that what "went awry was the balance between man and nature, between life and art, science and music, civilization and culture—that balance which was the living strength of the great Humanist movement."

In many Elizabethan plays, particularly in the comedies, one feels the very atmosphere almost to be suffused with music, or as though the spirits of joy and vitality themselves were immanent in them. In Milton, again, there is the timbre that in his longer works changes its resonance and strength but remains constant throughout. The sustained and vibrant music in these instances, although they may be chance products of individual genius, may be also expressions of cultural harmonies and beliefs. If they express the temper and harmonies of a culture, they may be seen to contrast with the kind of harmony expressed in long Victorian poems. The harmony, or music, of most Victorian poetry, it would seem, is not one that arises from the harmonies of a culture. It is an enervated, other-world music, frequently a kind of wail for the imagined world of Arthur and his court. It does not express, in virile forms, a society with a sense of large harmonies. Even the more virile language of Hardy often has its harmony in terms of the *Weltschmerz* that dominated a part of the nineteenth-century literary mind. Sometimes, however, his language is tortured and roughened for the purpose of slowing the reader and making him experience strongly what the poet would have him understand. In this, Hardy, like Hopkins, does not seem to be representative of his period. Modern poetry, like modern music, with its dissonant and cacophonous sounds arises from a more honest admission that post-Renaissance society is somehow out of balance. To put it another way, modern poets broke with a poetry that could express harmony only by ignoring many problems and questions. Therefore, our poetry tends to be analytical, intellectual, and, more recently, conversational. At its best it is a profound criticism of the society.

To put it more bluntly, Victorian poetry, for the most part, had lost its intellectual fiber. Problems with which there was any deep concern were usually treated in prose.[2] What was known as the real world was discussed in prose. If poetry was to recover vitality and intellectual strength, it would, in breaking with Victorian diction and rhythms, have to build upon prose structures. This recognition would appear to explain such concerns as that with vers libre, sprung rhythm, and alliterative verse, all efforts to break with the melodious meters of Tennyson and Swinburne. Auden, to return to our example, has been one of the chief among the later experimenters.

Auden, again, has been among those who brought many of the concerns and much of the vocabulary of prose into poetry. He wrote about his contemporaries, discussed Freud, sociology, and economics either in large abstractions like History, Justice, and Life, or in commonplace references to tennis courts, whirring propellers, and motorcars. In his poetry one could find the modern world as one might actually know it. Auden did these things easily and well. Behind him, however, was a generation of poets who had struggled to free poetry from the Victorian rhythms and idiom.

## 2

The Victorian poet who was concerned to repeat the principles furnished him by his mores inclined to write a descriptive, expository, narrative, or didactic poetry. These were the practical functions of his medium. There was yet another direction, an emphasis upon the dream-reality which the Victorian poet might evoke by employing an exclusionist diction and a misty subject matter.[3] The two emphases are not so contradictory as they appear at first glance. They exhibit the Victorian separation of the heart and head. They imply the rigidity of Victorian categories and the difficulties faced by the poet who wanted to use his medium, uniting thought with feeling and expressing reverie. Its history can be traced from the Keats of "La Belle dame sans merci" through Tennyson Swinburne, Morris, and the Pre-Raphaelites. Thus the young Yeats, the inheritor of the tradition, could say, "All art is dream."

The poetaster, like Arthur O'Shaughnessy, a man, as Leavis points out, with no real sensibility and nothing of his own to communicate, turned quite naturally to the dream-world genre.

> We are the music-makers,
>   And we are the dreamers of dreams,
> Wandering by lone sea-breakers,
>   And sitting by desolate streams;
> World-losers and world forsakers,
>   On whom the pale moon gleams. . . .

T. E. Hulme was among those most articulate about what was wrong with poetry and how a more balanced view of the subject matter and the writing of poetry might be restored. His position comes clear from a comment like this:

> What I mean by classical in verse, then, is this. That even in the most imaginative flights there is always a holding back, a reservation. The classical poet never forgets this finiteness, this limit of man. He remembers always that he is mixed up with the earth. He may jump, but he always returns back; he never flies away into the circumambient gas.

Hulme's objection to a preoccupation with the infinite is a part of the general objection to the dream-world literature. The only way, he believed, to turn poets and their public from the vague and the mysterious was to establish a new convention. This convention, as he defined it, would require poets to employ "accurate, precise, and definite description." It would be an effort "to prove that beauty may be in small dry things."

It does not follow that Hulme had narrowed the problem to accurate description, attained by the employment of ordinary language. The ordinary phrases and the commonplace sequences of words seemed to him singularly inappropriate to poetry. "Never, never, never, a simple statement. It has no effect. One must always have analogies, which make another world. Through-the-glass-effect, which is what I want." Language, he felt, would be strengthened if poets could point to their meaning by indicating new analogies between actual objects. "The process of invention," he said, "is that of gradually making solid the castles in the air," a statement very like Marianne Moore's observation that the poet should put live toads into his imaginary gardens.

Ezra Pound's influence, possibly greater than Hulme's, was in the same direction. "Go in fear of abstractions." And much of his criticism was concerned with the image, its nature and function. Again, Pound emphasized the need for writing poetry out of one's own environment—each "age demands an image." Many in the generation of Hulme and Pound, then, were trying to bring poetry back to the commonplaces of experience.

Pound, with his sense for the startling, dramatized the need for precision in poetry by saying that Ford Madox Ford realized "poetry should be written at least as well as prose." One hesitates to believe that Pound considered Ford an important poet. He was important historically—and it was this which Pound emphasized:

> I find him significant and revolutionary because of his insistence upon clarity and precision, upon the prose tradition; in brief, upon efficient writing—even in verse.

The employment of precise diction was a way of purifying the medium, ridding it of the otiose, poeticisms, and vagueness. A few months after writing about Ford, Pound praised Robert Frost's *North of Boston* for similar reasons:

> Mr. Frost has dared to write, and for the most part with success, in the natural speech of New England; in natural spoken speech, which is very different from the "natural" speech of newspapers, and of many professors.

Frost has consistently held to traditional metrics over which are set conversational rhythms. His diction is further allied to the prose idiom through his dry understatement and economy of phrase. Pound found it necessary to emphasize the prose element in Ford and Frost in order to dissipate the mists which had come to inform and to surround poetry.

The prose language of the Victorians, like that of Mill, Newman, or Huxley, could be precise. But, having developed its character as an analytical instrument, it was not suited for poetic purposes. The poetic language of Eliot, on the contrary, is both precise and suggestive. His meaning is clearly perceivable and at the same time can be *experienced*, felt through the agency of his images and symbols, his employment of paradox, contrasts, and appropriate rhythms. The meanings of Victorian prose writers were clearly perceivable. Yet they could hardly be experienced—they could not, as Eliot might put it, become "states of mind." The diction of Victorian poetry, on the other hand, was not used for analytical purposes. It was used for inducing feelings. In Swinburne and Dante Gabriel Rossetti the tendency achieved its purest expression. "The Pre-Raphaelites," Bateson writes, "do not deal in revelations but in the *feeling* of revelation. There are no statements, in the ordinary sense, in their poems at all. What they communicate, with untiring artistry and superb *élan*, is a state of mind—the state of mind of a dreamer." The two impulses in the Victorian mind were separate. Mill and his fellow prose writers represented the real intelligence of the period. The poet either, like Browning, re-expressed the attitudes and beliefs of the mores or, like Swinburne, withdrew into a misty region of sweet melodies and the feelings that ill-defined phrases might be made to induce. (Even an intelligence like Arnold's was a partial victim of the diction and manner of poetry.) If the poetic revolution was to restore mind to poetry, it had to recover precision, clarity, the power of analysis, and a closeness to the physical world. To do this it had to use, at first, the language of prose. It had, that is, to do in poetry what could be done in prose. Thereafter, it could transmute the language of prose into that of poetry. In turning to the prose idiom, the modern poet could feel himself on surer ground. The temper of the age is "scientific," and its image is prose. In a poetry arising from a prose idiom the poet might achieve his purposes as a poet without foregoing the advantages of prose.

Pound felt it necessary to throw over the whole rhetoric of the Victorian idiom. One could not very well attack Victorian values in the sweet and honeyed language of the dream vision. Before poets could examine our world, they had to have an idiom capable of suggesting the feelings a contemporary has or might have in moving among real objects, in experiencing actual situations. There had to be an idiom composed of words which define solid objects, catch the significance of our reactions, and do so in appropriate rhythms. Pound in "Hugh Selwyn Mauberly" managed such an idiom.

The poems in this sequence cumulatively are an ironic evaluation of the life of a poet, one who has spent his years in search of artistic perfections, in what he sees as a "botched civilization," as "an old bitch gone in the teeth." The critique is neither so complex nor so searching as that of *The Waste Land*. Yet it is an effective indictment of a materialistic society with many tawdry values—

> What god, man or hero
> Shall I place a tin wreath upon?

The idiom for the most part is from contemporary speech. But it is a speech with considerable range, biting, contemptuous, mocking, pathetic, and poignant. Each subject is examined with a kind of objectivity and detachment. Pound's language is concentrated, rarely padded or loose. He uses the vocabulary, even the clichés, of common speech—but incisively, ironically, to intensify his meaning.

It is Eliot, of course, who has done most with the prose idiom, raising it to music and ordering the words and phrases in such ways that new meanings are found and overtones stirred up. Sometimes he uses a learned vocabulary, words which Victorian poets would have thought appropriate only in scholarly treatises. His learned vocabulary is the counterpart of his erudite references. But any subject, any experience, any thought, may be alluded to or drawn into his sensibility. He may refer to the singing of mermaids, smells of steaks in passageways, or a "five per cent Exchequer Bond." In a passage treating of Mme Sosostris and the curious Tarot pack of cards we learn that the "famous clairvoyante"

Had a bad cold

Again, there is the announcement, in colloquial speech, that the pub is closing—

HURRY UP PLEASE ITS TIME

The meaning of the line, in the context of "A Game of Chess," is, of course, twofold—that the pub is closing and that purposeless lives are being used merely to consume time. And, of course, the various conversations reflect the respective social levels of the speakers.

There are still other elements relating Eliot's poetry to a prose idiom. He employs transitional phrases as in

We have been, let us say, to hear the latest
Pole.

Frequently he repeats or plays little variations around a word or idea as people do conversationally.

For I have known them all already, known them all
Have known the evenings, mornings, afternoons. . . .

He has in these lines managed an effective rhythm and evoked a melancholy feeling by repeating vowel sounds, but the surface structure is a prose idiom.

But vocabulary and prose mannerisms alone do not explain the prose element in Eliot's work. His meter completes the pattern. His prosody depends, as he says that of the Metaphysical poets does, on the "constant evasion and recognition of regularity." Even in the "freest" of free verse there should lurk the ghost of some simple meter "which should advance menacingly as we doze, and withdraw as we arouse." The poet, he is saying, should avoid "tom-tom" beats, on the one hand, or the multiple irregularities of prose rhythm, on the other. The modern poet can lean on prose rhythms —he should not be dependent on them. Eliot's are conversational rhythms drawn taut.

Others roughly of an age with Eliot, like Marianne Moore and E. E. Cummings, compromised, each in his own way, with contemporary language. Once poets broke with the Victorian lilt, insubstantial and narrow subject matter, they were forced to examine the objects and concepts of their own time and to examine them in contemporary language.

Marianne Moore not only refused to write an evasive idiom; she even chose a subject matter traditionally reserved for textbooks, the columns of statisticians, or the notebooks of specialists. She chose for the most part a subject matter which had a rigid, exact, or, as she herself said, "literal" objective existence. She is not, however, in the prose tradition of broad abstractions, of easy generalizations. Her generalizations, if stated at all, are seen against the context of conflicting opinions, discriminations, and suggestive metaphor in which they were begotten. Her ideals appear to be those of the prose stylist who is also scholar and critic. Each detail, from the commonplace which is seen as though for the first time to the erudite and exotic, is examined dispassionately.

There is little of the mythmaker about Miss Moore. She does not transcend, at least to any great extent, the categories and stereotypes of the scientific emphasis by creating categories of her own. In her lines the objective world is not to be seen through the distortions of a highly personal imagination. She avoids, on the other hand, the standardized responses and attitudes which many of the objective-minded somewhat naïvely accept as their reasoned opinions. Like them, she holds to the objective world. Her distinction from them rests in her ability to see many facets, to make subtle distinctions, and to project clarifying analogies. She is an objectivist and a precisionist whose feeling for prose rhythms and heightened phrasing and whose ability to isolate key words and images enable her to transform prose into poetry. Even her employment of rhymes seems in imitation of the unwitting use of it in prose. Only occasionally does she use end-stop rhymes or rhyme words which are pivotal in the meaning. They seem, when one is aware of them at all, accidental, as they are in prose.

Morton Zabel, by giving a prose arrangement to one of Miss Moore's poems, shows that her syntax is a prose syntax. Yet without the stanzaic form one is likely to miss much of the exquisite detail, the nuances and studiedly appropriate, conversational and melodious, rhythms. Yeats showed by arranging in verse form lines from the study of the Mona Lisa that Pater, for stylistic purposes, thought in phrases. At least his attention was not on the general thought of his sentence at the expense of the individual word or phrase. Miss Moore, too, regards the thought of her sentence—but not at the expense of any of its parts.

Miss Moore accepts the prose ideal, exactness and strict intellectual control. Her imagination is never indulged for its own sake, nor does she allow—if only, as some artists do, for the sake of contrast with their technical excellence—imperfections a place in her delineations. Hers is a studied excellence, even to the extent that words and objects sometimes seem to be merely *objets d'art*. Yet she has shown that insight and rationality may have a spirit of their own and, when properly objectified, that they may be made into poetry.

E. E. Cummings, too, attempts to catch the surface effects of physical actuality as it appears to him. The language he employs is largely that of contemporary America. In poems like "Portrait" and "Poem, or Beauty Hurts Mr. Vinal" he catches the rhythms of American speech.

> . . . A
> mer
> i
> ca, I
> love,
> You. And there're a
> hun-dred-million-others. . . .

His typography suggests in objective fashion the actual cadences we use. Like Anderson and Hemingway in prose and Sandburg in verse, he knows the American idiom. He is alone perhaps in his ability to indicate its rhythm and stresses. Cummings enables the reader both to see and to hear it.

This is not to say that Cummings transcribes the American scene. He satirizes, adulates, and interprets it. Not least among his contributions is his use of verbs and subordinate parts of speech as nouns. He uses them as a part of his campaign against the prosaic characteristics of existence, against what he calls *un-ness*. It is as though he were saying, look, here are the parts of speech which symbolize your *un-ness*, your acceptance of stereotypes, your myopia, your submission even to language. They are alive if you look clearly at them, feel them, and imagine them in new contexts.

> My father moved through dooms of love
> through sames of am through haves of give,
> this motionless forgetful where
> turned at his glance to shining here . . .
>
> and should some why completely weep
> my father's fingers brought her sleep. . . .

Commenting on this poem, Theodore Spencer has said: "In an age when language tends to become platitudinous and anemic, it is a splendid thing to have a poet take the most colorless words of all . . . and suddenly give them character and responsibility." Cummings accepts, as it were, the prose character of our language and life and shows that they need not fix our lives and character.

## *3*

The compromise with prose implies, it is evident, what estheticians have called a "reformulation of the differentia of art." An aspect of this reformulation is the new realism, or naturalism, somewhat romanticized and sentimentalized, associated with the "Chicago Renaissance." The poets in it, Carl Sandburg and Edgar Lee Masters among them, broke much more sharply, in a sense, with the Victorian theories of the beautiful than did the poets in the tradition of Pound and Eliot. And in the effort to emphasize the realistic they slighted the esthetic. Their work, indicating only an incidental concern with form, is much more literally in a prose idiom.

The "real" for these poets is likely to be the isolated incident or surface history. In lieu of the delicate, they usually offer the muscular. Nuance and subtle insight are sacrificed to directness and physical immediacy. Thus Sandburg's lines from "Jazz Fantasia"—

> Moan like an autumn wind high in the lonesome
> treetops, moan soft like you wanted somebody
> terrible, cry like a racing car slipping away
> from a motorcycle-cop, bang-bang!

Or Masters' from "The Hill"—

> Where are Elmer, Herman, Bert, Tom and Charley
> The weak of will, the strong of arm, the clown,
>   the boozer, the fighter?
> All, all, are sleeping on the hill

Sandburg's long sentences, loosely strung, seem intended merely to hold together the details which impinge upon his sensibility. The details have their relevance in relation to the feelings they arouse in Sandburg. In the lines quoted, the motive behind the selection (hardly the ordering) of detail appears to be his zest for violence. There is no intellectual evaluation, no analysis of his materials. There is, of course, a socialist emphasis which occurs occasionally in his work. But it does not come into clear focus against the objects and situations which most stir his sensibilities. Object and idea do not sustain each other. Form is the objectification of idea, and its excellence, it would seem, depends upon its appropriateness to the idea. Eliot's "I have measured out my life with coffee spoons" may be taken as an instance of appropriate form. It unifies several strands of Prufrock's thought, giving it, too, emotional strength. For the poet, like Sandburg, who is objectifying large emotions, there can hardly be appropriate form. In other words, there has to be precision of thought before there can be appropriateness of form. A loose prose idiom is for Sandburg most "appropriate."

Masters, too, prefers the immediate magic of physical reality, as Conrad Aiken long ago observed, "to what is indefinitely called the sense of beauty." In his most compelling work Masters is concerned with human actions. His "facts" are those of the naturalistic storyteller. It seems merely accidental that he chose verse as his medium. "He is by nature extremely loquacious and discursive—it appears to be painful for him to cut down to mere essentials—and prose would seem to be a more natural medium for such a mind."

It is hard to agree with Aiken, however, that Masters' poetry is the result of a "cold hunger" for understanding human character. None of his characters are more than types. He evidences no insight into the complexities of character. He merely accepts the formulas of reductive naturalism which gave such a uniform grayness and deadliness of tone to much fiction in the twenties. He is Sherwood Anderson in verse. Ironically, when Masters attempted lyric writing, he was quite as Victorian in manner as any of his Georgian contemporaries. Sandburg's sensibility has a far greater range than that of Masters.

The unwillingness of Sandburg and Masters to use a tighter prosody is a part of their uneasiness with form. Rhythm, properly controlled, is among the chief techniques the poet may employ for precise expression. If the subject matter and consequent emotions of their poetry are ill defined, there can be no appropriate metric. A frankly prose rhythm is inevitable. Unfortunately, this is sometimes rationalized, in free-verse discussions, as a preferable form by those who do not recognize the place of analysis in poetry. The analytical mind makes insights possible. And these insights are turned into "states of mind" when caught in appropriate rhythms.

The irony inherent in the overthrow of Victorian metrics in favor of completely free verse is that one form of sensibility largely divorced from intelligence was being substituted for another. If the greatest precision in capturing idea, mood, tone, and emotion is possible in prose rhythms, then the poetic forms, quite obviously, need not be employed at all.

The developments of the Imagists and Objectivists gave further impetus to experiments with the prose idiom, both in rhythms and in the physical reality of their subject matters. Amy Lowell, John Gould Fletcher, Richard Aldington, and F. S. Flint were most explicit about their vers libre, which they defined as the marriage of prose and verse rhythms. They emphasized the term "cadence," the natural rhythmic flow of the language. (The emphasis was not new, as Eliot pointed out. Appropriate rhythms might be irregular, as they were in some earlier English poetry. But there was no such thing as "free" verse. Lines written without a conventional metrical pattern are not really verse; freedom, he said, "is only truly freedom when it appears against the background of an artificial limitation.") And the Imagists believed, as Fletcher put it, that in poetry as many gradations in cadence are possible as there are in musical time. The metric the Imagists talked so much about may not have been new, but it implied that poets were searching for more subtly appropriate rhythms. Again, verse metric and prose metric were consciously brought together.

Other emphases of the Imagists caused less of a furor, but they, too, were a part of the general effort to come to terms with the "real" world. They wanted poets to use a diction composed of words from common speech, to write about any subject matter, and to avoid what Hulme called "cosmic poetry." Their principles are operative in much of the best work of poets like Pound, Eliot, and Marianne Moore.

The principles of the Objectivists were far narrower than those of the Imagists. These principles, at least as stated by Louis Zukofsky in *An Objectivist Anthology*, seem mere parodies of the modern fallacy that individual facts, *particulars*, are ultimate knowledge. "It is impossible," Zukofsky writes, "to communicate anything but particulars." The long poem, "Prolegomena to a Theodicy" by Kenneth Rexroth, illustrates the theory. There are lists of unrelated or only slightly related images—

> The revealing eye
> The crazed pane
> The revelation of the lamp
> The golden uncials
> The revelation of the mirror. . . .

And so on. Sometimes, of course, there is more than a catalogue of objects—but almost never does the poet suggest an insight in terms of his object. It is a drugged, curiously nihilistic kind of poetry, in which people, as in this poem by William Carlos Williams, live but have no meaning—

> On hot days
> the sewing machine whirling
> in the next room
> in the kitchen

and men at the bar
  talking of the strike
  and cash.

The ideal of objectivity, the presentation of uninterpreted facts, reaches its *reductio ad absurdum.* The Objectivists not only compromise with the prose ideal; they turn their medium over unquestioningly to its service. The poet as *maker* abdicates. He merely objectifies the external world in his poetry.

CHAPTER FIVE

# *The Influence of the Symbolists*

*La poésie en Amérique aujourd'hui parle français.*—RENÉ TAUPIN

THE influence of French symbolism upon modern English and American poetry is difficult to assess because it is all but impossible to follow a specific influence through the unique and subtle transformations it undergoes in a poet's mind. One may merely note the most obvious borrowings and surface similarities. The profound influence which one can hardly note, however, may work indirectly, possibly, even, in ways the borrowing poet does not fully understand or acknowledge to himself. Again, a small aspect of any poet's work—a way of shifting accents, a preponderance of certain vowel sounds, a way of subtly relating connotations, etc.—may be borrowed and then absorbed into what is generally a quite different esthetic. The influence of Poe, for example, through Baudelaire and the Symbolists, returned to modern American poetry in a concretized language which is quite different from Poe's own vagueness.

The debt of modern poets to the nineteenth-century French group and their successors is nonetheless real and significant.[1] Despite the appearance in the mid-nineties of a movement self-styled "American symbolism," the actual use of Symbolist techniques did not begin until the second decade of the new century. In 1912 Amy Lowell's first published collection, *A Dome of Many-coloured Glass*, shows a faint reflection of the poetic practices of men like Francis Jammes, Albert Samain, and Henri de Régnier. With the formulation of Imagist principles, however, modern American and English poetry began to show a clearer relationship to symbolism. Pound, one of the most influential though not the first of the spokesmen, wanted to purge poetry of nonessentials, to render language precise, vision distinct, and thought concentrated into image. This, too, was the program set forth by T. E. Hulme, the English critic, who had gone deeply into current French poetic theory and practice and who shared, in the main, Rémy de Gourmont's critical theories. It is fundamentally from Gourmont, particularly from his *Problème du style*, that the important precepts for Imagist and Imagist-influenced poetry came: the idea that an analogy should be free from the rigors of the reason, that an image should be fused from two different things seized upon by the imagination, and that the style is primary, the subject secondary. The Imagists, however, never really employed symbols in the Symbolist sense, having been concerned primarily with the precise rendering of a natural object, especially as that object appears to the eye, and so were, indeed, nearer to the French Parnassians (except for vers libre experiments) with their emphasis upon an austere, objective art devoid of practical intent and devoid of romantic self-revelation. The French Symbolists, in spite of many differences in theory and technique, were agreed in the use of the natural object as a symbol, to make it, that is, the means whereby the reader moves toward the mystery and suggestiveness which inhere in it and lie beyond it. This is not to say that the object is always presented explicitly and cannot be misunderstood by the reader. By the Symbolists, words were used not for their representational value but to create states of mind. A portion of the manifesto as stated in *Figaro* (1886) commits the Symbolist poet to the tenet that "all concrete phenomena are mere sensory appearances destined to represent their esoteric affinities with primordial Ideas." The philosophy is strongly reminiscent of the Neo-Platonic writers of the Renaissance, but the symbols are not their traditional ones. The use of all known objects as symbols with private meanings and significances was the first major step toward the obscurity that became a distinguishing characteristic of Symbolist poetry. The next step was the endeavor to employ synaesthesia, whereby all sense perception is interchangeable and unified. The third step was to dispense with logical sequence, in order to allow the extra-rational faculties and experiences full play in poetic expression.

Stéphane Mallarmé illustrates the vagueness and fleeting quality of the sense perception in Symbolist poetry as opposed to the exact perception of the Imagists (although Mallarmé is capable, in such a poem as "Herodiade," of the severe architectural design the Imagists desired):

SOUPIR

Mon âme vers ton front où rêve, ô calme soeur,
Un automne jonché de taches de rousseur
Et vers le ciel errant de ton oeil angélique
Monte, comme dans un jardin mélancolique,
Fidèle, un blanc jet d'eau soupire vers l'Azur!
—Vers l'Azur attendri d'Octobre pâle et pur
Qui mire aux grands bassins sa langueur infinie
Et laisse, sur l'eau morte où la fauve agonie
Des feuilles erre au vent et creuse un froid aillon,
Se traîner le soleil jaune d'un long rayon.

It is translated by Roger Fry:

SIGH

My soul towards your brow where dreams, my calm sister,
An autumn scattered with freckles of russet
And the wandering heaven of your angelic eye
Mounts up as in some melancholical gardens
Faithful, a white jet sighs towards the Azure!
—Towards October's tender, pure and pale Azure
Which reflects in great basins its infinite languor
And lets, on dead water where the tawny death-throes
Of leaves wander windswept and scoop a cold furrow,
The yellow sun creep of a long-drawn-out ray.

The technique in its general aspects is readily enough defined. Mallarmé contemplates his subject, in this instance a sigh, finding in it many ordinarily unsuspected relationships. "His poetry," says Roger Fry, "is the unfolding of something implicit in the theme." He inclines to repeat certain terms, like *Azur*, which he believed have an incantatory power. His symbols or images suggest the mood and tone but lack a precise definition of their own. The imagery becomes meaningful only when we grasp the theme of the poem. Lastly, Mallarmé used words for their connotative rather than for their denotative meaning. "Straight denotation," Francis Golffing writes, "was incompatible with the language of poetry, for *poetry should not attempt to communicate rational experiences*. For the latter purpose, prose was the proper vehicle; verse should carry with it the vagueness of dream and create in the reader a state of enchantment. Hence the numerous incantatory lines in Mallarmé, which though not wholly without meaning need the support of the context to be clearly apprehended." The successful writing of such poetry depends, it would seem, upon how coherently the poet can arrange his own highly personal associations with the implications of his subject and at the same time offer his reader sufficient clues so that he can discover the coherence for himself.

H. D. in "Pear Tree" illustrates the objective, precisely rendered description that was the aim of the Imagist group:

Silver dust
lifted from the earth,
higher than my arms reach,
you have mounted. . . .

O white pear,
your flower-tufts,
thick on the branch,
bring summer and ripe fruits
in their purple hearts.

It is evident, even from such slight examples, that the Symbolist poet gains in range and multiplicity of impressions through using a succession of images and through following their implications as these are organized in terms of the personal associations and meanings the highly subjective mind of the poet gives them. Beside such poetry, the clarity and completeness of the *one* image faithfully presented in and for itself seems a strangely shrunken sort of art. Yet the insistence of Gourmont upon the exact word possibly helped cause the second-generation Symbolists to move toward the *real* rather than continue in the Baudelairean tradition of using symbols for their "liberating value," of probing subjective levels of consciousness and unconsciousness for poetic material. It is ironical that Gourmont should have played the role he did, since it is he who so stresses the importance of the *vision* element in poetic composition, pleading with the poet to raise his perception of the natural object and the actual experience to the level of a vision. (Quite possibly Eliot's concern with the precise image that is also unconsciously general is his answer to Gourmont's demands.)

The Symbolist conception in the 1880's of the symbol as the essence of poetry was, of course, related to the modern psychological notion that the symbol is the prime expression of the unconscious, the emotional. In the pure sciences the atomistic nature of life was being revealed; and in philosophy, especially in that of Bergson, intuition was considered a mode of metaphysical perception and reason was being relegated to the sphere of the merely practical. These parallel developments in the intellectual milieu, expressing themselves most noticeably in the idealism of late nineteenth-century philosophy, were supporting arguments for the role that French symbolism had assigned itself—that of being a mystic revelation of the universe. The Baudelairean idea of breaking up the world of appearances and rearranging its fragments according to a new order determined by the mind and sensibility of the artist who is seeking a superior reality is, according to Georges Lemaître, the basis for all the developments in modern art.[2] From this plane, where literary art attempts to solve one of the profoundest problems—the nature of reality itself—French symbolism rapidly devolved into mere estheticism, into a cult of literary technicians. So extremely subtle had to be the ways of following in words and rhythm the elusive movements of the subconscious, of the imagination freed from the rigidity of reason, that an overconcern with the medium, a fascination with the virtuosity necessary to capturing a new vision of the universe, developed quite naturally in the Symbolist group. Consequently, a too narrowly esthetic emphasis, the public-be-damned attitude, and a toying with obscurity for its own sake reach their ultimate and inevitable end in the Dadaists.

The poetry of Pound, and that of the Imagists generally, owed something to the Symbolist experiments with metrics. The free verse, by which they stirred so much controversy, was little like the rhetorical, ocean-rhythms of Whitman. The theories behind this free verse come, René Taupin says, from Vildrac and Duhamel's *Notes sur la technique poétique*. The principle is that of a concern for accent, not the counting of syllables—the count of ear, not eye. Attendant upon such scansion came a freer syntax, an emphasis upon cadence. Pound looked especially to Gourmont for instruction in versification, believing that he knew more about it than "anyone alive." Gourmont's *Livre des litanies* was especially fruitful to English-speaking poets interested in the metrical discoveries of the French Symbolists. But, in this connection, Edmund Wilson's comments upon the American Francis Vielé-Griffin's importance as an innovator reveal the obvious nature of free verse:

> He had succeeded in wrecking once for all the classical Alexandrine, hitherto the basis of French poetry—or rather, as an English reader at once recognizes, he had dispensed with it altogether and begun writing English metres in French. The French called this "*vers libre*," but it is "free" only in the sense of being irregular, like many poems of Matthew Arnold and Browning.

Vers libre, then, for English poets, was nothing new. *Ripostes* reveals Pound's mastery of the Symbolist technique of establishing a perfect harmony between cadence and vision. Especially does Pound employ Henri de Régnier's pattern of resting long, regular lines on shorter ones as a hinge. In "The Return" and "The Alchemist" Pound is using rhythms learned from Régnier and Gourmont, respectively, as Taupin shows by extensive quotation. Later, as Pound turned from imagism to vorticism, he turned too from the French lyricists who had served as his masters earlier to find in Tailhade, Corbière, and Laforgue the style of the ironist he has become by the time of *Lustra* (1917). The trenchant, "sawtooth" effect of Corbière, fashioned upon the use of many consonants, becomes his ideal. This stanza from *Les Amours jaunes* is somewhat illustrative:

> Ange, viens pour ton hère
> Jouer à la misère
>       Des dieux!
> Pauvre diable à ficelles,
> Lui, joue avec tes ailes,
>       Aux cieux!

Pound admired in Tailhade what he called the "prose quality of poetry." The best-known work of Tailhade was in conventional rhythm (and even rhyme), but its syntax is that of prose.

Much has been made by critics of the importance of Laurent Tailhade, Tristan Corbière, and Jules Laforgue in the formulation of the conversational ironic genre in modern poetry, particularly Eliot's. Students of symbolism have noted that Eliot's diction in "Rhapsody on a Windy Night" and "Gerontion" is much like that of Corbière. (Interestingly enough, other influences upon "Gerontion"—certain Jacobean dramatists, *The Education of Henry Adams*, and possibly Newman—can be established quite as readily.) Yet Eliot's irony is less the play on words that Laforgue's is than the irony of situation, and it has little of the attention to self, the subjective lyricism of Laforgue. Treating the same themes as Laforgue—the streets of a great city, the manners, drawing-room affairs, and trivial intercourse of a society, with the central focus a human being and his passions—Eliot has, we feel, the more complete vision (close to Baudelaire's demonic city), the more telling historical sweep and contrasts, and the more finished art. The tone of a few of Eliot's French poems and of his "La Figlia che piange" is like that of Laforgue, but it is only in a poem like "Conversation galante" that his Laforguean manner is the dominant impression. And Eliot turned to Corbière and to Laforgue because, as he himself admits, he found them nearer to the poetic school of Donne than were any of his own English contemporaries.

In the Sweeney poems, too, there is a resemblance to the work of other French Symbolists, early and late. For instance, André Salmon's "La Maison du veuf" and Guillaume Apollinaire's "Tiresias" have a decided kinship to the group. Salmon's penchant for strange, violent facts, for situations symbolic of modern restlessness, is shared by Eliot. Apollinaire's use of café talk, overheard and shuffled around, objects like tobacco tins or newspaper headlines, his abrupt changes of time and place, and his juxtaposing of diverse objects are familiar techniques in Eliot's poetry. Both poets, Eliot and Apollinaire, depend upon an orthodox rhythm, created for special effects; but that, of course, is true of many other modern poets.

Hart Crane, though he read French only slightly, studied Rimbaud and Laforgue. By the time his "In Shadow" was published in the *Little Review* in 1917, Crane had passed beyond imagism and had become more of a Symbolist. In "Repose of Rivers" Taupin finds echoes of *Une saison en enfer* and in "Voyages" echoes of "Bateau ivre."

In "Voyages II," for example, some of the techniques and effects developed by certain Symbolists are readily evident. The theme is quite simple—that the sea as a symbol of eternity suggests the relationship of man to the flux of nature into which he will be reabsorbed.

And yet this great wink of eternity,
Of rimless floods, unfettered leewardings,
Samite sheeted and processioned where
Her undinal vast-belly moonward bends,
Laughing the wrapt inflections of our love;

Take this Sea, whose diapason knells
On scrolls of silver snowy sentences,
The sceptred terror of whose sessions rends
As her demeanors motion well or ill,
All but the pieties of lovers' hands.

And onward, as bells off San Salvador
Salute the crocus lustres of the stars,
In these poinsettia meadows of her tides,—
Adagios of islands, O my Prodigal,
Complete the dark confessions her veins spell.

Mark how her turning shoulders wind the hours,
And hasten while her penniless rich palms
Pass superscription of bent foam and wave,—
Hasten, while they are true,—sleep, death, desire,
Close round one instant in one floating flower.

Bind us in time, O Seasons clear, and awe.
O minstrel galleons of Carib fire,
Bequeath us to no earthly shore until
Is answered in the vortex of our grave
The seal's wide spindrift gaze toward paradise.

The "cumulative effect," to use Fry's term, is not simple. The elements of the poem, emphasizing and merging with one another, objectify the theme. The sea, from which life springs, is in its impersonality, vastness, and annihilating power a good symbol of eternity. Yet, compared with eternity, it is merely a "great wink." The second line is an exploration of its vastness. Thereafter the poem investigates the sea, and, by implication, life, as flux. The glistening water suggests happiness and love, as well as terror; only love endures. The sea is prodigal in throwing up life, in change, and in taking away. Death in the sea is appropriate because the "meaning" of existence is flux. The last line is a statement, a kind of cosmic irony, of the always unanswered question.

Like Mallarmé, Crane uses images which merge with one another and dissolve, only to recur in other forms or by implication. The values of life and the final peace are suggested in the recurring flower imagery. Whiteness, a symbol both of happiness and of terror, is explicitly and implicitly employed—"Samite sheeted," "scrolls of silver snowy," "lustres of the stars," "spindrift," etc. The meaning is sustained obliquely and in the overtones. Like Baudelaire, Crane suggests the unifying power of the mind by the use of synaesthetic meanings. The sea laughs and gives forth a full diapason of sound over its written sentences. The specific and sometimes warm associations around words like "sessions," "demeanors," "Adagios," or "Bequeath," are used to enrich strange contexts. New qualities in experience are thereby discovered. Like the more ironic Symbolists, he uses economy of phrase ("sceptred terror") and paradox ("penniless rich"). The complexity of the entire poem raises the relatively simple meaning above mere statement, into esthetic experience. Many "obscure" poets, from Tate through John Wheelwright and Randall Jarrell, employ an esthetic in many ways similar to that of Crane.

Marianne Moore's exquisite discrimination in describing the world of art objects and catching subtle distinctions in human motives and actions seems to invite the finding of French models for her art, at least for its beginnings. Mallarmé, Rimbaud, and Laforgue have been suggested—but no case for their influence upon her can be easily established. She has the chaste intellectual and architectural precision that Mallarmé sometimes shows, without his music. Again, her work, in its epigrammatic terseness, is toward, not away from, rational control. Her sense for strong but delicate imagery and her intellectual resilience ally her to the later Symbolists. Yet these comments seem to be but the finding of excellences common to many different poets rather than any indication of the specific indebtedness of Miss Moore to the French group. Undoubtedly, she knows French poetry well and finds the techniques of certain of the French Symbolists congenial to her own practice, but apparently she is not greatly indebted to any one of them. (Her influence, in turn, may be traced in the poetry of Elizabeth Bishop.)

The exoticism, elegance, and keen awareness in the poetry of Wallace Stevens suggest the Gallic exquisiteness of taste commonly found in such "ivory tower" figures as Gautier, Mallarmé, Gourmont, Villiers de L'Isle-Adam, and the Comte de Lautréamont. Surely Stevens' subtlety is his own, but his knowledge of Symbolist poetry, especially Mallarmé's, quickened and refreshed his imagination and subtilized his phrasing, which is French in its rapid movement, its exclamatory and quizzical temper.[3] The sudden oscillations between joy and anger, the "bite" of even the briefest lyric, are akin to sensibilities expressing themselves in French Symbolist poetry. Even Taupin, however, does not press French influence in the case of Marianne Moore and Wallace Stevens. For William Carlos Williams he finds no French antecedents, merely a relationship with the Imagists.

The initial indebtedness of E. E. Cummings to the *Calligrammes* of Guillaume Apollinaire seems quite evident. The typography Cummings employs, however, has become for him the one way to express his insights and intense feelings. Through long association and the discovery of new usages the manner and method have become his own. The informing spirit is his. The externalities of the form merely remind us of the initial indebtedness.

The various influences of the Symbolists are so thoroughly imbedded in the matrix of the work done by the younger poets that nothing much is proved by indicating the specific or general indebtedness. It is relatively easy, on the other hand, to indicate ways in which the influences still operate. George Marion O'Donnell, in stating his indebtedness in matters of technique, states the general indebtedness of his contemporaries:

> It happens that for me, as for a great many other writers, the most usable poetic strategy is a modification of the French symbolist technique to the Anglo-American literary tradition.

Josephine Miles, for example, has learned both the Metaphysical and Symbolist techniques. Whatever her specific indebtedness may be, she has circumscribed the area in which she allows herself to work. Her subjects, never "large" ones, tend to grow from slight objects or situations against which her observation is held steadily but obliquely in focus. The Symbolist technique is uppermost in a poem like "Opal":

> The steamfitter had no notion of buying an opal,
> But a stone comes sudden in its meaning often.
>
> He looked for a new watch, that part of his life,
>   there was none,
> He had to furnish his own time sense.
>
> But this opal. Fire of time that burned in the
>   antique reaches,
> Roman omen, power of the sooth.
>
> How comes so much straight evil into an opal?
> Fix on a streak of bad luck, it goes out.
>
> How come so much red, then green, in an opal?
> There aren't these colors in a glass of milk.
>
> His wife didn't want the jewel but he bought it
> And took that burden on, which fate forbore.

No conscious influences seem to have gone into the poem. Yet it could hardly have been written had not Miss Miles learned her craft after the Symbolists had been studied by American poets. And, similarly, so excellent a poem as her "The Sun Is a Reagent" could have been written only by one who had learned the techniques of the Metaphysical poets.

One may point up the indirect way in which the Symbolist influence still functions (as one of many influences) by suggesting the relation between Hart Crane and Karl Shapiro. Shapiro, like Crane, has reacted strongly to the effects of city living (as did Baudelaire, Laforgue, and Apollinaire), to the dulled sensibilities, the frustrations, and the vulgarity; both have caught the sour little bars, the depression and unspoken horror of the slums, the pawnshops, the congested streets and alleys. And, coincidentally, they both associate the eeriness of Poe, who foretold the effects of the machine on the individual, with the slums of the eastern city. Apparently a certain kinship of sensibilities has operated in drawing Shapiro to Crane's work, just as a similar kinship drew Crane to the poetry he could find by Rimbaud and Laforgue.

One critic has said that Crane's "Idiot" is indebted to Laforgue. It so happens that Shapiro in his excellent "Mongolian Idiot" seems indebted to Crane for a part of his subject matter. In this instance we have a neat though tenuous illustration of the continued influence of the Symbolist poets. (Allen Tate's "Idiot" is also obviously modeled upon Crane's, even though Tate's surpasses Crane's in subtlety and sustained mood.) One infers the influence from such similarities as these: in both poems the idiot plays with children's toys, in one poem he is "Fumbling his sex," while in the other he is "Not ever father and never quite a son," etc. But the theme is handled differently by each poet, probably more movingly by Shapiro. Quite likely Shapiro was unaware that in "Mongolian Idiot" he was even remotely indebted to a poem by Laforgue.

Undoubtedly, however, it is unimportant that a specific subject matter originating with a French poet has been used by several American poets. The important matter is that Crane, whether from direct readings in Rimbaud or Laforgue (Tate, his friend, said he read some French, though neither critically nor systematically) or from Edith Sitwell, Stevens, or Eliot, developed a style indebted to the Symbolists. "He shares with Rimbaud," Tate wrote in the Introduction to *White Buildings*, "the device of oblique presentation of theme. The theme never appears in explicit statement. It is formulated through a series of complex metaphors which defy a paraphrasing of the sense into an equivalent prose." It is a poetry of great internal excitement, with strange new meanings being evolved in terms of the metaphors and newly discovered connotations. Crane, undoubtedly, needed to discover the Symbolists in order to free his imagination. Once he had learned the possibilities in his medium, he no longer needed them as models. Shapiro, in turn, we may assume, learned, in part, from Crane the ways in which imagination can inform a word or quicken an object into metaphor.

Through these French poets and theorists, the modern English-speaking poet could repossess the lyrical subjectivism of the native Romantic tradition without its uncritical self-revelation and its naïve lack of self-knowledge. Baudelaire, Rimbaud, and Laforgue, with their awareness of the deeper levels of the life of the ego, its evil and its irrationality, had followed upon Shelley's optimism, Wordsworth's conventional dedication to poetry as a means of moral safety, and Keats's groping toward a complete esthetic. The English and American poet in studying these French writers knew it was possible to repossess the mystery, the emotional and sensory content and organization of poetry, without having to sacrifice the intellectual firmness and satiric power which the earlier Romantics had found incompatible with their revolt against the eighteenth-century esthetic and without, on the other hand, falling back upon the explicit language of prose. The conscious intellectuality which Mallarmé, Laforgue, and Paul Valéry brought to the criticism and composition of poetry has helped to give to the poets of our time a poetry of high wit and seriousness and to check Victorian tendencies toward solemnity, vague emotionalism, and, often, mere fatuousness.

The symbol, as Mallarmé observed, is the way in which the synthesis of all the meanings and levels of perception may be set down, in a way that explicit commentary cannot do. Symbolization in poetry is the way of getting the utmost complexity, the farthest range, and the most nearly complete degree of feeling and gradations of meaning into language. The way of symbolization is also the way of reconciling the contradictory roles of intelligence and inspiration in the process of poetic composition. The English Romantics had placed the intelligence at the mercy of the poetic "demon," but the best Symbolist technique requires the intelligence to pattern the life of the imagination into highly conscious and concentrated art.

CHAPTER SIX

# *The Influence of the Metaphysicals*

*Something . . . happened to the mind of England between the time of Donne or Lord Herbert of Cherbury and the time of Tennyson and Browning; it is the difference between the intellectual poet and the reflective poet.*—T. S. ELIOT

THE influence of the Metaphysicals upon modern poets, which has been carefully studied and documented, is held by many critics to be no less significant than that of the Symbolists. Certain elements of these separate influences, in fact, are very similar if not identical. Eliot has pointed out that some of the French poets "are nearer to the 'school of Donne' than any modern English poet." The influences have merged and tended to lose their definable character in the modern idiom. And, to repeat, it is usually impossible to follow an "influence" through the maturing mind and the transforming imagination of a poet. It is possible only to suggest certain obvious effects of the rediscovery, by the generation of Eliot, of the Metaphysicals.

The conscious awareness by modern poets of the need for a blend of passion and thought in poetry goes back undoubtedly to Eliot's essays in his *Homage to John Dryden.* There he had pointed out that in Donne one might find a "direct sensuous apprehension of thought, or a recreation of thought into feeling." And it is this idea, as George Williamson observed in *The Talent of T. S. Eliot*, which "governs Eliot's poetic method and range of material found in his poetry." Nothing, he adds, seems to have influenced Eliot's work more than his recognition that "the poets of the seventeenth century . . . possessed a mechanism of sensibility which could devour any kind of experience." The rediscovery of Donne, that is, enabled modern poets to see more clearly the forms of English poetry which they inherited.

It then became apparent, to some, at least, that certain forces had operated in the interval since Donne to the detriment of poetry. Thought, in the service of scientific abstraction, had been separated from feeling. An absolute separation is, of course, all but impossible —but the effort to separate them had occurred, with several consequences. Intelligence, or rationality, was held to be viable only in the language of abstractions. The image and symbol, to which many meanings and connotations adhere, and in terms of which these meanings may be *emotionally experienced*, became suspect. The poet living in a milieu in which scientific language was believed to be *the* vehicle whereby reality might be discovered was encouraged to use images and symbols merely for decoration. Secondly, a poetry from which intellectual concerns had been withheld naturally developed, tending more and more toward an evanescent, dreamworld subject matter. Lastly, what may be called a feeling for categories developed. That is, categories tended to be seen as absolutes. High seriousness was high seriousness, the ugly was the ugly, the delicate was the delicate—each having, as it were, an eternal character. Donne and some of his contemporaries had perceived that the edges of certain attitudes seem to have a way of dissolving and flowing into other "opposed" attitudes. Wit, for example, was not restricted to a light subject matter but could give intensity to the most serious concerns; love could be at once physical and spiritual; or the ugly could serve an esthetic function quite as powerfully as the delicate could.[1] The recognition of the nature of the creative processes of the Metaphysical poets, however, helped to make evident that the native tendency of the poet's mind is to absorb varied and heterogeneous experiences.

"Donne introduced," Eliot says, "the natural or conversational style, which the Elizabethans at their best had excelled in producing in a highly sophisticated metric of blank verse, into the lyric; he first made it possible to think in lyric verse." In this one statement Eliot has included several very significant elements in his poetic theory. The employment of a "natural" or "conversational style" implies that the subject matter, too, is from a real, everyday world, not from a circumscribed area arbitrarily held to be "poetic." The "sophisticated metric" was among the techniques for raising the language to poetry. And, of course, the intellectual quality he emphasizes recovers the lyric at one stroke from the vague realm of sheer feeling. This statement of Eliot's implies his more embracing statement already quoted—that in Donne and certain others among the Metaphysicals there is "a direct sensuous apprehension of thought, or a recreation of thought and feeling." This understanding, it would appear, is the controlling principle behind Eliot's criticism and poetic practice. Because of Eliot's influence it has become, as well, a controlling principle in much modern poetry.

Hi Simons found (and probably overstressed) in the poetry of Wallace Stevens a certain kinship with that of the Metaphysicals, although he did not know, he said, of any evidence that Stevens "has been influenced by Donne and his successors." Simons found certain statements written about the "unified sensibility" of some of the Metaphysicals to be an exact description of Stevens' identification of ideas with figures—"to think them is also to feel them." Stevens' chief themes, concerned with the artist and society and with imagination and reality, are philosophical. But the expression is frequently in terms of repeated symbols, like music and the moon to symbolize imagination, and in terms of what Simons calls the "radical metaphor," the technique of using figures as discourse rather than embellishment of and forcing their implications to the utmost. Again, Stevens' lines are frequently witty, exhibiting a graceful yet serious irony. His is a poetry of good manners and of facility that is moored to intellect. In being among the very first to write intellectual lyrics, Stevens became "one of the originators of the metaphysical trend in the poetry of our time." In Stevens, as in Eliot, the intellectuality of the Metaphysicals is conjoined with the Symbolist language of implication.

The sudden contrasts, too, which Eliot finds necessary function somewhat like the conceit. Both, when appropriate, startle one into qualifying or changing attitudes; they make new recognitions possible and deepen older awareness. Their startling quality—as in Donne's "a bracelet of bright hair about the bone"—can clarify an old understanding that has become separated, as it were, from our sensibilities. We learn, that is, by perceiving and experiencing significant differences.

In discussing Donne, Eliot says that "a style, a rhythm, to be significant, must embody a significant mind," and, in discussing Marvell, he emphasizes that intellectual agility makes possible "an alliance of levity and seriousness (by which the seriousness is intensified)." These and similar statements he has made emphasize the need the poet has, particularly in a complex and confused society, for a mature and analytical mind, one that is capable of evaluating an experience in the light of "other kinds of experience which are possible." Wit is at once the intellectual agility that makes such evaluation possible, and the successful fusion of elements ordinarily considered foreign to each other, by which new attitudes are suggested. Brooks goes so far as to say that

> wit, far from being a playful aspect of the mind, is the most serious aspect, and that the only poetry which possesses high seriousness in the deepest sense is the poetry of wit. But some obvious reservations are to be made and some misapprehensions anticipated. We have defined wit in its most general terms. The wit of Donne or a Marvell is after all only one form, and an extreme form, which wit may take. There are obviously many fine poems, including some of Arnold's, which are not "witty" in the superficial sense at all. But if we are to understand the poetry of the Elizabethan and Jacobean periods we must discard the view that wit is to be associated with barren and shallow ingenuity.

In *The Achievement of T. S. Eliot*, Professor F. O. Matthiessen explains the appropriateness of these techniques at the same time that he indicates Eliot's indebtedness to and kinship with Donne. In the poetry of both men one finds recorded the "disintegrating collision" in sensitive minds "of the old tradition and the new learning." Both have written poetry arising from painful self-consciousness. That is, if one becomes acutely aware of the diversity of the world and experience, aware that man's role in the universe is not one of continuum (the chain of being, or the homogeneity and truth of a tradition), then whatever unity there is to be found must be personally found. This involves an examination of the actual processes of thought, "their rapid alterations and sharp antitheses." Our age, of course, is more keenly aware of the process of association and the utter diversity of things. But the "jagged brokenness of Donne's thought has struck a responsive chord in our age." In his poetry Donne caught the sense of the intricacy, the interrelatedness and dissonances of experiences as they flow through the mind. Through his ability to put down a "whole of tangled feelings," Donne appeals to the modern mind. The more specific influences he has had upon modern poetry derive from this ability.

Yeats somewhere observes that the dominant image of the poets of our time is bone. The subjects of poetry, it is said, are love and death. It does not follow that the treatments of death cannot differ significantly. Death, as in Shelley's *Adonais*, can be romanticized. And certain forms of belief and statements can lessen its starkness, its absolute contrast with exuberant life, its terrible finality. When the vision of death, in these latter terms, is held in a clear focus, the hard outlines of all our actions are more readily perceivable. More specifically, many Victorian poets tended to envelop death in a mist, using it to induce melancholy ruminations. The Metaphysicals tended, on the other hand, to see death and life in a kind of synthesis, the thought of death serving always as a kind of qualifying irony. Among the moderns the recovery of the sense of evil, the frank break with the supernatural, the experience of violent death, as well as a more intense intellectuality in examining all experience may have contributed to a similar awareness. That the moderns recognize this similarity, and may even have been influenced by Metaphysical expressions, is several times made explicit. Eliot refers to Donne as one who

> . . . knew the anguish of the marrow
> The ague of the skeleton;
> No contact possible to flesh
> Allayed the fever of the bone.

Tate, whose "Ode to the Confederate Dead" is an intense appraisal of the "heroics" of life examined against the death of heroes, employs, in his "Horatian Epode to the Duchess of Malfi," Webster as a text:

> The stage is about to be swept of corpses.
> You have no more chance than an infusorian
> Lodged in a hollow molar of an eohippus.
> Come, now, no prattle of remergence with the
> ὄντως ὄν

Dr. Henry W. Wells finds two volumes by Conrad Aiken, *Preludes for Memnon* and *Time in the Rock*, which are concerned with the theme of time and death, to be soliloquies "undoubtedly under the influence of the Elizabethan dramatic tradition." A similar note is almost constant in the poetry of Edith Sitwell:

> "Love my heart for an hour, but my bone for a day—
> At least the skeleton smiles, for it has a morrow;"

And in Yeats we find lines like these:

> "Consume my heart away; sick with desire
> And fastened to a dying animal."

The awareness of the skeleton beneath the flesh establishes, at least, a kinship between the Metaphysicals and the moderns.

Yeats is considered by Dr. Wells as among the spiritual heirs of

Donne. It is true, he says, that Yeats does not employ the elaborate conceits that Donne does in his longer poems; yet there is, he adds, a similar intensity to their lyrics. Both poets seem to be intellects "walking naked." Yeats's later style was metaphysical in its intellectuality sensuously stated. In it is caught a sense of physical immediacy, a feeling for the real world. Yeats explicitly confessed his faith in this emphasis:

> God guard me from those thoughts men think
> In the mind alone,
> He that sings a lasting song
> Thinks in a marrow-bone.

There is, of course, a conscious eloquence in Yeats's diction and manner, but it is strengthened by his determination to be always virile, alive, and direct. Much of his persuasiveness seems explicable in these terms.

The earlier poetry of Eliot—that which had such a large formative influence on other poets—is more akin to the Metaphysicals than his later poetry in which religious orthodoxy is behind the greater coherence and order. Even so, much that has remained constant in his poetry is indebted, or at least akin, to the Metaphysicals. His ability to turn an idea into sensations, "an observation into a state of mind," has never lessened. His intellectuality has continued to be expressed in ironies, paradox, the contrast of the colloquial and the bizarre, wit, intensive, and subtle analysis. Matthiessen finds the influence of Jacobean dramatists upon Eliot greatest in "Gerontion." The disillusionment and the sense of harsh realities troubling and disrupting the idealisms of Middleton, Marston, Webster, and Ford is repeated in Eliot. His language, like theirs, is colloquial, realistic, highly imaginative, and caught in a similar metrical pattern. These dramatists, like Donne, experienced the tensions inherent in a society that is troubled by growing disbelief and shifting attitudes.

In the essay he contributed to *A Garland for John Donne*, Williamson finds the influence of Donne in modern American poetry mostly in the work of the Fugitives. In commenting on John Crowe Ransom, however, as illustrative of the group, he finds the influence less obviously Donne's than that of "a Cavalier heir of Donne." Ransom's poems have what Eliot calls the "tough reasonableness beneath the slight lyric grace." There is frequently a strong tension between the easy precision of his lines or the elegance of his texture and the sometimes macabre or always serious subject matter. His wit, appropriating conceits and controlling his rhetoric, rarely fails him. The play of levity and seriousness one finds in Marvell—

> The Grave's a fine and private place,
> But none I think do there embrace—

is quite as constant in Ransom's poems. Human capacity for exaggeration and for mixed motivations finds an ironic recognition. Thus of the woman with the china-blue eyes—

> A woman shooting such blue flame
> I apprehend will get some blame
> On her good name.

Or the messenger carrying a girl's venomous and angry letter, which she half-wishes unsent, to her lover—

> Away went the messenger's bicycle,
> His serpent track went up the hill forever. . . .

Quite possibly the tension between the romantic and the real in Ransom's poems is the basic reason for his kinship with the Metaphysicals. He attacks the romantic South, with its religious belief and chivalry, in a gentlemanly manner, employing as his weapons the language of realism and a scientific viewpoint. The individual battles are not waged with battering rams and machetes, however, because the poet is not a fanatical enemy of those values. His skepticism forces him to probe, or qualify, rather than to demolish them. To maintain his position, he requires a constant intellectual awareness, the manner and some of the techniques of the Metaphysicals.

The influence of the Metaphysicals upon Robert Penn Warren's work is exhibited in more ways than that on Ransom's. In Warren's poetry there is the constant awareness of doom, the terrors we carry within us, the sense of innocence irretrievably lost. Where Webster, as Ruth Herschberger notes, has

> All the flowers of the spring
> Meet to perfume our burying,

Warren has

> She blinks and croaks, like a toad or a Norn
> in the horrible light,
> And rattles her crutch, which may put forth a
> small bloom, perhaps white.

The forms of evil are always in the background, qualifying, as the awareness of death, say, qualifies and helps to define all actions and significances. The cold finality of the tomb is suggested by the themes, the imagery and symbols—

> Listen! the poor deluded cock
> Salutes the coldness of no dawn.

Like Donne, he can employ the harsh line, varying his accents to make the sound and rhythm appropriate to his meaning. And sometimes the language is reminiscent of Donne—"on easy axle roved" or "iron to the magnet yearns." And, like Marvell, whose "Garden" he has imitated, he can create a coherent body of imagery and conceits, which intensify and enlarge the meaning of the poem. Again, like Marvell, he can employ symbols that dramatize his meaning. In Marvell's "Garden" the mind is an

> ocean where each kind
> Does straight its own resemblance find;
> Yet it creates, transcending these,
> Far other worlds, and other seas,
> Annihilating all that's made
> To a green thought in a green shade.

In Warren's "Monologue at Midnight" there are these questions:

> The hound, the echo, flame, or shadow . . .
> And which am I and which are you?
> And are we Time who flee so fast,
> Or stone who stand, and thus endure?

And, like Marvell, Warren repeatedly employs the symbols of light and shade. However incandescent the light becomes, one is aware of the shadow that gives it focus; or however learned the terminology or shrewd the insight in certain poems, its meaning is bathed in a submarine light. Yet the mysteriousness arises out of the immediateness of the presented symbols. And analysis is at the heart of them, quickening them, as in

> Season by season from the skein
> Unwound, of earth and of our pleasure.

That the influence of the Metaphysicals is now a part of the growing and developing body of modern poetry is illustrated by its presence in the work of a poet as young as Robert Lowell. In his *Lord Weary's Castle* one finds the elements that characterize the metaphysical moderns—the ease in incorporating the antipoetic into the poetic structure, the unexpected but appropriate adjective, the ironic and analytical mind, the varied but strong metrical pattern, and the constant awareness of the bones beneath the flesh. The mood and manner is in these lines from "The Drunken Fisherman":

> Is there no way to cast my hook
> Out of this dynamited brook?
> The Fisher's sons must cast about
> When shallow waters peter out.

The tension between the traditional ideals and the modern sense of formlessness and heterogeneity is especially strong in Lowell's work, because of his sense of his age and his own religious orthodoxy.

Elinor Wylie, like certain other poets of the twenties, was a willing student of Donne. In her *Angels and Earthly Creatures* she attempted to approximate his temper and mood. "That her study of Donne was not an assimilation, an incorporation," Williamson comments, "is apparent in the way in which his actual vocabulary peppers her page. We find the familiar 'ecstasy,' 'anatomy,' 'shroud,' 'metempsychosis,' and 'element.' " To put it more bluntly, Miss Wylie's sensibility was far from being similar to Donne's. However frequent her references to deaths, the real world of her poetry, as it is reflected in her most persistent imagery, is glittering, sophisticated, romantic. Hers is a poetry of delicate strengths, finding its major symbols in crystal, silver, glass, lightning flashes, and flame. And hers is a romantic attitude and subject matter. The distinction she has earned is in large part the result of her technical control. A conceit—like this from "Let No Charitable Hope,"

> I live by squeezing from a stone
> The little nourishment I get

—is likely to be followed by a Housman-like brand of irony, as

> In masks outrageous and austere
> The years go by in single file;
> But none has merited my fear,
> And none has quite escaped my smile.

There were other poets not metaphysical by inclination, at least not strongly so, who also were affected by the critical interest in the Metaphysicals which followed upon Professor Grierson's edition of *Metaphysical Lyrics*, as well as upon Eliot's essays. An anthology was published which included "metaphysical" poems from Marvell to Edna Millay. "You, Andrew Marvell," by Archibald MacLeish, for example, is obviously indebted to "To His Coy Mistress." Similarly, John Peale Bishop's conceit

> I see a distance of black yews
> Long as the history of the Jews

seems indebted to Marvell's

> And you should if you please refuse
> Until the conversion of the Jews.

One finds the surface evidence of Donne's influence in a poet like Edna Millay. In his essay, "The Poet as Woman," Ransom examines the implications of placing Miss Millay in the tradition of Donne. He sets their poems side by side, then examines their underlying attitudes and resulting effects. He concludes that, despite the "parallel" passages, the two poets are not alike—"the gulf is too wide." The gulf between them is caused by Donne's hard sense of the real world and his intellectuality.

Further examples suggesting the influence or concern with the Metaphysical school might be multiplied. The extent to which a metaphysical manner was adopted in the twenties merely because it was fashionable is no doubt impossible to assess. Sophistication, of course, needs wit and an air of intellectuality to support it. Those who turned unquestioningly toward the social-minded and political poetry of the thirties, we may assume, had no felt need as artists to employ metaphysical techniques. Those, on the other hand, who could not appropriate another manner and idiom would seem to have found in those techniques the one way to express the tensions of our time.

## CHAPTER SEVEN

# *The Influence of the Pre-Modern Americans*

> *We can trace the developing self-consciousness of the American genius from the middle of the last century when we first really had a literature worth talking about to the moment toward the end of the second decade of ours when it was plain that, following the cultural slump of the period after the Civil War, a new movement had got under way.*—EDMUND WILSON

THE early complaints of Van Wyck Brooks and of Lewis Mumford that America was hostile to the esthetic emphasis are easily documented. America was hostile to the artist. Yet, despite their society being dedicated single-mindedly to practical affairs, there were a few—Herman Melville, Nathaniel Hawthorne, Emily Dickinson, Stephen Crane, Henry James, Henry Adams, and George Santayana—who did their part to keep the integrity of the artist alive as an ideal. The sudden flourishing of a mature poetry in the generation of Eliot, Pound, Marianne Moore, Ransom, *et al.*, and the concern of critics to relate it to Metaphysical and Symbolist poetry have caused many to lose sight of the native influences from the late nineteenth and the early twentieth centuries. These latter influences may not be so strong as the former two—but they are significant and should not be overlooked.

With the perspective we now have on American literature in the nineteenth century it is not difficult to understand groupings which similar interests and perceptions urged upon individual authors. We can understand the friendship of Hawthorne and Melville and of

Henry James and Henry Adams. We can understand the similar interests which drew Conrad, James, and the young Stephen Crane together. Nor is it surprising that two or three generations later poets like Hart Crane and W. H. Auden would be writing poems in honor of Melville, James, and Emily Dickinson. A community of spirit and craftsmanship establishes kinship. More specifically, we find the problems of artistry have been seen by all of them to relate to the peculiar problems of modernity. Morton Zabel has stated the problem in relation to James.[1] We can accept his statement, to a considerable extent at least, as relating to the other poets who have strongly influenced modern poetry.

At the beginning of the century James could sense the disintegrating forces that would afford an easy rationalization for formlessness in the coming literature. What he wrote in his critical prefaces for aspirants in his own profession was almost immediately focused against modern poetic theory, as Zabel states it, at four important points: "the motives of technique, the nature of artistic intelligence, the duty of self determination, and the character of modernity. All of them have been paramount in literature during the past half century, made so by the decline of the romantic principles and the resistance of creative integrity to the confusion which those principles induced."

Whitman, despite the intensity of his democratic visions, was a part of the gathering strength of the naturalistic overemphasis on detail for its own sake. Soon many would believe that the accumulation of facts and data in itself was explanation. Facts speak for themselves. The writer, who should be the central and controlling intelligence, becomes lost in the flux of detail he amasses. The poets in Whitman's wake are concerned with the geography, the history, and the myth of the land, with adding to a story already told. Their failure to interpret America in its complexities may be laid to their initial failure to bring a critical discernment and a will to profound imagination to their factual material. Constance Rourke, in 1931,



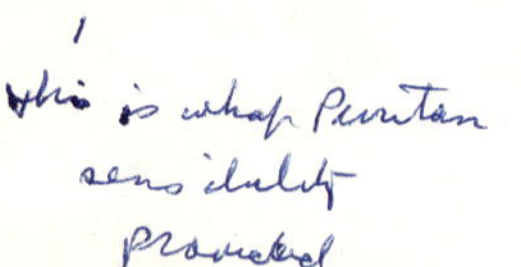

found that James, like "other primary writers in the American tradition, stood alone in his achievement. The prolific energies that create an entire literature were lacking in this long period, though a widely flung pattern had been created which had freshness and even magnificence." Miss Rourke found the implications of James's work fulfilled in Proust, Joyce, Dorothy Richardson, and Virginia Woolf, but, finding no American novelists who followed him, she assumed his influence slight. James, as Zabel has shown, was felt in another way—to the poets he became a model of discipline and discrimination. Nor was James alone. There has been a thin line of artists in his tradition who have made the work of their successors possible and easier. That a tradition has been maintained is indicated by the eagerness with which the modern poets have turned to Hawthorne, Melville, Emily Dickinson, Henry Adams, Stephen Crane, and, to a lesser extent, to some few others.

Despite the accusations that James lacks vitality and substance, he remains for most modernists their artist—"the poet of the difficult, dear addicted artist." The work of no other novelist or critic certainly has been the subject of such pious concern. The cultist appeal in this instance, moreover, lies deeper than the thin surface of the usual literary fad. This reverence for James has a longer history than Auden's "At the Grave of Henry James" (1941) and the recent reissues of certain of his novels and short stories. In the *Little Review* in 1918 Ezra Pound, with as much respect as he could muster, wrote a long and detailed study of, in Pound's own words, "the great man's work." And in the *Cantos* he caused James to take his place with other great ones in the timeless history—

> And the great domed head, *con gli occhi onesti e tardi*
> Moves before me, phantom with weighted motion,
> *Grave incessu*, drinking the tone of things,
> And the old voice lifts itself weaving an endless sentence.

In the same issue of the *Little Review* Eliot established the relationship between James and Hawthorne. "The really vital thing, in finding any personal kinship between Hawthorne and James, is what James touches lightly when he said that 'the fine thing in Hawthorne is that he cared for the deeper psychology, and that in his way, he tried to become familiar with it.' " Eliot's point is that the weight and strength of other nineteenth-century novelists lies in their "visual realism." (Eliot is not unaware of the dangers in the emphases of Hawthorne and James, nor is he maintaining that the "deeper psychology" is essential.) Hawthorne and James allow the reader to see only a minimum.

Eliot observes also that both men were able to establish the atmosphere of their societies, that Hawthorne does "get New England, as James gets a larger part of America, and as none of their respective contemporaries get anything above a village or two, or a a jungle." Both were able to get the "tone of things." Through the indication of nuance, movement, and manner, through the selection of detail, the complex attitudes that give a society its character were evoked. In his *Instigations* Pound said that the emotional center of James "is in being sensitive to the feel of the place or to the tonality of the person." The poets, with Pound, know that this ability to transcend a merely naturalistic representation lies in their grasping the "tone of things." It becomes an appropriate detail of history that another critic, Allen Tate, writing, in turn, of the *Cantos* of Pound, said that "they should be read every few weeks just for the tone." The Symbolist formula, so far as the novel goes, is found to some extent in James, and it allies him with the poets who look to him. His technique included a "minimum" use of "architecture" and a tendency toward dealing with "barely ponderable motives." For James, like the Symbolists, investigating areas of understanding and expression not available to discursive language, knew that tone can be only evoked, not described.

That not only Pound and Eliot accept much of the "poetics" of James is indicated by the continued and scrupulously attentive study of him by Auden and other younger poets. Auden presents James as the master to whom all writers should turn:

> O with what innocence your hand submitted
> To these formal rules that help a child to play,
>   While your heart, fastidious as
> A delicate nun, remained true to the rare noblesse
> Of your lucid gift and, for its own sake, ignored the
>   Resentful muttering Mass
>
> Whose ruminant hatred of all which cannot
> Be simplified or stolen is still at large. . . .

The influence of Herman Melville spread more slowly than that of James.[2] Broadly speaking, Melville's reputation, other than in England, had to await the publication of his biography, which followed by several years his centenary in 1919, and the intensive interest of the critics and poets of the twenties. An English writer caught the explanation of the recovered reputation. Melville's contemporaries tended to see the world as a "perfectly clear-cut and comprehensible affair. . . . We feel that Melville's oceans and leviathans are credible symbols. That man hunts through a great deep who looks into himself." In Melville the moderns found an artist profoundly concerned not only with the metaphysics of evil but with its representation in pervasively meaningful symbols.

The awful heritage of evil, which Melville caught in his symbols of the sea, is carried into modern poetry by Hart Crane. The wretchedness and terror of Crane's life, and his death by drowning, give ironic overtones to the kinship of the two poets. Crane never recognized, as Melville did, in a profound or ordered fashion the essentially tragic theme he wrestled with, but perhaps his own life, which Philip Horton has recorded and interpreted so movingly, is sufficient commentary. And Melville's poem "Art" would have been strongly meaningful to Crane, had he known it, who suffered intensely, before the period of his relatively quick and complete disintegration, to organize his frequently violent imagery and strangely appropriate associations into coherent esthetic form:

> In placid hours well-pleased we dream
> Of many a brave embodied scheme.
> But forms to lend, pulsed life create,
> What unlike things must meet and mate. . . .

An artist like Melville, who strove, when he could gather his imaginative strength, and in the face of public indifference, to create, was sure to find his most reverent and respectful audience in readers like Crane. The last seven poems of *White Buildings* (1926), the best Crane wrote, are about Melville and the sea—

> High in the azure steeps
> Monody shall not wake the mariner.
> The fabulous shadow only the sea keeps.

Throughout *The Bridge* one senses the presence of Melville, and Crane, we can imagine, was highly pleased when certain of the best critics saw in his first book poetry of an order to rank him permanently as an artist with figures like Melville.

Hart Crane may also be taken as a significant example of the eagerness with which the poets of the twenties assimilated the esthetic of Emily Dickinson's poetry. All his published lines referring to her—in "Quaker Hill" and "To Emily Dickinson"—center on her exquisite isolation of spirit in song. And, however dissimilar they were as persons and as poets, both were "mystics" and both felt the need for expressing themselves through an individually discovered esthetic. Both persisted in holding to the line of their own development. In their best poems they held close to the exploratory metaphor and to conciseness of imagery and statement.

Students of Emily Dickinson have recorded the early history of her literary reputation, the initial warmth and flurry, then the years after the turn of the century when the references to her seem few. William Dean Howells, appropriately, in reviewing *Poems of Emily Dickinson, First Series* (1891), placed her as certainly, if not as definitely, as any later critic of the new poetry. In *Ancestors' Brocades* there is ample testimony to the interest, popular and critical, which her poems and letters caused. Nor did publication, in 1896, of the third series of poems harm her reputation. "Altogether," a critic in the *Chicago Journal* wrote, "the first impression of Emily Dickinson's writing is repeated and emphasized." So far as the anthologies and magazines of the first fifteen years after 1900 give evidence, however, her reputation and actual influence were slight. Until publication of *The Single Hound* in 1914 her name is not mentioned in *Poetry*. At that time, however, Harriet Monroe labeled her a modern because of her love of economy and epithet.

Sometime during the middle of the Victorian period a few poets initiated an effort to withdraw from the vaguely ideal and the cloyingly sentimental. The shift, encouraged by Browning, Meredith, and Hardy, was eventually to become a landslip. Intellect, analysis and insight, was to be freed, made a vehicle for discovering the legitimate sources and justifications for emotion and sentiment. Mind, held in new respect, would function integrally with feeling. The vision of *The Waste Land*, product of a profound analysis of tradition and the elements that compose a society and culture, was a long way off. But a beginning, like that of Emily Dickinson's self-analysis, could be made. Through her the ironic intelligence, the line charged with meaning, and the insight embodied in metaphor were irrevocably opposed to the evanescently romantic, the exclusively "poetic" and sentimental. She was, for whatever reasons, sufficiently aside from the literary culture of her time to initiate techniques and a manner of expression that generations of poets following her would find not only appropriate but inevitably right for their poetry. When Edward Sapir reviewed her *Collected Poems* in 1925, he felt in her work the possible destroyer of our late romantics and "vendors of jeweled bindings." Sapir viewed her as a kind of "primitive, a forerunner of a spirit in American poetry that had not as yet quite succeeded in shaping itself."

If we assume for Stephen Crane very much influence on the poetry of the twenties, we should credit him with advancing the influence of Emily Dickinson. Her elliptical and sometimes cryptic lines made possible an idiom taut with implication. Crane, according to Ford Madox Ford, never "tired of exasperatingly declaring it was his unattainable ambition to make every one damned word do the work of six." The long elemental lines of Whitman are suited to large, almost primitive emotions, and the lines of Poe are built upon the careful balance of an "exclusive diction" with mournful and melancholy rhythms. The followers of both poets would oppose the "epigrammatism" of Dickinson and Stephen Crane.

Hamlin Garland, who eventually arranged for the publication of *The Black Riders* (1896), and to whom it was dedicated, later recalled his first sight of Crane's poems:

> I was astounded by their power. . . . They were at once quaintly humorous and audacious, unrhymed and almost without rhythm, but the figures employed with masterly brevity were colossal. They suggested some of the French translations of Japanese verses, at other times they carried the sting and compression of Emily Dickinson's verse. . . .[3]

Garland was not a highly perceptive critic and does not seem to have been troubled by the fairly general disinterest of Crane in the discipline and techniques of the craft of poetry. He marveled at Crane's ability to compose poems "without a moment's hesitation." Crane knew Miss Dickinson's work. He had heard a part of it read one evening when visiting the home of William Dean Howells. He participated in the first burst of enthusiasm and wonder that began when Mabel Loomis Todd and Thomas Wentworth Higginson issued some of her poems. For some reason or other, the popular interest in her work diminished after 1900 and almost died—until in 1924, after, that is, the modernist movements had begun to gain the ascendancy in the United States, several works placed her again in the foreground, and detailed study and criticism re-established her position. Her reputation and influence seem to have lagged behind that of Crane, who was studied by the Imagists and epigrammatists writing their elliptical free verse. Her reputation, which should greatly have exceeded his, was to some extent prepared for by his. Both had striven for an esthetic emphasis, and both made the dominance of it in the twenties possible.

According to Thomas Beer, the critics of Crane, except for Howells, failed to see the "ironies chasing themselves" throughout *The Red Badge*. The early response of reviewers and readers generally to Crane's work indicates that he had to face a straitened single-mindedness in his audience. Both books of poems bewildered reviewers. "Mr. Crane's sense of humor," one wrote, "is of a mystifying kind. He deliberately shows us the horrors of war and then entitles his work 'War Is Kind.' " The negligible notice, during these same years, given to Edwin Arlington Robinson's *The Torrent and the Night Before* (1896) and *The Children of the Night* (1897) implies a part of the reason for the reception given Crane's poems. With *The Man against the Sky*, in 1916, Robinson won his first notable attention. "Richard Cory," which had appeared in his second volume, found its audience twenty years later. In England the themes of irony which Crane handled so roughly—*tedium vitae*, the revolt against God, and the view of man as a speck in an indifferent universe—had been treated with more subtlety and artistry by James Thomson, Swinburne, and Fitzgerald. In *The Mauve Decade* Beer interpreted the craze for the *Rubáiyát* as a "symptom of mental growth, a fleet glance out of so much bawling optimism at things insoluble." Crane, too, was symptomatic. After the turn of the century England and America were to allow Hardy to become a major figure and to read Housman with something more than wistful attention. Even so, Crane's audience in the nineties was not prepared for the bad-tasting "pills" which Crane himself acknowledged to be "pretty darn dumb, anyhow." And in 1919, when Harriet Monroe was attempting to relate Crane to the new poetry, she found his God-baiting (she had heard Ingersoll) merely sophomoric and dated. In this respect, Crane seems more prophetic, indicative of a changing temper, than influential.

Miss Monroe took notice of the "persistent assertion" that Crane "forestalled and outdid the vers-librists of these days." She pointed out that his sententiousness is not so very different from that of the Victorians, but without observing that he was sententious after the fashion of the moderns, using their prejudices and biases. She was more willing to accord Emily Dickinson a place as a pioneer but did not add that in some respects Crane was in direct line of descent from Miss Dickinson and was, through the very success of his techniques as a modern, instrumental in preparing a later audience for her. Miss Monroe did, however, admit he was something of an innovator. "His free verse was different from Whitman's, his use of the short line especially was a presage and it may have influenced some of the poets—the Imagists, for example—who are now trying out its tunes. Ezra Pound, indeed, has somewhere spoken of him appreciatively." He did not, she said, become a master of the new instrument and will longest be remembered for his prose. Both of these statements seem true enough, but one should add that Crane's work made the development of the modern idiom and esthetic easier. Without examples of the kind he afforded, the formulations of the poets and critics who followed him would have been perhaps greatly delayed. Glances through the book news and literary columns of American magazines after 1900 reveal a continued interest in his work. When Ford reviewed *Some Imagist Poets* (1915) for *Outlook*, he quoted Crane's "the waves were barbarous and abrupt," calling it "the real right thing." Ford in successive and repetitious articles never tires of praising Crane's genius in creating appropriate analogies through images and of "placing" him as an innovator.

If Crane had been born a generation or so later, or if he had lived longer, he might well have turned his major energies to poetry. His gift was not reportorial or even an ability with discursive expression; it was one of intense perception which expressed itself most readily and clearly in images. If he had lived only a few more years he might have joined with Pound, who went to England in 1909, where he found the criticism of James, Rémy de Gourmont, T. E. Hulme, and Ford germinal and provocative. Crane had associated with James and Ford as a kind of schoolboy genius. Yet Crane anticipated, though without raising his *aperçus* as a practicing craftsman to a coherent theory of criticism, the concern of Hulme with images. He is therefore a forerunner of the poets who under the influence of Hulme attempted to create an "Imagist" poetry. Hulme, according to Herbert Read,

> was always haunted by a suspicion of the futility of logic. He despised "words," regarding them as mere counters in a game, "beads on a chain," mere physical things carrying no reality. Against words he opposed the *image* as a unit and the *analogy* as an instrument of thought. . . . Thought, he argued, was prior to its expression in language, being the simultaneous presentation to the mind of two different images: thought was the recognition of their analogy.

Valuations put on the poetry of the Imagists should not influence judgments of the value of Hulme's theories. It remains that much of the esthetic we call "modern," the concern with concretion, ellipsis, reflexive explosion of meaning, and suggestive detail, was first formulated by him and his associates. In the light of Pound's theory of the image functioning as a vortex, derivative certainly from Hulme's position, it is possible to characterize not only modern poetry but much modern prose. A consideration of Crane in the light of the history of the image in modern literature established beyond doubt his break with the novelists who preceded him and the debt owed him by both poets and novelists who followed him.

Joseph Frank, with conclusive use of detail, has shown that Pound's definition of the image as "that which presents an intellectual and emotional complex in an instant of time may serve as a principle for more than adequately characterizing a major aspect of modern prose and poetry. Pound defines an image not as a "pictorial reproduction"—the degree beyond which certain Imagists could not move—but as a "unification of disparate ideas and emotions into a complex presented spatially in an instant of time." Even a brief examination of *The Red Badge* establishes Crane's relationship with this esthetic.

Crane's novel of a battle is not discursive in the usual manner of fiction. It reveals the realistic details, catching always those aspects that reveal its meaning to the participants, and enlarging continuously through the exploration of images the horror and "red sickness of battle." The characters are barely identified, and their personal histories seem all but irrelevant. They contribute to the artist's presentation of an "intellectual and emotional complex" but are not investigated individually and sequentially. Only what is relevant to the "complex" is allowed. Whatever might distract or disconcert is ignored. The technique here is not so complicated as it was to be in *Ulysses*, in which fragments and allusions must be kept in mind until, by "reflexive reference," they can be linked to their "compliments," but his technique is nonetheless modern. And as the technique of *Ulysses* is related to the technique of modern poetry, so is that of Crane's *Red Badge*.

In this brief history also belongs the name of George Santayana. No other American of his age was so free to participate in American life yet remain distant enough to focus against it a shrewd and brilliant philosophical commentary. He restored idealism, Mumford put it, "as a mode of thinking creatively." *The Sense of Beauty* was published in 1896, and thereafter the aspiring artist had a strong philosophical position from which to view and assess America's literary expressions. Santayana made basic distinctions. The pleasure derived from beauty, he said,

> must not be in the consequence of the utility of the object or event, but in its immediate perception; in other words, beauty is an ultimate good, something that gives satisfaction to a natural function, to some fundamental

need or capacity of our minds. . . . Morality has to do with the avoidance of evil and the pursuit of good.

The dignity of this kind of philosophy—it was the beginning of critical maturity—must have given hope to at least a few. It was followed almost yearly by book-length statements evolving his full critical and philosophical position. His poetry, because he was not born to English, did not offer a parallel influence—but by 1912, when the poetic renaissance was under way, he had helped in the best way he could to prepare for it. And a fuller understanding of his "The Poetry of Barbarism" (1906) would have saved the experimenters of the twenties from exploring certain blind alleys in the Whitman tradition.

The Spanish birth of Santayana and his continued dependence on an Old World Catholic traditionalism separated him from his contemporaries but allowed him to understand them better. In a letter discussing *The Last Puritan*, he said that

an important element in the tragedy of "his hero" is drawn from the fate of a whole string of Harvard poets in the 1880's and 1890's—Sanborn, Philip Savage, Hugh McCullough, Trumbull Stickney, and Cabot Lodge. . . . Now, all those friends of mine . . . were visibly killed by the lack of air to breathe. People individually were kind and even appreciative to them, as they were to me, but the system was deadly, and they hadn't any alternative tradition (as I had) to fall back upon. . . .

Henry Adams wrote the biography of one of these poets, *The Life of George Cabot Lodge*. In it, as Edmund Wilson points out, the deadliness of Adam's world is pervasive, expressing itself through a double-edged irony of which Adams seems sometimes hardly to have been aware. The irony was the sharp doubt which Wilson says "peeled the gilt from the Gilded Age." Adams expressed, as few contemporaries could, the effects of the loss of faith. The later concern of Eliot with tradition and the need for a society sustained and given dignity by spirituality derived in good part from the preoccupation of Adams with the Virgin at Chartres. F. O. Matthiessen, as we have noted, quotes a passage from *The Education* which obviously served Eliot in "Gerontion." A slightly earlier study by R. P. Blackmur explains Adams' inability to accept a faith that had made the literature and sculpture of the Virgin possible. If we grant significance to Eliot's statements of the essential dilemma of our time, we must observe the part Adams played in preparing for them. And we should note that, without his persistent awareness of the need for the esthetic emphasis, Eliot's own expression of the dilemma would have been more difficult and perhaps less perceptive and moving. Considerations of Adams as historian tend to blur our recognition of his part in the development of later artistic awareness. Adams found that the most profoundly cultivated reaches of the mind demand the same treatment that the artist strives to give.

> The pen works for itself, and acts like a hand modelling the plastic material over and over again to the form that suits it best. The form is never arbitrary, but is a sort of growth like crystallization, as any artist knows too well, for often the pencil runs into side paths and shapelessness, loses its relations, stops or is bogged. Then it has to return on its trail, and recover if it can, its line of force.

Adams, like Pater and James, emphasized the function of mind in establishing the relationships between perceptions and appropriate expression. Without these proper relationships the historian, philosopher, or artist will not properly objectify his perceptions.

CHAPTER EIGHT

# *The Imagistic Symbol*

> *We have elected to know the world through our science, and we know a great deal, but science is only the cognitive department of our animal life, and by it we know the world only as a scheme of abstract conveniences. What we cannot know constitutionally as scientists is the world which is made of whole and indefeasible objects, and this is the world which poetry recovers for us.*—John Crowe Ransom

William Butler Yeats turned to the doctrines of symbolism, as he understood them from Arthur Symons' *The Symbolist Movement in Literature*, because he saw therein a possibility of recovering the inspiration which he felt lies in the personal depths of every artist. "The scientific movement," he wrote, "brought with it a literature, which was always tending to lose itself in externalities of all kinds, in opinion, in declamation, in picturesque writing, in word painting." Yeats hoped that a poetry might develop which would move us because of its symbolism, a poetry to be contemplated and experienced because therein the phenomena of the world are captured, refracted rather than reflected. In more recent years, Allen Tate has examined Yeats's thesis and pointed to two kinds of poetry that have arisen as a result of science: the first kind appeals through abstract ideas, is a poetry that "looks from explanation to action"; the second is a poetry in revolt against the dominion of science, a poetry which gives us "the emotion known as 'romantic irony.' " A third kind has no "practical utility"; it presents, as in a play like *Macbeth*, "the whole created image which is neither true nor false, but exists as a created object."[1] It is this last kind of poetry which Yeats wished to see. His concern with symbolism implies an effort to recover, as it were, the soul of poetry.

The process of recovery is necessarily difficult because our preconceptions about ourselves and our world are cast in terms which the scientific view and emphasis have made inevitable. If we recognize, as Tate has recognized, a poetry that has assumed a guise of science and proceed to put it out the back door, we should expect to see it, in a variant guise, coming in at the window. Knowledge has been directed toward the external world and toward controls. We might expect, as Arthur Symons complained, that poets would strive to "build in brick and mortar inside the covers of a book."

The scientific disciplines have discouraged the use not only of an emotional language but of a language not thoroughly subject to controlled meaning. There has been, consequently, an avoidance of imagistic symbols, other than as supplementary to an abstract denotative language. As a part of the modern philosophical effort to restore the "human response to a place of dignity," however, there has developed the recognition that the human mind constantly creates symbols, many of which cannot be used in the service of discursive, logical language. Perhaps the simultaneous concern of artists and philosophers with a study of symbols is not fortuitous but represents an effort to readmit subjective expressions. As such, this concern would imply that all cognitive expressions cannot be made to fit the traditional rules of a scientific language.

Modern poetry, it might be said, develops from symbolism, through imagism, objectivism, surrealism, and the rest, in the sequence of a withdrawal from "scientific" to subjective attitudes. The beginnings of this poetry should be examined in the light of these recent philosophical analyses of symbolism. If the study is "the seed of a new intellectual harvest, to be reaped in the next season of human understanding," the poetry Yeats desired will in the future be more easily written. For the historical moment, we may observe that philosophy has given the symbolistic and imagistic language of the poets a clearer and more readily acceptable justification.

## 2

Since an understanding of poetic language, indeed of all language, must be arrived at through a study of symbolism, at least a brief recapitulation of the subject must be undertaken. Mrs. Langer, in *Philosophy in a New Key*, gathers up an imposing array of philosophers, psychologists, and philologists who are agreed that "symbolism is the recognized key to that mental life which is characteristically human and above the level of sheer animality."

A distinction between "sign" and "symbol" is prerequisite to any full understanding of mentality at the human level. The use of the sign implies a mental function at an elementary, even at an animal, level.

> As soon as sensations function as signs of conditions in the surrounding world, the animal receiving them is moved to exploit or avoid those conditions. The sound of a gong or a whistle or a word, itself entirely unrelated to the process of eating, causes a dog to expect food, if in past experiences this sound has always preceded dinner; it is a sign, not a part, of his food. . . .
>
> Even animal mentality, therefore, is built up on a primitive semantic; it is the power of learning, by trial and error, that certain phenomena in the world are signs of certain others, existing or about to exist. . . .

Man uses signs also, sometimes in the way animals use them. In addition, he uses them in a way peculiar to him: Man uses signs "not only to *indicate* things, but also to *represent* them." The animal mind directly transmits messages to its "motor centers." Many words, however, are not signals of something about, or likely, to happen. They *remind* us of things rather than *announce* things. "Signs" of this latter kind are more properly considered symbols. Symbols and signs, then, may be seen to differ in this wise: signs are proxy for the objects they represent; symbols are "vehicles for the conception of objects." One reacts toward a sign or is aware of it; one conceives a symbol, and it is this conception that the symbol directly "means." The single word, of course, can be both sign and symbol: the sign indicates the object, whereas the symbol allows of a conception of the object. "Water" to a child at an early stage of development means "to drink;" to a more mature mind "water" means a name by which a substance can be thought of, and remembered—an instrument of thinking. A distinguishing quality of the human species, Mrs. Langer points out, is man's need of "symbolization." Symbolization is *the* characteristic act of the human mind, as primary and as constant as the receiving of sense impressions.

Only a part of the symbol-making process, however, is related to the canons of discursive reasoning. The tremendous treasure of nondiscursive symbolic material is often not being used in any way at a given moment; but, as the product of spontaneous and undirected brain activity, it does provide the mind with reserve material always accessible at need. And this need does not arise in connection with symbolic presentation of logical concepts. The reserve is drawn upon in those moments of extralogical, nondiscursive perceptions of meanings and significances.

The brain has been called a great transmitter: the stimulus-word, the sign, represents a message from the world to this "motor center." The conception of mental life as symbolic activity requires a new figure, the transformer: the "current of experience that passes through it undergoes a change of character." These experiences become symbols, the characteristic constituents of the human mind. The transmitter image implies a *rational* act. But, as popular semanticists are eager to point out, certain signs (words) set up highly indirect currents through the circuit and often cause garbled messages. The transformer image does not necessarily imply a rational act. Brain activity goes on continuously: some symbols merge into a composition of dreams, of fantasy; others become a part of ritual or myth; still others become connotative parts, or even parts which defy verbalization, of artistic expressions, as in poetry.

The use of the term "symbol" to indicate abstractions like communism or Christianity, however useful to semanticists, is almost a secondary usage so far as the criticism of poetry is concerned. Symbols that are also images are, if not the poet's most immediate concern, at least a primary contemporary concern, because the image as a form of knowledge and artistic expression has for several centuries been suspect.

Yet it is exactly this mode of knowing that is most significantly human, most fundamental to the processes of man's mind. A glance at any poetic image will reveal how basic is this form of communication between man and man.

> Old pond,
> Frog
> lapsing into water—
> noise.

Dr. Loewith has translated this imagistic scene in these words: "Life is like the sound caused by the leap of a frog, foolish, pathetic, and transient. It causes a little noise that is soon over. And the perfect silence once again settles over the old pond." There is no reason for holding up this interpretation as the sole meaning of the poem. Quite possibly it had no such meaning for the Japanese poet who wrote it. That is, its writing derived from no pre-analyzed and thought-out meaning. It is *presentational*, and what it means to the reader depends largely on his previous associations with the elements within the poem as well, of course, as on his response to the esthetic relationships established by the poet. One might find many and even divergent meanings in the image. Or, feeling no impulse to extract a meaning, one might quite unwittingly absorb the image as one receives impressions of certain wallpaper patterns or certain shades of color.

There is a point beyond which analysis cannot go. The experiences of shade and color and pattern are parts of total experiences and as such have meanings, however impossible the logical expression of them may be. Water and noise and frogs are a part of our common sense experience and contribute quite as much to our understanding of our world as do weights and measurements. Experiencing them sensuously as well as intellectually, we have a feeling of whole experience that is indiscoverable in bare statement. Nor does it follow that symbols can be broken into their elements and thereby explained.

Still, certain specific ambiguities are available to analysis. Thus one can explain how the crimson carpet in the *Agamemnon* organizes the play by bringing into focus, as Philip Blair Rice expressed it, "the blood-soaked deeds of Agammemnon's hybris—Oriental despots walk into their palaces on crimson carpets, which in Greece are spread only for the statues of gods entering their temples; and the blood feud whose struggle with civic justice is the main theme of the trilogy."

Taking a hint from this dramatic use of crimson, one may question the symbolic uses poets make of color. Among the most complete catalogues of the hues of whiteness man has experienced in symbols, perhaps, is found in Herman Melville's *Moby Dick*. "It was the whiteness of the whale that above all things appalled me." The nature of this horror of whiteness was all but ineffable. Yet Melville knew that the meaning of the entire prose poem would either find its center and source of artistic representation in the *whiteness* of the whale or fall away into separate chapters, with only heavy archeological meanings. He shows how the whiteness is "at once the most meaning symbol of spiritual things, nay the very veil of the Christian Deity; and yet should be as it is, the intensifying agent in things the most appalling to mankind." A passage, taken almost at random, exhibits the many and subtle ways in which whiteness can invest an object or scene.

> Though in many natural objects, whiteness refiningly enhances beauty, as if imparting some special virtue of its own, as in marbles, japonicas, and pearls; and though various nations have in some way recognized a certain royal preeminence in this hue; even the barbaric, grand old kings of Pegu placing the title "Lord of the White Elephants" above all their magniloquent ascriptions of dominion;—and though, besides all this, whiteness has always been even made significant of gladness, for among the Romans a white stone marked a joyful day; and though in other mortal sympathies and symbolizings, this same hue is made the emblem of many touching, noble things—the innocence of brides, the benignity of age. . . .

The anthologies of English poetry would give up hundreds of examples of the symbolic effects of whiteness. So instinctive a poet as Robert Burns wrote

> The white moon is setting behind the white wave,
> And Time is setting with me, O!

Yeats observed that if "the whiteness of the moon and of the waves, whose relation to the setting of Time is too subtle for the intellect" were taken from the lines, their beauty would be lost. We can establish no single logical relationship between whiteness and time, but long association with whiteness gives us certain hints. Whiteness suggests age (note the first passage from Melville) and the pallor of death and the unknown (note the symbolic usage of whiteness in Christian ritual and belief), with its mixture of fascination and terror. The use of "white wave" extends even further the area of associations by adding the powerful and infinitely varied symbol of the sea.

The psychologists tell us that the emotional response to objectless color is, like the response to music, impossible to express verbally in any of its subtlety. Statements about the feelings aroused thereby can be made only very generally—so, unless cultural or personal associations have caused special reactions, we may agree with the students of color in calling pure yellow "happy," deep blue "quiet and earnest," red "passionate," violet "wistful," and that, in general, "the brighter and warmer tones are joyful and exciting, the darker and colder, more inward and restful."

Oswald Spengler, among others, found symbolic expression of varied psychic interest in color as readily as in philosophy or architecture. And Havelock Ellis believed that the coincidence of the opening of the Christian Era and an awakened interest in blue is explained by men turning their eyes skyward as well as by the revulsion from red, the symbol of battle, and yellow, once the color of the bride but later the symbol of illicit love. One might assume, then, that the use of color in the poetry of various periods, as well as in individual poets, differs significantly.

Victorian developments, for example, based on a language of practical utility and science, on the one hand, and one of feeling and poetry, on the other, encouraged the use of such "musical" appeals as objectless colors. Thus Swinburne speaks of a land of "gold," a land hardly to be identified although associated with a color. All such usages might be disparagingly referred to as "romantic." Secondly, it is apparent that not all uses of color are tremulous or vague. It has been Eliot, for one, who, by insisting that the word be identified with the object (either, we might suggest, in regard to color words, in a concrete noun, or through an adjective that is not redundant), has helped make it possible for modern poets to avail themselves of the "unconsciously general" associations attached to colors without letting go of a definite meaning. Such usages, which are not, of course, limited to the moderns, may be thought of as imagistic or symbolic.

Modern poets have been very much aware of the importance of color, with no sense, certainly, of continuing a Victorian technique. In fact, William Carlos Williams has said: "As I look back I think it was the French painters rather than the writers who influenced us, and their influence was very great. They created an atmosphere of release, color release, release from stereotyped forms, trite subjects." Modern color usages when contrasted with those of the Victorians might, if properly analyzed, suggest profound shifts in "psychic interests." But this is a matter for the historian. We can note that the Imagists furthered the development of modern poetry merely by insisting that poets "render particulars exactly and not deal in vague generalities." Thus, as in John Gould Fletcher's description of the "effect of cloud shadows"—

> Silver filaments, golden flakes settling downwards,
> Rippling, quivering flutters, repulse and surrender,
> The sun broidered upon the rain,—

colors were restored to their objects. This might be considered an imagistic rather than a symbolic use of color. For the most part, as an admirer of the Imagists has said, imagism is "presentation, not representation." This is its limitation.

The poetry of Wallace Stevens furnishes excellent examples of varied worlds of color—peacocks, barbaric glass, Chinese umbrellas, melon flowers, red birds, and butterflies. It is Stevens who most strongly objects to the ascetic because he makes an effort to see the sky "without the blue." Of themselves, the colors Stevens uses are mildly exotic, suggestive of the effete and near-decadent. When used in "an image that is sure," that is, as a qualitative part of perceptions that express symbolic values, the colors become the difference between an abstract understanding and an experience that stirs us profoundly. Thus in "Sunday Morning" we are allowed to sense the old terror of the Crucifixion as the suggestion of it plays in the mind of an emancipated and privileged woman

> Complacencies of the peignoir, and late
> Coffee and oranges in a sunny chair,
> And the green freedom of a cockatoo
> Upon a rug mingle to dissipate
> The holy hush of ancient sacrifice.
> She dreams a little, and she feels the dark
> Encroachment of that old catastrophe,
> As a calm darkens among water lights.

The pungent oranges and bright, green wings
Seem things in some procession of the dead,
Winding across wide water, without a sound,
The day is like wide water, without sound,
Stilled for the passing of her dreaming feet
Over the seas, to silent Palestine,
Dominion of the blood and sepulchre.

In Stevens' poetry, color functions symbolically.

Other than for the Imagists, Stevens and Conrad Aiken, the American poets of Eliot's generation[2] seem not to have used color so extensively as their English or Irish contemporaries, the Sitwells, Walter de la Mare, or, most particularly, Yeats, although Marianne Moore has employed it in a muted fashion—"the elephants with their fog colored skin" or the "splashes of fire and silver on the pierced turquoise of the lattices." Cummings, too, should be mentioned because his exuberance frequently has found its expression in color. Many of the best of Miss Moore's contemporaries, Tate, Ransom, and Warren, are metaphysicals—and possibly there is a correlation to be made between a certain pallidity in color and metaphysical treatment of subject matter. Of the generation after Eliot, only Spender in any large way has been preoccupied with color. But with the generation immediately after his, color becomes, as with Stevens, an indispensable part of the poetic substance.

Many in this generation, dominated by George Barker and Dylan Thomas, write what Arthur Mizener has called "a decorative baroque style." The real interest, he says, is "not in the subject in the ordinary sense, but in the verbalized details of the subject; and the characteristic product of this kind of interest is a poem in which a very simple structure of meaning supports a vast and intricate elaboration of highly colored details." The American poets that Mizener finds most influenced by this style are Karl Shapiro, Robert Lowell, and, less evidently, Randall Jarrell and John Malcolm Brinnin. (This is not to say, of course, that these poets have not been influenced by other styles or have not developed personal idioms.) As lines from Lowell's "The Capitalist's Meditation by the Civil War Monument, Christmas, 1942" indicate, color words can strengthen an indictment just as surely as they can lighten tone.

> Union generals
> Perching upon a pillar of dead snow,
> Two cannon and a turdlike cairn of balls,
> Livid in unfinished marble, know
> Only the vulture's leavings of the warcloud:
> Their dead-pans bay the Wizard's Stars for blood.
>
> A blizzard soaps Christ's diapers, and all
> The crowsfoot feathers mossing Mars' brass hat
> Whiten to angels' wings and the War's snowfall
> Slogs down the philanthropic plutocrat
> (Who swished his whited blossoms of goodwill,
> Like sunlight on the hot-beds of world debt)
> And still the venery of Capital
> Freezes the Puritan virtues into gold,
> While Mars, pinched healer, taps their veins.

The Imagistic symbol may serve, even as the abstract symbol, as an organizing principle, a means of gathering up isolated strands into a pattern that is amenable to an act of perception. If this were its sole function, the abstract symbol, which is denotative and tractable, would be a preferable medium of expression. We have a need, however, for *experiencing* our knowledge. The function of the poet, as Eliot said, is to "transform an observation into a state of mind." The symbol is an expression both of thought and of sensibility, a vehicle for expressing understanding esthetically and movingly.

The realm of emotion, of feeling, has commonly been held to be inexpressible if it could not be projected into discursive language. Ludwig Wittgenstein's comment is characteristically positivist: "Everything that can be thought at all can be thought clearly.

Everything that can be said can be said clearly." If one accepts Wittgenstein's premise, then the poet may be said to join the mystics because he persists in a semantic that is not always accessible to the logical mind. What, in effect, the positivist-minded semanticist insists upon is the exclusive use of discursive symbolism. Discursive language, certainly, is not our only means of articulate thought; some of it is imagistic. And imagistic articulation draws upon a different pattern of experience from that of discursive symbolism. To put the difference in quasi-epigrammatic form: If, as Walter Pater said, "all art aspires to the condition of music," then all discursive thinking may be said to aspire to the condition of science. A recognition of the validity of both aspirations, that of logic and that of art, accounts not only for scientific and practical intelligence, but for artistic intelligence and expression as well. But this is to oversimplify. Language that attempts to divorce itself from perceivable meanings aspires to be music, not poetry. A precise, complex intellectuality has its place in art, but it needs sensuous objectification.

Language as the instrument of discursive reason has not been able to express the intricate interplay of feeling, impression, memory, and fancy. This language, admirable in its way, is the achievement of "scientific naturalism." To be reasonable, scientific naturalism must now enlarge its emphasis and give an account of itself in relation to the imagistic aspects of cognition. Each of us in the workaday world knows that all nondiscursive language is not irrational but that it is meaningful in many ways that discursive language cannot be.

In analyzing such a poem as Williams' "Queen-Ann's-Lace," one may observe that a specific complex of ideas, among those which inhere in the multi-meaningful symbol of whiteness, can be expressed only through reference to such a symbol as the one he employs.

Her body is not so white as
anemone petals nor so smooth—nor
so remote a thing. It is a field
of the wild carrot taking
the field by force; the grass
does not raise above it.
Here is no question of whiteness,
white as can be, with a purple mole
at the center of each flower.
Each flower is a hand's span
of her whiteness. Wherever
his hand has lain there is
a tiny purple blemish. Each part
is a blossom under his touch
to which the fibers of her being
stem one by one, each to its end,
until the whole field is a
white desire, empty, a single stem,
a cluster, flower by flower,
a pious wish to whiteness gone over—
or nothing.

The poem is not, of course, concerned merely with description of a field of Queen Anne's lace; it is a metaphorical expression of the specific nature of a woman's love for a man. Despite its being specific, the poem cannot be reduced to a few prose sentences. Our understanding of it depends upon our ability to follow the imaginative leaps of the poet's mind, and our ability to do this depends upon the nature of our experiences with, and understanding of, *whiteness*.

In a paraphrase we can approximate (and only that) the meaning of the poem. The woman is neither remote nor self-sufficient in a virginal beauty ("anemone petals"); her life centers in her love for a man, a love which admits of no distractions ("the grass does not raise above it"). Then the poet repeats his theme (ll. 7–9). Every beauty ("Each flower") she possesses has grown under his caresses. Every impulse of his love to which she has responded has carried her farther from her original state (ll. 11–12). Again (ll. 13–20), the theme is repeated, with the strongest possible emphasis being put upon her love as the entire reason for her existence. The phrase "a pious wish" seems to suggest that once her love was not so intense, may even have been "dutiful." Now she is so completely identified with it that her existence is her love for him—"or nothing."

The whiteness of the flower Williams describes draws upon experiences of such long standing, conceivably even atavistic ones, that our response to it is somehow more complete than our response to an analytical account of the woman's love could be. We absorb sense experiences constantly. Exactly what they mean we are not sure, nor are we often very conscious of their "having to mean" something. But the mind continues to absorb them. And in such a poem as "Queen-Ann's-Lace," we are suddenly aware that artistically employed—functioning, that is, as poetic metaphors—they quicken our awareness of centrally important experiences.

Philosophy has currently asked a new question of itself and of the scientific-minded world it has of late mirrored. It has admitted the vast realm of symbolism as a new semantic. But modern poets have for some time been concerned with a recovery of symbols. They have not waited for a theoretical rationalization of imagistic symbols.

Poetry, then, is concerned in part with symbols which do not lend themselves readily to discursive treatment. The meaning is intimately involved with the form. The import of the poem depends not only on what is said but on the way it is said. And the way it is said is, in part, the physical images employed. Yeats observed that "although you can expound an opinion, or describe a thing when your words are not quite well chosen, you cannot give a body to something that moves beyond the senses, unless your words are as subtle, as complex, as full of mysterious life, as the body of a flower." Passing over the apparent impossibility of experiencing something that "moves beyond the senses," we can observe that Yeats might have been concerned with what Mrs. Langer calls "presentational" images. Such images or symbols do not allow of a systematic breakdown of meanings. The relationships are seen simultaneously. "Their complexity," as Mrs. Langer says in referring to pictures, "consequently is not limited, as sheer discursive language is, by what the mind can retain from the beginning of an apperceptive act to the end of it." The associations we may have with a certain symbol may be so many and the feeling it evokes so elusive, for whatever reason, that the denotative and connotative elements will be too inextricably involved to allow of a ready statement of its meaning. Certainly a poem like Hart Crane's "Air Plant" is not completely analyzable in terms of its denotative or connotative meanings. Yeats, coming at a time when the scientific world view was still in mid-career, recognized the inadequacy behind an effort to understand the world solely in abstract terms. It can be adequately understood only through the functioning of the senses. Ordinary expression is inadequate for expressing emotional states. Language which systematically avoids imagistic symbols fails to catch the intricacies of meaning, shades of feeling, echoes of almost forgotten or of strong memories, or of unarticulated but real emotional reactions. The "only way," Eliot wrote, "of expressing emotion in the form of art is by finding an 'objective correlative.' "[3]

Professor Matthiessen, in *The American Renaissance*, has made evident the primary debt in matters of artistry that Eliot owes to Henry James, even perhaps to the point of having been free to derive his formulation of the "objective correlative." (Santayana also discussed the "correlative object" as early as 1900.) In discussing the *Sense of the Past*, James wrote that he seemed to see the story "in images." Not only certain passages in James, as Matthiessen notes, but many of his titles are imagistic symbols which function as "objective correlatives." A ready illustration is *The Beast in the Jungle*. The jungle is those dark parts of our lives that lie ahead of us and which we fear because someplace therein lurks a terror, the beast, which we cannot see until it springs at us. We may ask, however, whether the "objective correlative" is anything more than idea and emotion objectified, whether in metaphor or in drama. (The objectification may not, of course, always be appropriately motivated.) Passages illustrating it might be cited from Shakespeare or from many of his contemporaries. Blake's tiger is an "objective correlative," as is Williams' field of the wild carrot. The irony of Eliot's being obliged to formulate such a working principle stems simply from modern poets being obliged to recover a sense of the physical for symbolic uses.

It is demonstrable that a common characteristic of modern poetry is the frequency with which images carry the meaning, Mark Van Doren's "Down World" affords a ready example:

> No animal so flattens to the ground,
> Hiding and sliding, as clear water will:
> Its belly nowhere different from the back
> Of the slope earth it hugs, head downward still.

That the restoration of objects to language has been achieved and is central to the esthetic of modern poetry can be observed in the poetry of any of our foremost contemporaries. John Crowe Ransom mutually identifies word and object in "Winter Remembered." Parsnips as fingers could hardly have been seriously accepted by the Victorians.

> Dear love, these fingers that had known your touch,
> And tied our separate forces first together,
> Were ten poor idiot fingers, not worth much,
> Ten frozen parsnips hanging in the weather.

We accept the identification of parsnips and fingers. Ransom's idea and feeling are embodied in the image, which functions intensively by appropriating to itself the mood of the poem and becoming its "concrete objectification."[4]

CHAPTER NINE

# *The Quality of Irony*

*Human thought and conduct can only be treated broadly and truly in a mood of tolerant irony. It belies the logical precision of the long-faced, humorless writer on politics and ethics, whose works rarely deal with man at all, but are a stupid form of metaphysics.*—J. H. ROBINSON

IRONY is a mode of perception, as well as a temper of mind, which enables one to express insights without sacrificing their complexities. The quality of the irony in the poetry of a particular period will depend upon the nature of the period. In an age when the "real" and the "ideal" seem to be or are in balance, when the society's governing beliefs are conceived in such terms that men's moral, esthetic, and economic needs are more nearly served, the ironist can afford a relatively easy role, gently prodding his fellows into more civilized awarenesses and preventing their falling into a stultifying smugness. He functions to improve what, given the historical and not to be transcended premises of the age, is already a relatively satisfactory society. He is therefore a kind of arbiter as well as a gadfly. And for a time, at least, the society could survive his indifference to it. In an age, like our own, when the real and the ideal are out of balance, or in one in which the society is struggling to conceive its basic premises, the critical intelligence plays a central role. And irony is one of its chief instruments.

There seem to be two major causes for the ironic temper in modern poetry. First, the forces which helped develop the character of the middle classes—with their indifference to the esthetic and the imaginative and the directing of all energies toward the "practical"—alienated the artist. The irony deprecating these movements of our society could undoubtedly be traced in divers forms from Henry James and Henry Adams through many contemporary writers. The very isolation of the poet implies that he holds different values from those of his society and will therefore examine opposed values with amusement, contempt, or sympathy. A range of such ironic examination can be found in poets as different as Robinson, Pound, Eliot, Cummings, Fearing, and Auden. The ironic temper is almost constant in many of the best modern poets. Secondly, as we have already indicated, with the disintegration of the Christian vision we have lost our capacity for "absolute" judgment. As Kenneth Burke has put it, the "relativistic sciences," like psychology and anthropology, have undermined once stable values. It is no longer easy to say, " 'It is wrong in the eyes of God,' nor even, 'It is wrong in the eyes of human justice.' One can simply say, 'I do not like it.' " Yet, it is hardly sufficient for the poet to say, "I like it" or "I do not like it." He must examine his materials critically and publicly. By employing a tolerant irony, he can save himself from those commitments which allow neither of alternatives nor of qualifications. Thus we have a poet like Wallace Stevens who, essentially concerned with finding a moral focus as a center for his poetry, examines, as in "The Comedian as the Letter C," serious problems relating to the poet with the graciousness of one seemingly not involved.

Erasmus, accepting the "seriocomic" nature of man, exhibits the Renaissance awareness of irony. He knew that rigidity of beliefs inhibits a quality of mind that is opposed to the distortions of intolerance and cant. The attitude, manner, and tone of *Praise of Folly* are common to many Renaissance minds, from Sir Thomas More through Shakespeare and Donne. The successes of the Renaissance world were so sudden and so many that only an exquisite irony could have saved one from an obsession with power and hopefulness.

In no one, other perhaps than Shakespeare or Donne, does the ironic temper of the Renaissance find fuller expression than in Raleigh. The pride that sired both physical bravery and moral courage was kept from being monstrous by a subtly working irony, itself just short of being inordinate. The tremendous successes of the man, the daring of his intrigues, demanded a tragic awareness of the suddenness with which reverses might—and did—come. Raleigh's "The Passionate Man's Pilgrimage," for example, depends on the continued contrast of worldly strategems with the Christian's spiritual quest. His condemnation of the court becomes the image of "conscience molten into gold."

> For there Christ is the king's attorney,
> Who pleads for all without degrees,
> And he hath angels, but no fees.

The pun on "angels" serves as no extended comment could to state the irony of court justice being bought by gold. The Renaissance, for all its beaten gold and courtly trappings, rarely forgot its immediate medieval ancestry. The tension between Christian humility and the modern pride in personal success probably was read far more clearly and explicitly by Elizabethans than it is by us. Raleigh's fame now is as a courtier and an explorer. We look for evidences of nobility in his poetry. It is significant that he constantly employed the Christian virtues as the foil for the nobleman's values. Humility still maintained a place in the collective consciousness, a virtue related to the wry knowledge that success has failure as a counterpart. Raleigh was dedicated to certain ends, but not so single-mindedly that he was no longer free to maintain a degree of detachment or to see one object in relation to other objects.

Irony as usually found in Restoration plays is an expression of a knowledge of worldly ways. The irony of the sophisticate is merely at the expense of those naïve about such ways. Worldly knowledge is a kind of absolute value, and human motives are assumed to be low motives. The ironist working with these assumptions, themselves vulnerable to irony, may achieve great verbal brilliance. His irony is instructive to those wishing to understand the society, but it is severely limited as instruction in human motives generally. Irony in a polite society, as we may assume the eighteenth-century society to have been, has similar limitations. The society's ideal of avoiding enthusiasm, for instance, runs counter to human impulses. Profound feelings are a part of great actions. Great dignity or nobility seems hardly possible in individuals who have not felt deeply. The ironist who accepts the ideal of "sheer reasonableness" is likely to be concerned with manners and with verbal witticisms. He reconciles man to his society rather than to his fate. The eighteenth century seems not to have known tragic irony, at least in its own literature.

Cosmic irony and romantic irony, both reactions to the developments of rationalism, were relatively late expressions. Oddly, the breakup of the Ptolemaic world and the consequent effects upon Christian belief were, for the most part, realized slowly. Only in the nineteenth century did poets really discover a cosmos in which man was a speck. In their frustration some of them castigated a God who could put men in such a miserably low status; or they denied Him and took a hollow delight in pointing up the absurdity of man's self-inflation. Among the cosmic ironists were the young Shelley, Clough, James Thomson, Swinburne, Fitzgerald, and Hardy. In America the strain was developed briefly by Stephen Crane. One finds it even now, as in Osbert Sitwell's *Collected Poems and Satires*. But cosmic irony could be sustained easily only while there was a strong feeling that man had somehow been betrayed, badly treated by God, or misinformed about his place in the universe. Eventually the new cosmos became an unquestioned part of man's experience, and the poet who overstressed this awareness began to seem a little naïve.

The romantic ironist is also frustrated by the new knowledge. Allen Tate explains the origin of his frustration in these terms:

> Throughout the nineteenth century, and in a few poets today, we get an intellectual situation like this: there is the assumption that Truth is indifferent or hostile to the desires of men; that these desires were formerly nurtured on legend, myth, all kinds of insufficient experiment; that, Truth being known at last in the form of experimental science, it is intellectually impossible to maintain illusion any longer, at the same time that it is morally impossible to assimilate Truth.

The romantic ironist confesses his despair. He does not believe he can deny the picture of a world indifferent to man. Thus he finds himself, in Yvor Winters' terms, in "a state of moral insecurity," in a position which he finds insufferable but is unable to alter. The assumption of the romantic ironist is that poetry must present the same kind of knowledge that science presents. He would not make such an assumption, presumably, if he recognized that the scientific methodology is inadequate for the "study of mental phenomena"——imagination, values, and ideals. In brief, imagination other than in the affairs of science is generally suspect by a society preoccupied with "the control of the external relation of persons and things."

It has been observed frequently that the eighteenth century saw not only great numbers of middle-class writers but a literature directed at middle-class readers. (Writers moved from a dependence upon patrons to a dependence upon the reading public.) We might say that, excepting work like Swift's, literature progressively became a bourgeois expression. The process continued through Tennyson, who had the largest of middle-class audiences. Irony within the confines of the bourgeois perspective is as limited as that within the perspective of the sophisticate. Irony, that is, was relatively restricted until the poet, by the 1890's, rejected his middle-class ties. A fairly mild expression of the break with the American concern for material success is Edwin Arlington Robinson's "Dear Friends" (1897)—

> The shame I win for singing is all mine,
> The gold I miss for dreaming is all yours.

Thereafter, there is the irony directed against the middle-class world, and there is the irony employed by poets attempting to find premises upon which new and larger perspectives may rest. The latter, conceivably, may yet achieve a profundity that will rank it with the irony of the great tragedies.

## 2

The facets of irony, all of them forms of "simulation," are rhetorical devices which give emotional intensity to expressions otherwise direct and coldly intellectual. Wilson O. Clough defines irony as a "form of allegory, thinking one thing and saying another."[1] Language generally, he says, "resembles a free translation, offering the general sense, and acting both as obstacle and organ. But understanding surrounds language with waves of connotation, and supplies, corrects, and gathers meanings." Irony functions to "pierce those ambiguities, to track consciousness through the labyrinths, and to free it from premature assumptions." Irony through puns, paradox, understatement, conscious naïveté, litotes, oxymoron, through various forms of *indirection*, compensates for the limiting simplicities of most language, without sacrificing emotional impact.

A long anthology of poems dependent in some part on the ironic temper might be collected. Since Socrates, and undoubtedly before, some at least of the functions have appeared in all literatures. In English poetry one finds conscious naïveté in Chaucer's "My wit is short, ye may well-understonde . . ." or in Walter de la Mare's "Peeping Tom":

But what can Miss Emily
Want with a box
So long, narrow, shallow
  And without any locks?

Conscious naiveté is closely akin to understatement, perhaps the commonest of all forms of irony. The latter is a kind of reticence or modesty of statement that makes a strong affirmation while appearing to underestimate the significance of what is being said. In America there is a Yankee tradition of word parsimony and fear, almost, of giving in to emotion. The tradition has become associated with New England, so that some of her poets, like Frost, write characteristically in this manner.

Understatement indicates a wary intellect. By appealing to the reader to use his imagination in filling in the stratum between the level of actual statement and that of implied truth, the poet employing it increases the reader's awareness. Usually, too, understatement involves a dry humor and saves the poet from sentimentality. But constant understatement can become an annoying mannerism. The poet, like Wallace Stevens, who can achieve brilliant rhetorical effects yet hold them in check by an ironical awareness does not inhibit himself, as Frost unfortunately does, by infusing each line, as it were, with its measure of laconic humor or whimsy. There may be dangers in the grand manner—but the great subjects, on the other hand, cannot be treated in an idiom that threatens at each moment to become folksy.

The irony of circumstance, or situation, with its dramatic nature, seems common to all periods. It is a chief feature in drama, but it is found also in ballads, lyrics, and certain forms of narrative poetry. Hardy's "Satires of Circumstance" may be among the most successful of the modern uses of the type. Robinson, too, employed dramatic irony, as in "Richard Cory." Much of his success with short lyrics, in fact, depends upon the successful use of ironic situations. The use of ironic situations, coupled, of course, with employment of varied ironic attitudes (tone), might be traced through many poets: in Cummings, as when he has the ruddy Mr. Lyman coming from a funeral; in Van Doren, as in "Two of You;" or in Eliot throughout *The Waste Land*.

Among the more strictly verbal forms of irony is the employment of puns and paradoxes. Understatement is sometimes emphasized by verbal play, as when Mercutio, being near death, says, "Ask for me tomorrow, and you shall find me a grave man." Among contemporary examples is Shapiro's pun on "club" in his satiric "University." Social graciousness is a weapon to be used against those who do not "belong"—thus "Poise is a club."

Each of the parts, or the single part, in the statement of a paradox is usually so well understood in its ordinary contexts that it is accepted as a truism or a commonplace. Seen in a new context, there is a tension established between the newly suggested and the older meaning, or meanings, that creates an ironical contrast. Thus the surprise of Eliot's line, "Liberty is a different kind of pain from prison," or of Stevens' poem, "Theory":

> I am what is around me.
>
> Women understand this.
> One is not a duchess
> A hundred yards from a carriage.

That strong intellectual emphasis in poetry all but requires employment of paradox is suggested by the frequenty of its usage by the Metaphysicals and the moderns.

The commentaries of I. A. Richards, particularly in his *Principles of Literary Criticism*, have served to bring to the forefront of critical discussions the awareness of the contrast between poetry easily vulnerable to irony and poetry that can withstand "ironic contemplation."

> There are two ways in which impulses may be organized; by exclusion and by inclusion, by synthesis and by elimination. . . .
>
> The difference comes out clearly if we consider how comparatively

unstable poems of the first kind are, They will not bear an ironical contemplation. We have only to read *The War Songs of Dinas Vawr* in close conjunction with the *Coronach*, or to remember that unfortunate phrase "Those lips, O slippery blisses!" from *Endymion* while reading *Love's Philosophy* to notice this. Irony in this sense consists in bringing in of the opposite, the complementary impulses; that is why poetry which is exposed to it is not of the highest order, and why irony itself is so constantly a characteristic of poetry which is.

The sentimentalist inclines to express greater emotion than the occasion warrants and to find satisfaction merely in indulging his feelings. The sentimental poet achieves his effects by narrowly selecting detail that will intensify the emotional impact, by treating an experience more seriously than it deserves. The weakness of many a poem, as Cleanth Brooks has demonstrated in his *Modern Poetry and the Tradition*, is exhibited when it is examined in the light of Richards' principles. In a period when poetry has been put to the service of ideologies, when poets must work out their private systems, and the multiplication of sensation is a chief "value," a critical awareness of the danger of oversimplification is of great importance. But the writing of a poetry invulnerable to irony requires more than a fear of falling into sentimentality. It requires a great deal of intellectual agility, a capacity both for seeing one idea in terms of its opposite or of other ideas which qualify it and for creating a mood and tone which do not belie the recognition.

## *3*

The ironist, because of dependence on his own mental agility, risks backing himself into a corner. The most obvious danger perhaps is that, in feigning indifference and in striving to see what is irrational, he will become passionless and come to suspect all reason. Irony, according to one of its students, being "relative and negative, more tolerant than generous, may reduce all to probabilism and atomism." The line between a positive critical irony and a contemptuous distrust of human understanding and motives is a thin one. One may find "in a nightmare world of relativity that nothing is worth doing, *all things considered*." The habit of irony, as David Worcester has put it, may be an escape from responsibility, for the inveterate ironist

> can expound the good side of cannibalism as well as the bad, explain why it is inevitable that Oxford Groupers and atheists should think as they do, and point to his own failures as interesting examples of the mechanical operation of heredity and environment.[2]

Irony thus shades into cynicism. As such, it is committed to the view (although rarely, if ever, in an absolute way) that everything is wrong, in the worst of all possible worlds. Irony need not be thus committed—it may be a mode of operation which has a secret alliance with positive goals. As such, it is a creative force despite its sometimes pretended liaison with mockery and ridicule. Indeed, certain forms of irony, romantic irony and cosmic irony, as well as the constant air of ennui or of whimsical amusement should, it seems, be categorized under some heading other than irony. They express a negative impulse and themselves invite ridicule. They spell frustration or megalomania as well as the persistent need for "debunking."

Conrad Aiken is perhaps the greatest of the modern cosmic ironists. He treats the theme subtly and in detail. But the theme is essentially that of post-Renaissance ironists who saw in a seemingly infinite universe no possible sanction for man's "sentiments, faith and morality." Man has dwindled to less than a speck. His speech, as it were, thins out suddenly, as though caught in a gust of wind and whipped wildly out into space and timelessness.

> No language leaps this chasm like lightning:
> Here is no message of assuagement, blown
> From Ecuador to Greenland; here is only
> A trumpet blast, that calls dead men to arms;
> The granite's pity for the cloud; the whisper
> Of time to space.

There is no attempt in this poetry to interpret the meaning of a society. There is, rather, the effort to evoke a poetic awareness of the cosmos—so that even the irony of the human plight dissolves into a shimmering nirvana.

Cleanth Brooks finds a romantic irony suffused through the work of MacLeish. In poems like "Memorial Rain" and "The End of the World" there is the same kind of ironic acceptance as in Carl Sandburg's "Cool Tombs." Time and nature, rather than human intelligence, effect the reconciliation. Like Aiken, MacLeish is a master of evocative detail. Except for his more recent large and loosely stated faith in "the people," however, he seems incapable of achieving a balance within a complex of principles or attitudes. Brooks follows Tate in defining the romantic ironist as one "defiantly or in disillusion" in revolt against science and the optimism generated by the concept of inevitable progress. The irony of Sandburg, Aiken, and MacLeish, however, seems less a revolt than a pathetic acceptance of the cosmos that science has shown us. Tate's thesis is more neatly illustrated in Hart Crane's harrowing cry in "The Tunnel," in those moments before he turned back again, from his vision of a society with no "rational order of value," to the vision Whitman had believed would become a living actuality.

Crane, we may believe, was taken in by the then current talk about science and industry being harnessed for man in a brilliant future. But he could not reconcile his vision of a mechanical hell with Whitman's vision, although he tried by apostrophes to Whitman to recover his optimistic faith. It is less easy to sympathize with the romantic ironist in the Fitzgerald and Housman tradition, those who have made self-pity the central theme of their poetry. All is tragicomic. Man sees himself as a pathetic victim.

"They sneer at me for leaning all awry;
What? did the Hand then of the Potter shake?"

All events are to be seen against inevitable disappointment and defeat. Whatever the subject, the theme remains the same. One builds a romantic hope and collapses in romantic despair.

'Is my friend hearty,
  Now I am thin and pine,
And has he found to sleep in
  A better bed than mine?'

Yes, lad, I lie easy,
  I lie as lads would choose;
I cheer a dead man's sweetheart,
  Never ask me whose.

This extravagant self-pity is a permanent viewpoint. It is indifferent to irony as a way of seeing around and behind opposed attitudes. It is pleased to manufacture small tragedies because its chief delights are the wry smile, the pose of long-suffering, and the affectation of superior knowledge. The Housman manner and idiom were readily assumed by those who had discovered that ennui, a blasé air, and the habit of "debunking" either satisfied a need or were pleasant forms of self-indulgence in a society that could not discover a way of establishing a system of values to replace that which had been undermined and, in part, discarded.

Perhaps this is to overstate the case against the romantic ironists. There are many poems, of course, informed and controlled in part by the spirit of romantic irony that are moving and convincing, successful in stating a tenable view of experience and successful as poetic expression. In Keats's "Ode to a Nightingale," Housman's "To an Athlete Dying Young," and Yeats's "A Dialogue of Self and Soul," the same theme is investigated, death as a release from pain, humiliation, and the sense of impermanence. Each is successful in terms of the situation or complex of attitudes investigated. In none of the three poems, however, is there the implication that *all* human experience ends in despair. The death of the athlete is seen by Housman as a matter for congratulation because the young man died at the height of his renown. The poem does not mean that it is better to die young rather than old. The context justifies the point of view. In the other two poems the attitude of the romantic ironist is entertained, tentatively accepted, but then rejected. In the third and sixth stanzas of his poem Keats wishes for death—but in the final stanza we learn these were wishes expressed while under the benumbing influence of reverie. In coming back to his "sole self!" he recognizes that

> the fancy cannot cheat so well
> As she is famed to do, deceiving elf.

Yeats, too, quite willingly admits all the frustrations the romantic ironist sees—but, when remorse is cast off, he reaffirms the sense of vitality and strength that sustain him. The pure statement of romantic irony implies absolute frustration. The romantic ironist has no center of positive belief or value that he is attempting to strengthen or to promote an awareness of. He merely cherishes, in Babbitt's terms, "the illusion that to be a spiritual vagrant is to be exalted on a pinnacle above the plain citizen." The pure romantic ironist uses his belief in the aimlessness of the universe and his own futility as the excuse for his "hot baths of sentiment, . . . followed by cold douches of irony." Romantic irony is a negative impulse.

There would seem to be a connection between the convictions that produced at least some of the modern poetry of ennui and those that produced the narrowly conceived naturalism that saw man a victim of his environment and heredity. In any case, it is observable that the revolution in manners and morals which found its major expression in the twenties was a product of this naturalism. Worcester has pointed to the use of irony in Hemingway's *The Sun Also Rises*. "An impotent hero held in thrall by sexual passion; a useless lover attending his lady through her promiscuous affairs: here is the apotheosis of irony, designed to draw iron tears down Pluto's cheek." The situation is such that any further frustration would dissolve the pathos into absurdity. And that the pathos was not to be taken too seriously is suggested perhaps by a passage in the same novel:

'What's all this about irony and pity?'
'What? Don't you know about Irony and Pity?'
'No. Who got it up?'
'Everybody. They're mad about it in New York. It's just like the Fratellinis used to be.'

The same crude conception of man determined and defeated which gave fiction writers an enormous new area to work had its effect on poets. Edgar Lee Masters' *Spoon River Anthology* affords the prototype. In verses like "Washington McNeely" it is as though each human being were, in effect, a drunken blind man running into walls, stumbling against tables and chairs, before finally falling down two flights of stairs.

> Rich, honored by my fellow citizens,
> The father of many children, born of a noble mother,
> All raised there
> In the great mansion-house, at the edge of town. . . .
> They were strong children, promising as apples
> Before the bitten places show.
> But John fled the country in disgrace.
> Jenny died in child-birth—
> I sat under my cedar tree.
> Harry killed himself after a debauch,
> Susan was divorced—
> I sat under my cedar tree.
> Paul was invalided from overstudy,
> Mary became a recluse at home for love of a man—
> I sat under my cedar tree.
> All were gone, or broken-winged or devoured by life—
> I sat under my cedar tree.
> My mate, the mother of them, was taken—
> I sat under my cedar tree,
> Till ninety years were tolled.
> O maternal Earth, which rocks the fallen leaf to sleep!

The irony of Housman or Hart Crane implies at least that man has dignity. His great hopes go awry, but a suggestion of nobility is offered as a counterbalance. The despair could not be so great if the hope had not been so strong. But in the view of the naturalistic ironists man is so much the *ingénu*, so much without any power of interpenetrating or controlling his environment or the objects he lives with, that ironic contemplation of his plight is his only pleasure.

The vision of the universe which science has presented to us is such, apparently, that man can now be regarded, in Carl Becker's terms, as "a chance deposit on the surface of the world, carelessly thrown up between two ice ages by the same forces that rust iron and ripen corn, a sentient organism endowed by some happy or unhappy accident with intelligence. . . . The ultimate cause of this cosmic process of which man is a part, whether God or electricity or a 'stress in the ether,' we know not." The insights afforded by science make it appear that he is "unassisted and undirected by omniscient or benevolent authority." He must "fend for himself, and with the aid of his own limited intelligence find his way about in an indifferent universe." The way the poet, we might add, employs irony, in the direction of despair or as a positive mode of perception, is a test of his sheer pragmatic value to a society which envisions the universe as flux.

## 4

The part the modern poet plays as ironist has a curious similarity to that of the *eiron*, a stock character of early Greek drama, from whom our word "irony" derives. *Eiron*, an underdog, was set against *alazon*, a boastful character greatly given to exaggeration. The pride of modern man arises from his exaggerated notions of the power inherent in his scientific knowledge and in his secular, materialistic values. The poet is opposed to those emphases which see in values merely hollow ways of making the society "work" and in imagination functioning for esthetic purposes merely illusions.

Consequently, we have an irony, frequently merging with the satiric, aimed at ridiculing the ends the society accepts as ideals. At its best, this irony functions as a mode of perception. We have, for example, Eliot employing a large dramatic, as well as incidental, irony to characterize his world, Ransom employing a pleasant mockery to indicate that esthetic considerations run counter to certain "rational" ideals, and Stevens employing a self-satire that enables him to see personal problems as though through another's eyes. All three of these poets, as well as those with similar esthetic ideals, move warily from fact to fact, attempting to discover the point of view most tenable.

The chief mode of Eliot's irony, which is dramatic as well as verbal, may be suggested by the words Kenneth Burke uses to characterize the method of irony employed by Anatole France:

> He wrote his books on the top of other books, that his might share the quality of theirs; he found that by "scribbling upon the margin of books" he could restore for us some of the gentler existences out of which these other books had arisen. Like an archeologist, he found a calm Atlantis, which had heaved a huge geologic sigh and sunk slowly to the bottom of the sea, where it now lay, its temples still standing, its marbles posturing, and mournful fishes peering upon those dead splendors.

The theme of *The Waste Land*, of course, is the plight of a society attempting to live by secular values. "The values of the past" were thought to be, as Tate puts it, "pretty, absurd, and false; the scientific truth is both true and bitter." The society which the poem characterizes was holding close to the principles of a reductive naturalism. Consequently, love was to be understood as biological necessity, and individual nobility of spirit as an illusion of a world that had not known about genes and chromosomes. Sophistication had replaced the ideal of charity or selflessness. Eliot's task was to show those in his society who accepted these secular values unquestioningly that they were merely assuming that they understood the nature of man. If man had once been capable of spirituality in love and in his individual character, he still was.

Thus in "The Fire Sermon" Eliot uses Tiresias, who in *Oedipus Rex* had understood that the sexual relations of Oedipus and his mother had caused their land to be cursed, as a witness of the loveless relation of the young man carbuncular and the typist. These two have no sense of sin—they are merely bored. The succeeding incidents and comments serve to emphasize that the traditional values have broken down. Each has its measure of irony, through being contrasted with a historical incident or through the poet's indirect way of showing that the young man and woman are less than complete human beings. In other sections of his poem, as in "A Game of Chess," Eliot examines further aspects of his vision of modern man.[3] Professor Brooks has also shown how Eliot's irony operates to achieve a complexity of detail, to the end that his positive beliefs are made clear. This is not always recognized, with the consequence that Eliot's poem is sometimes held to be something it is not—as romantic irony, "a world-weary cry of despair or a sighing after the vanished glories of the past." The paradox upon which the entire poem is built is the ancient one of life growing out of death.

Another illustration of the ironic temper among the modern poets is the work of John Crowe Ransom. Southern poets and critics have quite rightly pointed to his poetry as an instance of the use of irony as a means of restoring a sense of equilibrium between the awareness of the irrational or evil inherent in the physical world and the rational order we must follow in the guidance of our affairs. As a man of sensitivity, he is constantly aware, to a greater degree than the scientific-minded, of those points at which the rational affords an incomplete realization; yet he cannot return to a complete acceptance of the physical and the irrational which would be primitivism. His ironic attitude, a kind of whimsical self-deprecation and an offhand and indirect way of suggesting that the rational approach has rigorous limitations, is his way of reconciling the discordant elements. For irony, in one of its aspects, is merely a way of resolving, in so far as it is possible, opposed attitudes. In "Janet Waking," to take an example, we may observe one or two aspects of his ironic manner.

> Beautifully Janet slept
> Till it was deeply morning. She woke then
> And thought about her dainty-feathered hen,
> To see how it had kept. . . .
>
> "Old Chucky, old Chucky!" she cried,
> Running across the world upon the grass
> To Chucky's house, and listening. But alas,
> Her Chucky had died.
>
> It was a transmogrifying bee
> Came droning down on Chucky's old bald head
> And sat and put the poison. It scarcely bled,
> But how exceedingly
>
> And purply did the knot
> Swell with the venom and communicate
> Its rigor! Now the poor comb stood up straight
> But Chucky did not.
>
> So there was Janet
> Kneeling on the wet grass, crying her brown hen
> (Translated far beyond the daughters of men)
> To rise and walk upon it.
>
> And weeping fast as she had breath
> Janet implored us, "Wake her from her sleep!"
> And would not be instructed in how deep
> Was the forgetful kingdom of death.

There is a pleasant domesticity which suggests a rationally ordered world, under intelligent control. To it is brought the sudden realization of the chief of all irrational elements, death. The term "transmogrifying," a learned term, mocks any emphasis that overestimates the importance of the rational. (In "Here Lies a Lady" the line, "After six little spaces of chill, and six of burning," more definitely mocks a scientific exactness.) The reader is jolted by the sudden shifts from ordered domesticity to the unalterable fact of death. Janet, too, who would not be instructed, may be thought a symbol of all of us who are insufficiently aware that any rational order is subject to the eternally unconscious, which is nature.

Wallace Stevens, who in his controlled delicacy and elegance is akin to Ransom, is also an able ironist. He sustains, for example, the fairly long autobiographical poem, "The Comedian as the Letter C," without mawkishness or distortion. His theme is the relation of the poet, both himself and the poet in general, to the society. The theme tempts one to large generalizations, attacks upon the society, ridicule of the poet for believing either that he can effectively reshape the society or that his being articulate about it will interest or move more than a very few, or, even, ridicule of the notion that a poet really has anything to say to a practical-minded society. Again, the poet actually writing is concerned with his personal life as well as with the theories of the poet's relationship to his milieu.

If the poet were to assume the role of sage or wear the silk-lined cape of the romantic figure, he would invite attack. He assumes instead the role of the *eiron*, the mild and questioning figure. The *alazon*, as it were, is all those exaggerated attitudes and pretensions which he reduces to reasonable proportions. The reader's sympathies and attention focus against a poet who introduces himself as the traditional valet-comedian, and not only as a comedian but as the "merest minuscule," the single letter of a word. Yet, quite obviously, this self-satirizing poet is capable of nimble verse and quick insights. The reader assured of the humble yet aware intelligence is thus prepared to follow carefully the jest, the exaggeration, and the plainly serious—to see what final perspective the poet evolves.

The poet tells, in the six sections, how Crispin has come to see his art, the history of the experiences, including his marriage, which led him to reduce the magnitude of the role he had once assigned himself, to adopt a greater conservatism, and to see the world, in its colors, to be sure (that is, imaginatively), more in the way the "stiffest realist" sees it. For Stevens the poem did not represent, as Yvor Winters has said it did, "a tentative leave-taking" from his art. It represented the history of a poet's adjustment to his society. It simply shows him giving up his dream of building "Loquacious columns by the ructive sea." The decision, he says, is no excuse for scrawling a "tragedian's testament." Indeed, it would seem most likely that Stevens chose wisely. In any event, the poem is not a "curious variant" on romantic irony. There is neither self-pity nor despair. The irony, which is operative from line to line almost, is that of a shrewd and perceptive mind, not one which attaches itself to a single attitude and holds on blindly.

Irony is a kind of guaranty against deception. It protects one against "microscopic tragedies," bathos and sentimentality. Used so that it does not betray the ironist, it encourges modesty, carefulness, and good will. It enables one to arrive at a reasonable mean. But it is not an absolute, a scale against which everything can be measured. It is a *way* by which the intellect assists itself toward the best perspective. In a time when all values are held to be relative, the poet would seem to be almost as greatly in need of a sense of irony as of a nimble imagination.

CHAPTER TEN

# *Tension and the Structure of Poetry*

*Without internal tension there would be a fluid rush to a straightway mark; there would be nothing that could be called development and fulfilment. The existence of resistance defines the place of intelligence in the production of an object.*—John Dewey

Early in his theorizing about the writing of poetry, Ezra Pound said that the chief problem was to recover "intensity." Most of the criticism since then has been concerned directly or indirectly with intensity or with what has been called "tension," which Allen Tate has defined as "the full organized body of all the extension and intension that we can find" in a poem.[1] The "meaning of poetry is its 'tension.' " The repetition of sound and sense, the contrast or comparison of part with other parts or with the whole, and the interfusion of sense and feeling into each part simultaneously—all are ways of increasing tension in the poem. The pronouncements of various critics usually relate at some point to this statement. Thus T. E. Hulme's account of the poet's imagination:

> A powerful imaginative mind seizes and combines at the same instant all the important ideas of its poem or picture, and while it works with one of them, it is at the same instant working with and modifying all in their relation to it and never losing sight of their bearings on each other—as the motion of a snake's belly goes through all parts at once and its volition acts at the same instant in coils which go contrary ways.

A more recent pronouncement, indebted no doubt to statements of Hulme, Pound, and their generation, is by Joseph Frank:

Since the primary reference of any word-group is to something inside the poem itself, language in modern poetry is really reflexive: the meaning-relationship is completed only by the simultaneous perception in space of word-groups which, when read consecutively in time, have no comprehensible relation to each other. Instead of the instinctive and immediate reference of words and word-groups to the objects or events they symbolize and the construction of meaning from the sequence of these references, modern poetry asks its readers to suspend the process of reference temporarily until the entire pattern of internal reference can be apprehended as a unity. This explanation is, of course, the extreme statement of an ideal condition, rather than an actually existing state of affairs; but the conception of poetic form that runs through Mallarmé to Pound and Eliot, and which has left its traces on a whole generation of modern poets, can be formulated only in terms of the principle of reflexive reference.

The reason for this type of organization is twofold. The precise meaning of the poet cannot become clear until it has been explored and stated in terms of all the elements in the poem. Secondly, since the meaning is to be experienced, as well, it should "strike the reader's sensibility with an instantaneous impact." Through this impact, says Pound, we receive "that sense of sudden liberation; that sense of freedom from time limits and space limits; that sense of sudden growth, which we experience in the presence of the greatest works of art."

In his *Principles of Literary Criticism* I. A. Richards has made quite explicit the notion that the poetic experience, at its best, is the harmonizing or reconciling of inharmonious elements. He discusses the poetry that synthesizes heterogeneous elements and the poetry that is composed of natively harmonious elements. The latter poetry is likely to be "poetic" in the sense that it is built upon an exclusionist diction, given over to an otherworldly, misty, or consciously romantic subject matter. And it is likely to be nonintellectual. Richards seems to have derived the suggestion for his theory both from Coleridge and from considering the elements composing dramatic tragedy. He might, as well, have derived it upon examining the willingness of many modern poets to introduce elements into the poetic structure which their nineteenth-century predecessors had been careful to exclude. That is, he could have seen elements, transmuted into poetry, which some earlier poets had been unable or unwilling to accommodate. Among these elements are intellectual subtleties, meanings lurking in obscurities of various sorts, an apparently offhand, conversational, and sometimes ironic manner, prosaic or even antipoetic terms, startling contrasts of various sorts and frequent shifts and variations in tone, and a compromise with the rhythms of prose.

If the poet must work through a context of conflicting and heterogeneous elements, the resulting structure will of necessity be dramatic. His "perspective of perspectives" will be the result of examining his point of view or attitudes in the light of ambiguous shadings of meaning, conflicting evidences, and ironical contemplation. The final perspective will be achieved through the examination of connotations and questioning of the validity of certain metaphorical or symbolic representations, as well as the appropriateness of certain rhythms and the ultimate tone of the poem. Kenneth Burke has called this process the submitting of a limited version of the truth to the ordeal, as in drama, of "unending conversation." Warren calls it coming "to terms with Mercutio." By coming to terms with Mercutio, he means that the intensely romantic love of Romeo and Juliet is subject to the ironic barbs and naturalistic qualifications of Mercutio. If the poet's "proposition," the worth and value of romantic love, is justifiable, it can withstand the ridicule. It will, in fact, be stronger if seen for what it actually is, partly naturalistic and partly spiritual. The Victorian romanticizing of love was readily vulnerable because of the pretense that love exists in a purely spiritual, idealized realm. The ablest poets arrive at an attitude or point of view as the result of the most scrupulous examination possible through the use of their medium.

Tension, then, serves the double purpose of presenting an attitude or statement precisely (not necessarily simply) and making possible the experiencing, or re-creating, of it by the reader. The attempt to achieve tension helps keep the poet from falling into sentimentalities, irrelevancies, exaggerations, unqualified moralizing, formlessness, vagueness, and incoherencies. Tension is not a foolproof formula, however; it is merely the able employment of a group of techniques which, like the ironic attitude, help the poet make an intelligent use of his medium. Warren refers to these techniques as "resistances" which the poet must overcome. As examples, he suggests the "tension between the rhythm of the poem and the rhythm of speech; . . . between the formality of the rhythm and the informality of language; between the particular and the general, the concrete and the abstract; between the elements of even the simplest metaphor; between the beautiful and the ugly; between ideas; . . . between the elements involved in irony; . . . between prosisms and poeticisms." To these, which Warren does not present as an exhaustive list, we might add the tension between specific opposites, as in oxymoron or in paradox; between repetition and variation upon repetition; between an intensive image and the rest of the poem; between the ambiguities and connotations of a word and between these and the rest of the poem; between the argument, or tenor, and the diverse suggestions latent in the images or symbols of the poem; between chains of evidence, as in metaphysical poems, that lead to different conclusions; between exaggerated statement, rhetoric, and simple, direct statement; and between the entire form of the poem and the elements that compose that form. If these, or some of these, tensions are achieved at the pitch of passion and reconciled, then exquisite poetry may result. This will be the reward, as Henry James says of the artist, for the poet's infinite curiosity and incorrigible patience.

## 2

Didacticism, the characteristic fault of much eighteenth- and nineteenth-century poetry, implies a thought-out, predefined conclusion to a poem, an evaluation which is often an extension of the poetic materials and therefore irrelevant to them. When poetry is deliberately didactic, the imagination becomes the tool of a predetermined attitude. Characters in drama then become figures of useful abstractions, and images in poetry become mechanical and decorative. Eighteenth- and nineteenth-century poems, particularly in America, frequently end with moral injunctions, and the poems "justify" themselves by their conclusions. The value, that is, is in the ease with which the moral can be pointed up.

When images function, not through the suggestions latent within them and meanings to be reconciled with the "logic" or "argument" of the poem, but as illustrations of a consciously striven-for poetic mistiness or moralism, the images will be superimposed—and often mixed. In James Russell Lowell's "Commemoration Ode" the confusion of images results from a confusion of rationalizing and preaching with what should be a simple reconciliation of poetic elements:

> A seed of sunshine that can leaven
> Our earthly dulness with the beam of stars,
> And glorify our clay
> With light from fountains older than the day.

Sunshine, stars, clay, and fountains are conglomerately set against one another and through some imagined quality expected to elevate the basically prosaic teaching. The elements do not converge. This is not to say, certainly, that diversified images cannot be used side by side. But, when so used, there must be points of similarity, of relationship to each other or to the central theme which justify their being brought together. Emily Dickinson, living in the same preacher-conscious New England, could in such a poem as "The Chariot" handle the theme of mortality—a temptation to moralizing—and succeed in making all the images intensify and relate to the dominant metaphor.

The kind of writing in which a situation is not examined in terms of its own character or attributes but in which it is merely associated with certain attitudes and feelings normally foreign to it is well known to propagandists. The attitudes are not generated by the subject working up, as it were, through the medium. They are, following a kind of sleight-of-hand identification, assumed to be related to the subject. Yvor Winters calls this sort of writing "pseudo-reference."

The opening verse of Hart Crane's "The Air Plant" indicates one way in which the imagination may investigate an object:

> This tuft that thrives on saline nothingness,
> Inverted octopus with heavenward arms
> Thrust parching from a palm-bole hard by the cove—
> A bird almost—of almost bird alarms.

First, there is the metaphysical element, the thriving on nothingness; second, there is the thematic relationship of saline, octopus, and cove; third, there is the sudden shift from octopus to bird—but with the justification that the uplifted, poised-for-flight appearance of the air plant makes the transition an easily acceptable one. Similarly, that the succeeding verses are developed always in terms of the air plant itself (not merely through the use of it as a rhetorical point of reference) makes the poem an instantaneous whole. Whatever the poet has to say is said within a frame of reference, within the stated subject of his poem.

The poet may, of course, examine a moralistic dictum or a platitude, subjecting it to various kinds of questions and examining it when it is caught in figurative expressions or in certain rhythms. Marianne Moore, among the moderns, does these things in much of her poetry. Or a poet may examine, in terms of his medium, as

Wallace Stevens does in the final section of "Peter Quince at the Clavier," the truth of an abstract statement.

> Beauty is momentary in the mind—
> The fitful tracing of a portal;
> But in the flesh it is immortal.
>
> The body dies; the body's beauty lives.
> So evenings die, in their green going,
> A wave, interminably flowing.
> So gardens die, their meek breath scenting
> The cowl of Winter, done repenting.
> So maidens die, to the auroral
> Celebration of a maiden's choral.
>
> Susanna's music touched the bawdy strings
> Of those white elders; but, escaping,
> Left only Death's ironic scraping.
> Now, in its immortality, it plays
> On the clear viol of her memory,
> And makes a constant sacrament of praise.

The first four lines are a statement of the poet's theme. The following six lines are explorations in figurative language of the truth of his abstraction. The constant flux of delicately beautiful things is figuratively caught up in the deepening green cast of evening light. The light becomes associated with an interminably flowing wave—thereby extending the idea of flux. Then the poet takes up a new image, the garden, the sweet breath of which scents the cowl of winter, thereby giving the changes of season a kind of approbation. The cowl of winter is an excellent intensive image. All the somberness and chill of the cloister, its suggestion of sequestered retreat, inhere in it. Another change of figure in the next two lines states indirectly that beauty lost in death of maidens merely takes another form. The final six lines are the exploration of a single metaphor, ending in the intellectual resolution of the poem. There is a series of symphonic changes implied in the music of Susanna touching the bawdy strings of the elders, rising to the shrill ironic scrapings of her death, and finally settling into a gentle paean of praise. Here there are sudden shifts, through association, of images (ll. 6–10); sudden shifts in tone from "maiden's choral" to "bawdy strings"; the intensive image; the reordering of words in unexpected relationships, such as "green going"; ellipsis, such as "white elders"; the exploration of single metaphor; etc. All are tools which shape the poetic structure and make the final statement just. Or, to change the figure, they are "resistances" which the initial statement overcomes in the process of stating and proving itself.

The tension, on the other hand, between the rhythm of the free verse of Whitman and the ordinary rhythm of spoken language is slight.

> The blab of the pave, tires of carts, sluff of
>   boot-soles, talk of the promenaders,
> The heavy omnibus, the driver with his inter-
>   rogating thumb, the clank of the shod horses
>   on the granite floor,
> The snow-sleighs, clinking, shouted jokes, pelts
>   of snow-balls,
> The hurrahs for popular favorites, the fury of
>   rous'd mobs,
> The flap of the curtain'd litter, a sick man inside
>   borne to the hospital. . . .

Here there is little of the tension Eliot implies in saying that the "ghost of some simple metre should lurk behind the arras in even the 'freest' verse; to advance menacingly as we doze, and withdraw as we rouse." The looseness of such lines derives from more than an indifference to formal metrics. Whitman did not attempt to organize his lines into a structure. He accumulated homogeneous elements and allowed them, as it were, to speak for themselves.

A great deal of contemporary poetry in the Whitman tradition —that, for example, written by Sandburg, Masters, and, more recently, Paul Engle and Struthers Burt—fails in tension for the same reasons that Whitman so often fails. There is no discoverable rhythmic pattern pulling against or drawing taut the phrases from common speech which these poets so frequently use. Again, the homogeneous elements of their poetry never face, as it were, their antitheses. Usually it is a poetry of impulses, to use Richards' term, moving easily in the same direction. Even writers as dissimilar as Jeffers and Frost, though Frost to a lesser degree, frequently write a poetry dependent upon carefully considered exclusions.

Form functions with intensity when a significant attitude is given an appropriate objectification. Form as form has no significance. Thus the inclination of many Victorians to shy away from analysis in poetry is an indirect confession of futility. Their dream-world poetry is concerned with feeling alone, with escaping from significance. Poetry that attempts to exist only as feeling is amorphous. It will have only a cotton-candy kind of substance, which dissolves when touched by analysis. Swinburne, of course, is the cardinal example. But a reading of much of Tennyson, most of Poe, almost all of Arthur Symons, and much of the early Yeats would indicate a similar absence of tension. The effect of such poetry is quite different from that in the Whitman tradition, but the principle of organization is much the same. Both depend upon the employment of homogeneous elements, on the studied avoidance of contrasts. Both avoid analysis. One invites a readily apparent formlessness; the other, what is in effect, because of its insignificance, formlessness.

Tension is also a matter of the relationship or interdependence of line with line. An image or conceit may be meaningless (although not necessarily) if wrenched from its context in the poem; so, too, may the individual line. If the lines or stanzas can be easily detached from the poetic structure without harming the structure, then it probably is essentially a prose structure—a progression from point to point in description, in exposition, or in argumentation. Poetic structure implies a single theme so that the completed poem becomes an instantaneous whole. An illustration of the prose structure vitiating the poetic structure is Tennyson's familiar "Break,

Break, Break." In his first verse Tennyson states his wish that he could utter the deep thoughts he has within himself. In the second verse he says nothing further about his deep thoughts; he simply notes that the sailor lad and the fisherman's boy and girl are at play. In the third verse he introduces ships and a memory of a beloved one who is dead. Then in the fourth stanza he reverts to the waves breaking against the crags and to days of happiness that are gone. The second verse could be left out entirely, as well as the first two lines of the third verse. In Tennyson's mind apparently there was some connection between the fisherman's boy and his own nostalgia. Perhaps the reader can guess at a connection; none is suggested. If the ships are symbolic of a movement through existence, the permanence of impersonal things in contrast to the impermanence of persons, or whatever, the reader can hardly know. The poet's nostalgia is obvious enough, as is the somberness of the sea; but these are commonly associated, and the poet has in no way distinguished his nostalgia or the specific way in which the sea induces it.

A contrast of Tennyson's technique in "Break, Break, Break" with that in a sonnet by Wyatt suggests the importance of the relationship of the individual line to the entire poem. Wyatt frequently presents his image in the first four lines, as in this instance wherein he compares his state to the troubled ship, and then investigates the implication of the image as symbol. Each line catches or explains a new implication.

My galley charged with forgetfulness
Through sharp seas, in winter nights, doth pass
'Tween rock and rock; and eke my foe, alas,
That is my lord, steereth with cruelness;
And every oar a thought in readiness,
As though that death were light in such a case.
And endless wind doth tear the sail apace,
Of forced sighs and trusty fearfulness;
A rain of tears a cloud of dark disdain
Have done the wearied cords great hinderance;

Wreathed with error and with ignorance,
The stars be hid that led me to this pain;
Drowned is reason, that should be my comfort,
And I remain despairing of the port.

It is, of course, a conceptual image through which each abstract statement is played off against a concrete figure. The symbol of the ship—the ship of state, life as a ship, or Wyatt's personal fortunes—furnishes levels of meaning enough to keep William Empson himself well occupied. Essentially, Wyatt's is a tension of phrase or line, as well as image, in relation to all other phrases or lines in the poem, and with, of course, the stated theme. The closeness and interrelatedness of the imagery make for a more intensified effect. In metaphysical poetry the complexity of imagery is, usually, even more marked.

The conceit is necessary to the expression of the metaphysical substance of much of Donne's and Marvell's and Herbert's poetry. We may examine one from "A Nocturnal on St. Lucy's Day":

But I am by her death (which word wrongs her)
Of the first Nothing, the elixir grown.

"Of the first Nothing" gathers up a seemingly inexpressible emotion and gives it being by indirection. The conceit holds more than the paradox of someone's being nothing: he is the Nothing that partakes of the first nothingness. And then, in extension, the seemingly violent contradiction, "the elixir grown." In him the darkness of nothing is changed in the sense that in his holding the profundity of nothingness in himself all other nothingness loses its absolute character.

The tension in such conceits is the consequence of the sharply unlike elements that make for a newer unity. Some conceits, of course, fail to exhibit tension. Crashaw's conceit, from "The Weeper,"

Two walking baths, two weeping motions,
Portable and compendious oceans,

is deservedly notorious. The excesses are characteristic of much post-Elizabethan verse.

> Had I a voice of steel to tune my song,
> Were every verse as smoothly filed as glass,
> And every member turned to a tongue,
> And every tongue were made of sounding brass. . . .

These forced comparisons of Giles Fletcher's spring from the same decadence. The reader turns away from the forced unions. Johnson wrote that a successful comparison is like the intersection of two lines, noting always that "the comparison is better in proportion as the lines converge from greater distance." In Crashaw's and Fletcher's comparisons the elements are parallel lines, which never meet.

Such images are not sufficient unto themselves and therefore cannot become integral in their poems. An intensive image, on the other hand, not only is a unity itself but in a measure gives rise to the poem's unity.

Ezra Pound, as we have noted, has referred to an image as an intellectual and emotional complex presented "in an instant of time." The term "complex" is appropriate if we consider the intensive image a complex in little; that is, the poem and the image bear a macrocosm-microcosm relationship. Such a complex is seen in Warren's image, "twin atolls on a shelf of shade," in the poem "Bearded Oaks":

> The oaks, how subtle and marine,
> Bearded, and all the layered light
> Above them swims; thus the scene,
> Recessed, awaits the positive night.
>
> So, waiting, we in the grass now lie
> Beneath the languorous tread of light:
> The grasses, kelp-like, satisfy
> The nameless motions of the air.

> Upon the floor of light, and time,
> Unmurmuring, of polyp made,
> We rest: we are, as light withdraws,
> Twin atolls on a shelf of shade. . . . .

A reading of the poem discloses that the poet is attempting to create a sense of timelessness, of eternity, and to draw some knowledge therefrom. If his image is appropriate, its compressed meaning will relate to and enrich the rest of the poem.

One can almost wrest the poem's meaning from an analysis of this image: the coral, to the building of which slow ages have gone, rests quietly in the sea. Yet it is not a quiet of whose origins one is unaware. The coral that is stone quiet is a memorial to the life and violences that begot it. Throughout the poem one finds emphasis on this: the preternatural stillness is most intense because of the violences it contrasts with. Further, "the shelf of shade" is rich in suggestion: the word "shelf" gives the *feel* of a physical body, of something actual, tactile, while "shade" suggests the intangible, the eerie, the mysterious. Together the words afford an appropriate contrast: the reader's sense that eternity, of which he knows nothing, is both real and unreal, like Yeats's "artifice of eternity." The image may be seen, then, to relate intimately to the setting, mood, tone, theme, and other images in the poem.

Tension implies the inclusion of all the related considerations the poet can discover. We have seen that denotation falsifies our understanding of a total experience. The diction of prose is necessary for recording and analyzing experience on one level; the diction of poetry is necessary on another level for the expression and fullest possible exploration of the total experience. In reading prose, one is aware of the writer's compromising with the actual nature of the experience being discussed. Many thought-situations apparently come into the mind with explosiveness: the necessity for prose expression, the breaking-down into a series of statements an experience that is not simple, belies the instantaneous quality of the thought-situation. Both prose and poetry compromise with the fulness, but poetry does so to a lesser degree. In expressing an isolated thought, one not threading its way through a tightly related context, there is a compromise—the implications, the suppositions, the contradictions, the ambiguities, the ironies beg for consideration. To prevent his lines from being taken in isolation, the poet will not only play off element against element within his poem, as has been said earlier, but he will also try to bring into focus on his theme as many related considerations as possible.

The term "inclusive principle" serves to focus these considerations: the poet will not write at a point on the periphery of his subject; he will not use his subject for tangential departures. He will have a structure, however complex, to which each poetic element is related. It will be a complex as rich as his mind can make it. Quite possibly the poem will be simple, but delusively simple in that it is not easily ridiculed or demolished by an ironic intelligence. Otherwise, as Morris Schappes has written of one poet, in his failure to "unify these disparities" the writer has become "subservient to every passing scene and impression."

An illustration of the inclusive principle is suggested by the frequent contrast between denotative and connotative meaning. This point may be illustrated by Emily Dickinson's "The Brain Is Wider than the Sky":

The brain is wider than the sky,
For, put them side by side,
The one the other will include
With ease, and you beside . . . .
The brain is just the weight of God,
For, lift them, pound for pound,
And they will differ, if they do,
As syllable from sound.

The denotative meaning of the entire poem does violence to our understanding of natural law. Physically, of course, the brain is smaller than the sky; metaphysically, the sky is nonexistent unless it is encompassed by the brain. Similarly, the line "The brain is just the weight of God" denotatively is sacrilegious; connotatively, it is the *beginning* of theology. (The study of connotative meanings, of ambiguity, has been done in such great detail by William Empson in *Seven Types of Ambiguity* and *English Pastoral Poetry* that almost any brief examination of the subject would be repetitious and incomplete.)

This usage of opposed principles in Miss Dickinson's poem may seem little more than a simple series of paradoxes. Yet it stems from a fuller recognition of experience than do most statements, prose or poetry. It exhibits tension. That it is humanistic may be seen by relating it to H. J. Muller's recapitulation of the humanistic position:

> But through "planned incongruity" and the principle of ambivalance or polarity, one may set platitudes in a richer context, restore the living truth in truism, at times even startle. One may locate the good in the bad and the bad in the good, and then make for better.

## *3*

The concern of modern poets with tension may be examined from two different positions, the esthetic and the moral. (This is to use moral in the large sense of what the poet basically believes.) The recovered esthetic emphasis implies a concern with tension. All artists, of course, are concerned with generating esthetic *qualities*, unique or startling effects, which impel interest and feeling. The techniques, of course, which establish tension—contrasts of various sorts, as between the beautiful and the ugly, a formalized and colloquial idiom, the concrete and the abstract, the connotative and denotative meanings, concentration and diffusion and so forth—can be considered merely as esthetic effects. They are methods or ways of breaking through the reader's unquestioning acceptance of the commonplace and the ordinary. Many of Pound's dicta, certainly, can be considered as representative of a concern with the esthetic problem of poetry.

In his frequently quoted "In a Station of the Metro"—

> The apparition of these faces in the crowd;
> Petals on a wet, black bough—

Pound appears to be concerned with tension in at least two ways. First, there is the startling awareness of the beautifully human in the swirl of the subway crowd. Second, in the two lines he has achieved a remarkable concentration, making possible for the reader a harder impact and deeper awareness. In fact, as a number of critics have pointed out, modern poetry at its best has tended to move in the direction of the elliptical, of concentration, layers of meaning—intensity. The emphasis may be rationalized or explained in several ways. The most obvious explanation is that it is a reaction against the tendency toward diffusiveness, or the mistiness or the platitudinous in much Victorian poetry.

The most startling experiments with concentration possibly are those in which Cummings has attempted to rearrange the ordinary sequences of language in order to achieve the immediacy and directness one can get from an actual scene or from a picture. In the latter half of Poem 81, he writes

```
                                look-
          pigeons fly ingand
whee(:are, spRIN,k,LINg an in-stant with sunLight
then)l-
ing all go BlacK wh-eel-ing
oh
          ver
                   mYveRyliTle
street
where
you will come,
                                at twi li ght
s(oon & there's
a                               m oo
)n.
```

Quite possibly experiments of this kind, like the attempts to build a poetry almost exclusively upon a language of connotation, have a periphery beyond which is merely confusion. Cummings, however, is trying to do, in this instance, with typography what his contemporaries are trying to do in other ways—to make the experience of the poem as concentrated and intense as possible. His poem is an example of what Frank has called "reflexive reference," the bringing-together of the elements of the poem in such a way that the final and complete meaning is seen at once, explosively. Eliot, too, seems to be pointing to this central concern of the poet with tension when in "Tradition and the Individual Talent" he says: "It [the process of creating poetry] is a concentration, and a new thing resulting from the concentration, of a very great number of experiences." In *The Waste Land* or "The Love Song of J. Alfred Prufrock," for example, the meaning is not stated explicitly. The elements converge always toward a meaning that is not stated directly but which is suggested, hinted at, symbolized. Again, when the meaning becomes apparent, it becomes an instantaneous perception.

This aspect of the esthetic concern of the moderns is, then, to be explained as a reaction against several kinds of poetry: against solely denotative statement, the loose accumulation of many details, as well as the careful organization of homogeneous "poetic" elements. In their reaction, as estheticians and historians have pointed out, they have been trying to restore the natural functions of their medium, to withdraw it from the service of explicit description and exposition.

The modern poet is also obliged to make a conscious use of the techniques implied in the term "tension" if in his poetry he is genuinely concerned with insights, knowledge, or a point of view. He does not live in a society that furnishes him with a ready-made vision of the universe, a steady scale of values or belief. Consequently, his point of view, if it is not to be easily ridiculed or overthrown, must be closely reasoned and justified in the ways made available by his medium. He must create a personal order in the disorder he finds about him, in the "destructive element." The modern poet, as Morton Zabel has said of Henry James, is aware that an age of "values" has begun. A poet's concern with values implies, of course, self-scrutiny, the attempt to understand the relationship of his medium to his belief, as well as an attempt to understand the "character of modernity." The poet thus aware is not likely to amass detail, however "poetic," for its own sake or to present a point of view detached from the experience from which it springs. Rather, he will examine his materials openly, however carefully or exquisitely, in the presence of his reader, who may—and indeed has to, if he would adequately understand—re-create the poem as he reads it.

CHAPTER ELEVEN

# *The Isolation of the Poet*

*I feel I am an exile here.*—HERMAN MELVILLE

THE isolation of the modern artist is a phenomenon that can be studied both in terms of the personal lives of many poets and novelists and as a theme running through much of their work. An aspect of the problem, related to what Mario Praz has called *The Romantic Agony*, can be traced from the late eighteenth century up through the various esthetic and decadent movements of the nineteenth century. Wordsworth, Coleridge, Keats, Shelley, and Byron looked upon themselves, in varying degrees, as outcasts, lonely men cut off from their society. Irving Babbitt, in discussing the melancholy of the Romantics, recalls that an old innkeeper remembered Wordsworth as a "desolate-minded man. . . . 'Twas poetry as did it." Coleridge, as Robert Penn Warren demonstrates in his study of *The Rime of the Ancient Mariner*, made the Mariner, "the outcast both noble-minded and accursed," a kind of prototype of the poet. Byron dramatized his role as rebel as though he were cast in a melodrama. Shelley, too, postured, emphasizing his isolation from "this hellish society of men." Keats, less given to the more violent dramatics, was nonetheless an outsider. "Chatterton," wrote Babbitt, "became for the romanticists a favorite type of the *poète maudit*, and his suicide a symbol of the inevitable defeat of the 'ideal' by the 'real.' " Poe, like Chatterton, was to become a symbol for Baudelaire and a later generation of French romantics.

Ultimately, the isolation of the artist is traceable to the dissociation of sensibility. As a result of the dissociation, all subjective projections, in terms of which ideals are expressible, became to a degree suspect.

Since the scientific revolution poetry has not played a vital role, or as vital a role as it once played, because, as Melvin Rader has noted, in "the main body of modern thought, it has been supposed that reality is the material of science and that values and concrete qualities are not ultimately real." Necessarily many have come to believe that the function of poetry is "simply and solely to entertain, not to heighten our understanding of man and his place in the cosmos." In our time only the hardiest attempt to hold poetry up as a form of knowledge capable of competing with the more scientific forms. (Among those who protest are those students of symbolism who believe that the language of metaphor and imagistic symbols has a nonexchangeable value of its own.)

Delmore Schwartz, among others, has assigned the initial cause of the isolation of the artist to the attempted split of thought from sensibility.[1] "There is a break between intellect and sensibility; the intellect finds unreasonable what the sensibility and the imagination cannot help but accept." Once, that is, reality and truth were held to be objectively verifiable, the truths of the imagination were held to be fantastic, chimerical. The truth was graspable only in terms of measurement. This premise gave rise to the belief that the truth was best communicated in abstract and denotative language. The symbols and metaphors of the poet were therefore untrue. And there was the further suspicion of language used to involve the emotions. In other words, the truth was to be sought not in the subjective but in the objective world. The poet's statements, however pleasant, were not ultimately true.

The consequences of this lopsided emphasis—the concern with fact at the expense of values and the refusal to accept imagined ideals as a part of the data—have been examined by observers like Toynbee and Whitehead. Among the consequences, as they point out, have been the tremendous successes of industrialization, the encouragement of specialization, and the growing desire for practical activities of all kinds. These developments, to a considerable degree, have been conducted along scientific lines, each problem being studied in isolation. The health and tonality of the culture has not been a basic consideration. These developments have not been adjusted to the esthetic needs or, we may put it, to the subjective life of individuals. Schwartz states the case very strongly: There "was no room in the increasing industrialization of society for such a monster as the cultivated man; a man's taste for literature has at best nothing to do with most of the activities which constitute daily life in an industrial society." Culture, he concludes, has become more and more autonomous, "removing itself all the time from any essential part in the organic life of society." Before poetry can become a part of the ordinary experience of society again, there must, of course, be an acceptance of the esthetic as an important aspect of experience.

The alienation of the artist from his society is less explicit in the major Victorian figures, like Tennyson, Browning, Arnold, Clough, or Meredith. They either glossed the dualities of the Victorian mind or made them the subject matter of their poetry. They may have suffered from the recognition of the inability of their age to reconcile the ideal with the real—but, whatever their criticisms of the society, they did not break with it. The English poets who play significant roles in Praz's study belong exclusively, except for Swinburne, to the later nineteenth century. And they, like Wilde, Dowson, and Lionel Johnson, seem to have more kinship with the French exiles, like Baudelaire, Verlaine, and Rimbaud. Isolation or exile became a distinguishing mark of the Symbolists. And it is their influence, as much as any other, which gives modern poetry its character. Many of the attitudes of the Symbolists toward middle-class values, of course, have likewise proved an important influence. Professor William York Tindall sees the exile of the poets as a break with the middle class.[2] "Accustomed to expressing feelings and ideas shared with their literate audience, poets slowly realized their disinclination or inability to express feelings so much coarser than their own. About the middle of the century Baudelaire looked out of his window and was filled with the 'immense nausea of billboards.' The rest follows from this."

Industrialization, we must remember, was possible because of techniques developed by science. Industrialization made the middle classes possible. And the chief middle-class ideal was practical knowledge, applied science. The philosophy of science, if we may put it thus, implies a suspicion of the whole range of subjective expression. The middle classes no doubt were unconcerned with the philosophy implicit in their attitudes. They could insist unquestioningly on the value and attitudes that had become a part of their mores. But the technical successes science made possible are behind their respect for practical knowledge. The emphasis upon practical knowledge should be seen as a result of the scientific emphasis. The isolation of the poet may be treated in a social context, provided it is not forgotten that the character of the society itself derives from earlier attitudes of the scientific mind about what is important and what is true.

The artist, as might be expected, reacted against the view that art is of negligible importance as well as against those expressions that were in accord with middle-class attitudes. If the artist could not accept middle-class values, he could hardly look upon himself as the articulate part of his society, as one whose duty it is to express its ideals and values. In taking this position, he isolated himself. Professor Tindall is right, however, in saying that "society exiled the poet before he exiled himself." And Schwartz is right in saying, "It was not so much the poet as it was poetry, culture, sensibility, imagination that were isolated." The varied isolation theories of art are a nineteenth-century phenomenon. Thus Whistler's self-satisfied pronouncement: "The master stands in no relation to the moment at which he occurs—a monument of isolation—

hinting at sadness—having no part in the progress of his fellow men." Thus, too, the later pronouncements of critics and estheticians like Fry, Bell, Ortega, and Bullough.

If the esthetic experience could not be rationalized in the mental climate which encouraged the growth of scientific and pseudo-scientific forms of knowledge, it could be cut off, as it were, from that climate and be encouraged to live a life of its own. Thus the doctrine of poetry for poetry's sake and the belief that poetry has no relationship to morals, politics, or practical activities of any kind. A consequence, as Santayana has pointed out, has been the attempt to purify the various media of art, to be concerned with what can be done technically in terms of a medium rather than with the values and ideas the medium might be used to serve.

Some who have written about the isolation of the artist treat it as though it were merely an American phenomenon. It is European as well. A more dramatic case can be made in treating the American aspect of it—because of the steady stream of Americans during the late nineteenth and early twentieth century moving to Europe, and because of the more flagrant indifference to the arts that a fast-developing society believed it could afford. The distinction is this: The poet in Europe, although isolated from his society, found his strength and sustenance in the considerable numbers of his fellow-poets and in the varied experimental movements. The poet or artist in America had neither strength of numbers nor local critical or poetic movements to sustain him. For both he had to go to Europe. The attitude that "culture and sensibility . . . did not fit into the essential workings" of a progressive society would in Europe find many opponents. And there were, as James was to note, the complexities of social existence and the subtle tones in the long corridors of history merely awaiting the artist.

## 2

In 1922 Van Wyck Brooks, in "The Literary Life in America," wrote bitterly of the impotence of the creative spirit in the America of the preceding half-century. Since then, as may be observed in *The Opinions of Oliver Allston*, he has recanted and noted in his early writing a tendency to attribute "to one's country the faults of human nature in general." Brooks at that time held that America always had an abundance of talent but that, once having "struck out with his new note," the American writer became "less and less himself." The "characteristic evolution of the European writer" toward "an ever increasing differentiation, a progress toward creation, the possession of a world absolutely his own," was denied the American writer because he was insufficiently nourished by the society in which he was obliged to live. Brooks objected that the up-and-doing drive inbred in Americans precluded personal growth and produced only "sharp-witted men of business." A people in whom the virus of ill-advised and often misdirected activity had so grown could not understand the need the creative man has to go his own way. Poverty was a cardinal sin in the society, and the artist, particularly one to whom greatness was not given, who could suffer the continued disapproval of his contemporaries was rare. And in America, unlike the London of Charles Lamb, poverty meant intellectual starvation as well. Sidney Lanier, for example, was defeated both by poverty and by isolation. Melville, too, given the "companionship of a friendly, critical, understanding sort," Brooks said, "might in London have carried his reflective vein to literary completion." The American writer was not made to feel that what he was doing *mattered*. "The hostility of the pioneers to the special career still operated to prevent in the American mind the powerful, concentrated pursuit of any nonutilitarian way of life."

American artists, at least until World War II was imminent, who nurtured an esthetic emphasis frequently were physical expatriates, like Henry James, Ezra Pound, and T. S. Eliot; spiritual expatriates, like Herman Melville, Nathaniel Hawthorne, and Sidney Lanier; or died young, like Hart Crane. "It is the particular tragedy of American art, a particular American tragedy," one of the most gifted young contemporary poets has said, "that our most sensitive poets exile or kill themselves." We can observe, in qualifying the implications of this comment, that many of our best poets, like Wallace Stevens, William Carlos Williams, Allen Tate, or Marianne Moore, have limited audiences and are considered the poets of the coterie or school intellectuals. Certainly most "educated" Americans do not think of these names when the question of "American poetry" is raised. They are more likely to think of those in the Whitman tradition who celebrate America's "westering," poets who somehow raise the geography of a continent to a symbol of hope and promise.

The history of poetry in America reflects a strong cultural conflict. Americans refer to "Old World beauty" with approval and to "foreign" with disapproval and sometimes with contempt. A part of the tension in American culture is our desiring a way of life "more definite, less atomistic and more patterned" than it is, "yet insisting on something new. Innovation is our ideal but conformity is our mentor." The manner in which the conflict is reconciled may in no small part put the stamp of success or failure on the experiment in culture that is America.[3]

Henry James knew as well as anyone the difficulties faced by the American writer. The exile in *Madonna*—in terms, except for the anguished tone, somewhat like those James himself might have used in a critical commentary—contrasts the European with the American writer:

> An American to excel, has just ten times as much to learn as a European. We lack the deeper sense; we have neither taste nor tact, nor force. How should we have them? Our crude and garish climate, our silent past, our deafening present, the constant pressure about us of unlovely circumstances

> are as void of all that nourishes and prompts and inspires the artist, as my sad heart is a void of bitterness in saying so! We poor aspirants must live in perpetual exile.

In his life of Hawthorne, James again contrasts the Old World with the New as soil for the artist—but he sees his America as a part of a necessary historical development:

> The flower of art blooms only where the soil is deep . . . it takes a great deal of history to produce a little literature . . . it needs a complex social machinery to set a writer in motion. American civilization has hitherto had other things to do than to produce flowers and before giving birth to writers it has wisely occupied itself with providing something for them to write about.

Nonetheless, James could not stay in America. Late in his lifetime, some thirty years after he had chosen Europe in preference to the United States, he spent a year rediscovering his native country, lecturing in cities in the Far West, Middle West, South, and East. He was eager, as he wrote to his brother, to see everything—the "actual, bristling U.S.A." What disturbed him most was the formlessness, growth, and development without plan. There was, he observed gratefully, a great lessening of poverty, and there were such conveniences as Pullmans and water closets. Yet at the center of the American consciousness was the all-controlling idea of money. A year was enough. He would be happier outside the "huge Rappaccini garden, rank with each variety of the poison-plant of money-passion." Upon returning to England, he gave many of his last years to his Prefaces—"a sort of plea for Criticism, for Discrimination, for Appreciation on other than infantile lines." The Prefaces were his effort to plug the hole in the dike. But he must have known that the changes he saw in America were changes affecting the whole Western world. The process was simply a little slower in England. There the inertia set up by the traditional forms working against the changes was favorable to the artist.

The expatriation of later figures, like Eliot, Pound, or Aiken, is similar, in varying degrees, to that of James. After World War I, in particular, there was a violent reaction against everything that had ever happened before the war. Eliot's great contribution, as Richard Aldington put it, was the "insistence that writers could not afford to throw over the European tradition." Pound, however incoherent he was in his pronouncements and manifestoes, went deep into old literatures for usable forms. Aiken merely preferred the temper and tone of life in England.

In 1926, several years before his suicide, Vachel Lindsay wrote with great bitterness about "What It Means To Be a Poet in America."[4] He was not concerned to examine the cultural context, to explain why the American attitudes toward the poet obtained. He was concerned with hitting back at the society and particularly at the groups who ignored or humiliated him because he was a poet. The argument as he rehearses it is familiar. Poetry has been taught like the multiplication tables. The aspiring young poets who are English instructors are frowned upon by their scholarly colleagues. The newspapers caricature the poet. The publisher tries to make him write novels or textbooks, not poetry. The raw material and elements of poetry, as found in songs or even in state papers, are not believed to have any relation to poetry published as poetry. There is a constant curiosity about seeing a live poet—but none about reading his books. The story is an old one. Many other poets, perhaps more capable of perceiving its causes and implications, have not reacted so violently toward it as Lindsay did. They either moved to Europe in the hope that their talents might there mature more completely or they remained in the United States. In either event their isolation from society was merely a matter of degree.[5]

Since the days when James and Adams needed Europe, and the days when Eliot, Pound, and Aiken and the others needed her in order to mature and grow as poets, and now, the cultural gap between Europe and the United States has gradually narrowed. The quality of the best poetry written currently in the United States is undoubtedly as good as any being written in England. Since the advent of Hitler, of course, the exiles, among them literary figures of all shades of worth, have moved to the west, to America. Americans no longer need Europe to find strength in numbers among their fellow-artists or to discover the moving currents of experimental forms. These they have at hand. The isolation of the artist is for them no longer a national affair—it is international and spiritual. The same mass indifference to the poetry that can be called modern as well as the occasional attacks from the middlebrows that beset Eliot or Spender or Edith Sitwell in England beset Stevens or Ransom or Marianne Moore in the United States. Genuinely important poetry in our time is nurtured in isolation or not at all.

## *3*

The isolation of the poet is not a matter limited in significance to whether the poet chooses to live in one place and not in another, a matter of patriotism or nationalism. If the best poetry is written, as it were, outside the society, then the society at large is not nourished or sustained by its best poets—it loses one of its chief civilizing forces.

The best modern poets are read, as everyone knows, by a very small audience. These poets look upon themselves as divorced or exiled from the middle-class culture. The kinds of poetry that are written for the middle-class audience compose a literature of epigonism which divides into several categories: There is the pseudo-Whitman poetry that sentimentalizes the American past and assumes a nineteenth-century-minded audience, an audience that has not experienced twentieth-century attitudes and tensions. There is a decadent romantic poetry, strong on sunsets, peaceful lakes, and the heart and other elements found in "poetic diction." There is the poetry in the Georgian tradition, written usually by elderly gentlemen to whom Eliot and his kind are upstarts. There is the poetry in a vein of highbrow sophistication and pseudo-modernity, of studied ironies and naughtiness. And there is, lastly, the poetry that apes merely the mannerisms of the avant-garde. These are the various forms of epigonism. They could hardly thrive in a society in which the poets who were expressing the real character of the age had a wide, discriminating audience.

Further, some of the aspects of modern poetry as well as the poets are to be explained in terms of this phenomenon of isolation. The preoccupation with traditionalism and with regionalism is an aspect of the isolation. The concern with tradition, as we find it in Yeats, Eliot, or Tate, is an effort to explain some of the values that are missing or which have but slight vitality in our society. Thus the care with which Yeats worked out a cultural history of sorts in *A Vision* and his frequent poems about and allusions to historical attitudes and belief:

> And what rough beast, its hour come round at last,
> Slouches towards Bethlehem to be born?

Eliot's poetry, quite obviously, is a kind of monument to much that is good in the cultures of the past. "This has been misunderstood very often," says Schwartz, "as a yearning to go back to a past idyllically conceived. It is nothing of the kind; it is the poet's conscious experience of the isolation of culture from the rest of society." Tate and some of his associates have likewise been concerned with the need for traditional forms, moral, esthetic, and social, particularly as these may be related to the culture of a region.

A related theme is that of dehumanization. The vulgarity and cold sensuality and the mild hysteria and frustration evident in so many of Eliot's characters symbolize the plight of individuals who are unable to find purpose or direction in their lives. Without a tradition which defines ideals and values most individuals are unable to define their personality or to maintain a strong sense of personal identity. The loss of respect for the concept and the person of man is the inevitable counterpart of the decline of values and ideals.

The isolation of the poet may be related also to the problem of obscurity in expression. It does not explain all obscurity—some of which is dependent upon the inherent difficulties of the subject matter, the unique workings of the poet's mind, and the imaginative leaps necessitated by the use of metaphor or symbol, etc.—but it may explain a part of it. Cut off from the culture of his society, the poet tends to go deeply into the workings of his own mind and sensibility—to make himself the subject of his poetry. Again, he knows he is writing for a highly specialized reading audience for whom obscurity has the interests of a highly intellectualized game. Some of the obscurity in our poetry, that is, is the consequence of its having become a highly specialized art.

The chief effort to break out of the circle of isolation came with the political and economic upheavals of the thirties. Unfortunately, the pendulum swung too far the other way. Poetry, in its political aspect, tended to become the poetry of a party. And politics tended to become the all-important, forcing out esthetic, philosophical, or even broadly human interests. The concern with politics, however, reminded some poets that their subject matter need not be intensive and narrow, that it may include anything with which the human being is concerned. The political upheavals taught the artist the danger of living and working in isolation from his society. The danger remains. Its solution, or partial solution, it would seem, must await the recognition on the part of society that it pays a penalty, in the form of synthetic art and sentimental values, for isolating its best poets.

CHAPTER TWELVE

# *Forms of Epigonism*

*The common reader with whom Dr. Johnson rejoiced to concur is as dead as Pan.*—H. M. McLuhan

In an essay on Yeats's concern to bring Ireland to a state of unity in which the artist and the populace at large might mutually sustain each other, Donald Davidson has outlined what the ideal relationship of the artist and society might be:

The popular lore ought to pass readily and naturally into the art; it ought not have to be sought out by specialists in special corners, collected, edited, published, and reviewed, and then, perhaps only through some accident of taste or fashion, be appropriated, at long range, by a very literary poet. The reverse of the process ought to work naturally. . . . The art ought to pass readily into the popular lore, and not remain eternally aloof and difficult. Unless both processes continue in mutual interchange, society as well as art is in a bad state of health; but the bad health of society is a cause not a result of this unfavorable relationship.[1]

The relation of the artist and his audience would thus be one of mutual dependence.

The ideal relationship which Mr. Davidson postulates does not exist for the modern poet, because he broke away from the middle-class society. First, he could no longer hold with middle-class values, as Yeats presumably could with those of the Irish peasantry. Second, he believed that his medium had become debased in the service of middle-class values—in the service of blatantly moralistic and utilitarian ends. A considerable part of modernism in poetry has been the concern with purifying the medium. The middle-class audience could hardly be expected to follow the experiments of poets who were often indifferent to the significance of a particular subject matter and consistently opposed to middle-class values. The middle class, however, has had several forms of epigonic literature designed for it. One is a continuation of Victorianism through Georgianism; its sponsors are openly opposed to modern forms. Another, using the nineteenth-century tradition of bohemianism and revolt, is superficially modern; the poets writing this form of epigonism usually do not use the modern idiom. A third form employs the modern idiom but in such a fashion that it is often fatuous, its intellectual fiber relaxed. Thus the particular forms, not the phenomenon of epigonism itself, are peculiar to modern poetry.

Clement Greenberg in "Avant Garde and Kitsch" has defined the avant-garde artist as one who has

> sought to maintain the high level of his art by both narrowing and raising it to the expression of an absolute in which all relativities and contradictions would be either resolved or beside the point. "Art for art's sake" and "pure poetry" appear, and subject-matter or content becomes something to be avoided like a plague.[2]

The avant-garde artist, according to this definition, has been more concerned with his medium than with his subject matter. In art this has meant a preoccupation with the nonrepresentational or "abstract." In poetry it has meant, at its extreme—but only at its extreme—an emphasis on the medium as medium, on rhythms, rhymes, symbols, connotations, associations, etc., rather than on the subject matter the medium is transmuting.

The cause of the avant-garde developments, according to Greenberg, was the crack-up of the old way of looking at society as something sacrosanct, "natural," and permanent. The "scientific revolutionary thought" of the "fifth and sixth decades of the nineteenth century" (the work of Marx and Engels presumably) soon was "absorbed by the artists and poets." The old verities of religion, authority, and tradition were seen to be without validity. The modern artist therefore has had little or nothing to say to a transitional audience. His task has been to keep his medium pure and intact "in the midst of ideological confusion and violence," for the day when the new society will present the artist with a new tradition, new axioms and values. His medium will then have new verities with which to work.

This explanation would undoubtedly surprise many avant-garde poets, particularly those like Eliot who have been at great pains to explain and characterize our society. Both the esthetic and the political questionings arose from a sense of the inadequacies in the society. But the artist and the revolutionary were not necessarily in agreement about what these inadequacies were. The social revolutionary believed that there should be a new distribution of wealth and opportunity. The artist believed that the function of art had been debased and distorted in the service of moralistic, practical, and sentimental ends. If the avant-garde artist thought that he was waiting out the transition of the revolutionary period, presumably he would take some steps to hurry the new order into existence. In his effort to restore his art to its original functions, however, he has, as Santayana has noted, frequently refused to have anything whatever to do with ordinary human interests, with morals, sentiment, or practical purposes of any kind. He has limited his attention to the art itself, concerning himself with subject matter only to the extent that his medium would have something with which to work. The phenomenon of avant-gardism, if the term is taken to mean solely experiments with the medium, is the result.

Seen from one position, then, avant-garde writing is merely experimentation with forms. As such it will be a literature for other writers and for students concerned with understanding what can be done in the new forms. Joyce, for example, has shown how many layers of meaning a symbol can sustain; Eliot, that an object or situation ordinarily unassociated with a poet's particular thought may be "the emotional equivalent" of that "thought"; Cummings, that the arrangement of words on a page can better suggest the *livingness* of words; Marianne Moore, that "human documents and school-books" can be made into poetry. The evidence is in. And the medium has been renewed and purified. One may ask, with all respect for Joyce's genius, what further evidence is needed beyond *Finnegans Wake*.

Dwight Macdonald, in "A Theory of 'Popular Culture,'" states that the avant-garde movements in our time have been the last stronghold of high culture.[3] He believes, with Aldous Huxley, that there is a Gresham's Law in cultural matters—the bad drives out the good. And he believes further that high culture, which he identifies with avant-gardism, is dying off. In proof of this thesis he evidences "the epigonism of the New Directions list, where the 'new' directions are those of Ezra Pound, W. C. Williams and E. M. Forster."

Although this general thesis may be correct, the weakness in Macdonald's argument, aside from his laying the blame for the "decline" solely in the laps of the "ruling capitalists," is in his failure to state that the poets he names are, or have been, avant-gardists. Pound and Williams, both important figures in the development of modern poetry, have helped to "purify" their medium. Nothing as violent as the break with a veristic art—which gave the experimenters their fame and notoriety—can be expected again soon. The new medium has not been with us long enough to decline in the service of any point of view. The chief difficulty, as we have suggested, is in the inability of the modern poets to accept the values of the middle-class society. The Shakespeare play, we must assume, brought popular and high art together, not because the entire audience was able to perceive all the subtleties presented, but because they held in common a body of beliefs and values which could be perceived at different levels in the play. The poet, that is, did not feel himself an exile from his society.

The problem, it would seem, is to find a subject matter that at once has significance, that can be best projected through the recovered or newly evolved forms, and that has a positive, not merely a negatively critical, relationship with the society. The "significant" subject matter is not something the poet is likely to find merely for the looking. The poet does not create a culture. He heightens, sustains and renews, or criticizes what already exists. A tragic poet writes a tragic drama only if his culture presents him with the materials, the temper, tone, and philosophy of tragedy. The most refined medium, at best a body of techniques, finds its ultimate justification in how well it can transmute the materials and interests of a culture into art expressions.

It would seem, further, that no poet who has learned how to use the purified medium has at the same time been so unquestioningly a part of a middle-class world that he could turn any of its values into poetry. Its complacency, material interests, synthetic entertainment, and glib pronouncements amuse or annoy him. The more positive virtues, such as thrift, sobriety, industry, and family affection, may be too easily sentimentalized or pushed to the point of being vices. Possibly the intellectual's position outside the middle class is still too heady an experience to allow his openly admitting any virtues in that class. At any rate, the poetry about the middle class has a satiric sting.

According to H. M. McLuhan, the present cleavage between intellectually honest artists and the society generally has a long history.[4] One "could say that after Jane Austen no serious artist exists save in drastic opposition to his society." He believes, further, that the cleavage may never be healed. It is evident, at least, that the modern poets are concerned, like Eliot, with the entire structure of Western history which "explains" our society, or, like Tate or Warren, with our incapacity for meaningful action. Again, serious modern poetry may turn on personal emotions, be concerned with heightening esthetic awareness, or with a fable or bit of history which relates only obliquely to our society. The point, then, is that our society is not such that the artist works easily and in conformity with it. Experiments like that with the folk tradition appear as efforts to find a way of using the society in some positive manner.

There have been a few attempts by formal high artists to cut a swath through middle-class art, which is usually seen as mummified and sentimentalized, as *kitsch*, to a vital folk tradition. Louise Bogan believes that only two modern poets, Lorca and Yeats, have succeeded in using a folk tradition.[5] "Lorca's genius was ignited in the most brilliant way by Flamenco tradition and Yeats was fortified and refreshed from the beginning by his close knowledge of the Irish peasant." But the cultural situations, she adds, in which the two poets found themselves were abnormal in an industrialized Europe. In America certainly the separation of a living folk tradition from high art is very wide. Indeed, industrialization, or the standardizations it has fostered, has all but killed off the folk traditions in America.[6]

The culmination of the folk song in America, Miss Bogan says, came with Stephen Foster. He represented the transition from an agricultural to an urban society. Eventually the folk tradition was superseded by standardized songs. The best contemporary forms of popular music, which make raids into classical music, are a long way from being "folk" forms; that is, the songs which grew from rural and regional attitudes and beliefs have been dropped in favor of those which arise from sophisticated urban attitudes. It is indicative of the nature of these sophisticated attitudes that the interest "in accident, sudden death, and the morbid in general (unlike American songs of an earlier day) has very nearly disappeared, along with the 'topical song,' that sister to the Broadsheet."

The poet can find little kinship with these popular forms. The vitality he needs was once expressed in the folk forms, which some have tried to recover because they expressed *lived experiences*—accident, sudden death, and the topical. The artist is, of course, usually a product of the middle class. His alienation from it stems from his inability to accept the sensibility and values which produce the "slick" forms, saccharined versions of human experiences and the devitalized characters and situations which serve the purposes of standardization. It may be enough to instance radio serials, the general run of movies, and most popular novels. The artist feels an integrity, honesty, and vitality in the older forms. Whereas the painter or sculptor attempts to find vitality in primitives, the poet sometimes looks to a folk subject matter. Since, however, we are a long way from the primitive sensibility as well as several generations from American folk poetry, neither probably can serve as more than a model of vitality.

## 2

There is, on the other hand, a body of contemporary verse which seems to be interpreting and refracting contemporary life—but does so through nineteenth-century eyes. In poems like Davenport's *My Country* and Burt's *War Songs* we, as Americans, find ourselves in some nonurbanized world, at the edge of a history of brave pioneers and an expanding economy. In such work there is no evidence that the tradition of satire, debunking, cynicism, labor and capital classes, close questioning of inherited values, etc., ever registered in the contemporary mind. It is a portrait of an America that no longer exists. Such a form of epigonism seems explicable only in that the authors, having no poetic sensibilities of their own, appropriate a poetry with which, presumably, they grew up.

An even less excusable form of epigonism is the fairly frequent decadent romantic poetry, sustained only by its artificial diction. It is a poetry which bears no relation to the time in which it is written. And therefore it has as little relationship to the sensibility of anyone alive in the twentieth century.

Progressively, particularly after the beginnings of the Romantic Movement, it became easier and easier to distinguish words used in poetry from those used in prose. The *peradventures*, *mayhaps*, *thrices*, as well as the *roseates*, *heavenlys*, etc., became associated with the poetic vocabulary. By the nineties a frequently quoted line could read—

> the viol, the violet, and the vine.

Since the resurgence of metaphysical verse in our day, with the renewed interest in commonplace things, there has come a renewal of everyday language in poetry. But a decadent romantic diction is still occasionally employed.

The body of epigonic poetry which now bulks largest is that which derives from Georgians like Rupert Brooke, Alfred Noyes, John Masefield, or W. H. Davies. For the most part the work of these poets—Leonard Bacon, Joseph Auslander, Robert Nathan, William Ellery Leonard, Genevieve Taggard, and others—is not characterized so much by similarities of style or subject matter as by the fact that little of it reflects the stress of the time in which it has been written. For whatever personal reasons, each of the derivative Georgians writes as though the wars, political revolutions, breakup of traditional beliefs, and the *terra incognita* of the irrational toward which scientific knowledge has been edged do not justify the alarms sounded by the modernists. By and large, they write a companionable poetry, shot through with a ready optimism. Frequently it is written around a country or suburban subject matter. It is a poetry which will satisfy the sensibilities of well-bred readers who have some knowledge of our literary past, buttress their sense of security, and shock them, if at all, only enough to ruffle their decorum. Robert Hillyer's "Night Piece" ends

> Frail are your stars, deep are your waters, mind;
> And the sound of falling waters troubles my heart.

While producing this sort of work, these poets have carried on a kind of rear-guard action against the modernists.

Poets like Dorothy Parker and Edna St. Vincent Millay, on the other hand, are likely to represent to a noncritical audience either avant-garde writing or something on the heels of it. Their audience is composed of those who want their disbelief and surface toughness expressed in brittle ironies. The inevitable counterpart to the irony of this poetry is its frequent warm waves of sentimentality. The mood is first apparent in the twenties, or even earlier, with the attempts to shrug off emotion, to establish sexual freedom for both sexes, and to dismiss the serious with flip *mots*.

The beginnings of the flippancy are apparent in Sara Teasdale's *Rivers to the Sea* (1915):

> You must love me gladly
> Soul and body too,
> Or else find a new love,
> And good-by to you.

Miss Teasdale was genuinely concerned, however, with the new freedom for women. More often she employed deadly earnestness in working out her theme. The pose of flippancy and worldly knowledge hardened in the twenties, finding its most effective statements in Dorothy Parker and Edna Millay. The wisdom of a woman of seventy, looking back on her years, is put thus by Miss Parker:

> For contrition is hollow and wraithful
> And regret is no part of my plan,
> And I think (if my memory's faithful)
> There was nothing more fun than a man.

McLuhan dismisses Miss Parker's work as a "tissue of hackneyed phrases held in place by a superabundant snobbery—sex snobbery, money snobbery, and social snobbery. To this array is commonly added an intellectual snobbery which has the same basis of imaginary superiority." The milieu of her stories and poems is a world that is chic, chromium-plated, and cut on modernistic lines. It is a world that the middlebrow, taking his cue from the ads in *Town and Country*, *Vogue*, and the *New Yorker*, believes is highbrow sophistication at its most expensively perfumed best. Middle-class virtue smells of kitchen soap and is therefore held to be vulgar. The reputation of Miss Parker may be simply a symptom of large groups who, culturally at loose ends, have felt a need for coming to rest in such empty values as calculated naughtiness and blatant snobbery. Miss Millay's literary reputation, though earned largely by her having become a spokesman in the twenties for the feminine rights of "intellectual and biological equality," is more nearly justified.

With the publication of *A Few Figs from Thistles* (1920), groping adolescence and naïveté had found a voice which held an assured tone of sophistication.

> I shall forget you presently, my dear
> So make the most of this.

The popular success of this theme encouraged Miss Millay to employ variations on it in later books, as in *The Harp-Weaver and Other Poems* (1923):

> I might as well be easing you,
> As lie alone in bed.

That Miss Millay, however, is not merely a *poseur* as a poet both Oscar Cargill and Ransom have been at pains to show. But her reputation and influence—which Mr. Untermeyer assures us was carried on by "a thousand imitators"—demand that the bulk of her work be placed in the tradition to which it belongs.

The all but exclusive preoccupation of most Americans with economic values and the general indifference to the spiritual need for awakening American art and poetry was the negative impulse, as it were, behind the rediscovery by serious artists of predecessors like Melville and James and the eager borrowing from the literature of modern France. The opening of these two doors changed the air. Thereafter, for example, poetry *as* poetry was to be the primary emphasis. The forms of bohemianism, the disavowal of many middle-class attitudes, and the personal license which accompanies all revolutions, however, now seem to some to be identified with modernism in literature. It is true that bohemianism was a part of the tradition of exile, just as it was a part of the twenties generally. But with a very few exceptions, like Pound or Cummings, the bohemian strain does not appear in the work of the more serious moderns. It appears not only as a manifestation of the twenties but as a nineteenth-century derivative in such work as Miss Millay's and Miss Parker's, where modernism seems to be a kind of veneer.

McLuhan traces the sophisticated "stereotyped social revolt" to be found in almost all the verse of Miss Parker and in some of Miss Millay's to "the Byronic strain of alienation" which had "important antecedents in the eighteenth century and interesting derivatives in the nineteenth and twentieth." Swinburne decried the gray pall which the Christian virtues and the Victorian mores laid on society. And Wilde, of course, announced the license of the artist. McLuhan observes that, whereas in the "last century artists like Tennyson and Browning were crippled, at least subconsciously, by conventional pressure, today the reverse is true." The mores are no longer so rigid, and bohemianism in letters has had a vogue. A romantic irony, usually in the Housman idiom, is alternated with a middle-class-morals-be-damned pose to form a poetry of protest which no longer has very much to protest.

It is an appropriate irony that this peculiar form of epigonism, with its modernist affectations, should be after a nineteenth-century manner. When the modernist pose is dropped, the diction is merely a romantic or Victorian derivative. Thus Miss Millay's "God's World":

> O World, I cannot hold thee close enough!
>   Thy winds, thy wide gray skies!
>   Thy mists that roll and rise!
> Thy woods, this autumn day, that ache and sag
> And all but cry with color.

Toward the end of the poem even the word "prithee" is used. There is no indication of a private sensibility. The imagery is loose, in no way refracted through the poet's mind. Miss Parker, too, uses the standard imagery of distress and sorrow:

So let a love beat over me again,
Loosing its million desperate breakers wide.

Both of these poets should be classified as traditionalists, though not in the sense that they re-examine those values from the past which the present so desperately is missing. They are traditionalists in the lesser sense of being purveyors of the sentiments from older poetry, simply giving it a contemporaneous glaze. Miss Millay has relied on the Cavaliers for such standard verse clichés as the inconstancy of lovers and the inevitability of the grave. Her idiom is much closer to Elizabeth Barrett Browning's than to Marianne Moore's. Miss Parker re-works the standard romantic ironies of Housman:

It's little in living I set my store.
There's many a maid would be flushed and glad
And better you'll knock at a kindlier door.

There is not even the attempt to vary the rhythm or the idiom. It is standard sentiment, sanctioned since the nineties by all who discovered the delights of self-pity. Unfortunately, both Miss Millay's and Miss Parker's brands of epigonism, because of their risqué and snob elements, are widely anthologized and accepted by many as genuinely modern expressions.

## *3*

The forms of epigonism mentioned thus far are relatively ineffectual. The latter-day Georgians are dying off. Miss Parker's muse appears to have retired, and Miss Millay's attitudinizing in *Conversation at Midnight* and mild hysteria in her anti-Axis (and anti-Roosevelt) verse undoubtedly disillusioned many among her audience. Still another form, which Macdonald has called "*l'avant-garde pompier*," has received less attention. It is a poetry which masquerades as experimental—but which is either patently derivative or imitative merely of the surface manner of the modern idiom. There is a danger, of course, in putting any poet, unless his history is clear, into either category. Yet there is an equal danger in refusing to notice what may be either a lack of integrity or an inability to employ the modern techniques other than as a mannerism.

The bulk of the poetry written by Archibald MacLeish has come to be seen as the *locus classicus* of pseudo avant-gardism in modern poetry. In the course of his extensive examination of the history of MacLeish as a poet and public figure, Morton Zabel[7] has quoted from a criticism by Rolfe Humphries:

> I do not mean that Mr. MacLeish is influenced by this contemporary, or borrows to advantage from that one; I mean much more; I mean that he depends on this one or that for his very existence. . . . But whereas the normal course of poetic progress is from imitation to originality, in the case of Mr. MacLeish, it has been from imitation to more extended feats of that art. . . . The whole complex of Eliot's language, tone rhythm, anthropological references, and symbolical allusiveness, has been elaborately imitated.

Zabel has documented the accusation, stating that the derivations are always self-evident:

> . . . The style and motivation of *The Pot of Earth* (1925) came straight out of Frazer and *The Waste Land; The Hamlet* (1928) was a deft enlargement of the motives of "Prufrock," "Portrait of a Lady" and "The Hollow Men"; *Conquistador* (1932) took the old-man theme of "Gerontion" and mixed it with the historical and anthropological images of Frenchmen like Apollinaire, Perse, Cendrars, Salmon, and Forgue; the general effects, contrasts, historical shifts, and colloquial structure of Pound's *Cantos* were freely diluted and made into easy reading not only in *Conquistador* but in the *Frescoes* (1933), *Public Speech* (1936), and *America Was Promises* (1939).

Edmund Wilson indicates still other influences in his "The Omelet of A. MacLeish":

> Leaves falling: and all of a flawless and hollow felicity:
> . . . And a wind out of Valéry's graveyard but it never blew anything loose. . . .

In addition to his vicious parody of the style, Wilson also points up the essential inability of MacLeish to write a modern poetry. The style is flawless but hollow, and the wind from it never blows anything loose. MacLeish, that is, chooses to explore only one side, rarely both, at one time. There is a critical alertness in Eliot's poetry, an awareness of the face value and the actual value of the situation examined, an understanding not only of what is present but of what is missing.

The passivity in much of MacLeish's poetry is the result of his failure to reconcile opposites, to achieve tension (a fault readily observable in *Conquistador*). In some lines he simply itemizes after the manner of prose:

> The pompous Latin the appropriate feasts
> The big names the imperial decorations
> The beautiful battles and the brave deceased. . . .

Other than for the missing punctuation, what is there to distinguish this from a slightly rhetorical prose? At its best, his poetry is smooth, a liquefaction of phrases:

> The quick loves: the sleep: the waking: the blowing of
> Winds over us: all this that we know:
> All this goes out at the end as the flowing of
> Water carries the leaves down.

The dramatic conflict of elements within the poem is consciously avoided, as lengthier illustration would reveal. Even his punctuation, and sometimes the lack of it, stems from a dependence upon an "exclusionist diction." His overuse of the colon, for example, seems to spring from a fear that the elements are not homogeneous enough, that they have individual edges and outlines. Through the colons their relationship is constantly emphasized.

A certain similarity in phrases and in general subject matter between *The Family Reunion* (1939) and *The Fall of the City* (1937) suggest a ready way of contrasting the styles of Eliot and MacLeish. The tautness of Eliot's

> Liberty is a different kind of pain from prison

has its counterpart in MacLeish's

> They wish to be free of their freedom: released from their liberty.

Both statements, of course, are paradoxical—but Eliot's is given a dramatic concentration through the words "pain" and "prison," whereas MacLeish's is distended and referred to no painful experience that might give it an emotional relevance. Again, Eliot in an entire scene and, as it were, obliquely throughout the play creates a sense of profound depths inherent in the things most commonplace, most unquestioned.

> Old age came softly up to now. I felt safe enough;
> And now I don't feel safe. As if the earth should open
> Right to the centre, as I was about to cross Pall Mall . . .
> But I remember now that I am always surprised
> By the bull dog in the Burlington Arcade.
> What if every moment were like that, if we were awake?

In *The Fall of the City* this awareness is stated more directly and flatly:

> We have seen the familiar room grow unfamilar.

That MacLeish's poetry has been paraded as a primary work of the imagination rather than as an example, for the most part, of the "forcible-feeble style" or of rhetoric blown up to unnatural dimensions is in large part due to the journalist reviewers and to the anthologists. The anthologists in particular, by bulking the good with the bad and the genuine with the pretentions, have done their part to cheapen tastes and dull sensibilities. An examination of Louis Untermeyer's criticism of MacLeish presents us with an aspect of the problem. We discover, for example, that Untermeyer appears to have no clear understanding of the contemporary idioms, that he does not recognize the all but frankly derivative nature of much of MacLeish's poetry. Here is a key sentence in his evaluation of MacLeish: "Alliteration and assonance take on fresh values in his vivid lines; brusque phrases alternating with long suspended sentences create a surprising tension."

Tension, if it means anything, means a context of resistances in terms of which an idea justifies and qualifies itself. The idea is seen in terms of an image or in relation to its opposite. The final statement, or the implication, is achieved in terms of contrasts. Alliteration and assonance function to preclude contrasts. Or, granted that MacLeish is a master of both tension and its opposite, we may glance at his characteristic work, "You, Andrew Marvell," "Immortal Autumn," "Epistle To Be Left in the Earth"—these are Untermeyer's selections, so presumably they illustrate the poet's mastery of tension. In the three poems there is a total of two periods (.). Even MacLeish's artful system of colons would have offered some resistance to the liquid flow. After these comments Untermeyer adds that these lines "transcend commentary"! They at least transcend any possibility of leading one to the tensional elements in MacLeish's poetry.

One of the publishers of Kenneth Patchen presents him as a poet who, in taking off from Cummings and Williams as well as from Freud and the Surrealists, goes on "to something that is all his own—something that may well be the trend of the future." It is noteworthy that the "something" is nowhere identified. An unsympathetic, perhaps even a sympathetic, reader will find little in his work that is even similar to Cummings or Williams, none of the former's sense of language alive or the latter's capacity for quickening imagery, and will find the Surrealist element merely a disjointed use of imagery with no discoverable center of meaning. Where the publisher finds "new forms," the reader will find merely formlessness. The occasionally brilliant phrase or good line is too infrequently a part of a worthy poem. Either the intensity of his anger or his indifference to ordered imaginings sends the phrases, some of them beautiful, some inane, into all directions.

Patchen has the merit of obvious, even dogged, sincerity. He strikes violently to the front and back and both sides of him at all forms of bigotry and injustice he can see—and at some apparently only he can see. His sincerity frequently causes him to be indifferent to the ideal of esthetic distance. One of his poems breaks off with

> I am tired of the lies . . . of the dirt
> And the murder
> I am too angry to bother with this poem
> About the beauty of the world
> Who cares a damn about that now.

He is obsessed with actuality to the degree that he sometimes hands it over piecemeal to his reader, forgetting apparently that many of the situations he has observed have been seen by others. Only his terrible anger seems to distinguish the quality of his observation—and one surmises its intensity, too frequently, not from the symbolic forms it assumes but from his use of repetition and his employment of upper-case letters, heavy type, and heavily inked illustrations. He employs, reminiscent of the editors of *Blast*, all possible devices for dynamiting the attention of his audience.

Patchen has been called, perhaps unfairly, a "professional literary rebel." His conscious evangelism and tremendous righteousness lead him into the sentimentality of grouping, but not identifying, his enemies as *you*. Thus his apocalyptic lines, which have a fiery intensity, are vitiated:

> O the lions of fire shall awake
> And the valleys steam with their fury
>
> Because you are sick with the dirt of your money
> Because you are pigs rooting in the swill of your war
> Because you are mean and sly and full of the pus of
> your pious murder
> Because you have turned your faces from God
> Because you have spread your filth everywhere

O the lions of fire
Wait in the crawling shadow of your world
And their terrible eyes are watching you.

One would incline to applaud a poet with the integrity, warmth, and compassion of Patchen if it were not for the strong suspicion that the fires of his anger are producing ash rather than purification. Even so, one may hope that his bewildered power will find a center, enabling his imagination to create a steady illumination in lieu of pyrotechnics.

There are also the pseudo-modernists who depend on the surface manner of the modern idiom but who fail to use the techniques in the expression of new perceptions or in the nurturing of generative ideas. Because obscurity has been accepted as a stylistic feature, as it were, of modern poetry, it has become relatively easy for the poetaster to pass off a manner for substance. One most frequently, perhaps, associates obscurity with a strong emphasis on the connotative power of words—but in the genuine poem the particular facet that is emphasized can be focused only because the related meanings are necessary if one is to understand the particular meaning refracted by the facet.

R. P. Blackmur, in reviewing Charles Henri Ford's *The Garden of Disorder* and Harry Roskolenko's *Sequence on Violence*, points out lines and words in which none of the ordinary centers of meaning are referred to. The poet can give disorder room, he begins, only within order. After six understandable lines in one of his poems, Blackmur says, Ford adds several of mere verbiage, two of which are

The robins of my eyes hover where
sixteen leaves fall that were a prayer.

One cannot relate the leaves to the prayer, or either of these to the robins in the eyes. Blackmur further illustrates his point with these two lines by Roskolenko:

"*You have seen* waves *and* rockets—*gerrymander*
the sightless shafts of air.

The italics are Mr. Roskolenko's. The word here in question is *gerrymander*. In another poem we find 'the spirit dismembered with élan,' where the important word is *élan*. No stretch either of word or context in either poem will bring these words into definable vital (or organic) relation with the meanings wanted." Neither word has its usual, commonplace meaning, nor does it carry a hint, to be inferred from its context, of having acquired a new or extended meaning. "When you find this type of writing expanded so as to be the only circulating element in long and obviously serious poems, you will conclude that the writer was not only not in possession of his subject but that he gave in only to its most obvious temptations: of verbal vanity—the fluxion of words without knowledge or assumption of the dictionary."

The margin of modern poetry in which this mannered manipulation of idiom is exercised may be slight, but toleration of it at all invites the widening of the margin and the publication of such hoaxes as Ern Malley's *The Darkening Ecliptic*. (It is worth observing that a portion of the Ern Malley matter was published in an American poetry journal before the Australian authors of the hoax made themselves known.)

As long, presumably, as there is a cleavage between the artist and the bulk of the society in which he lives, there will be varied forms of epigonism. Always, of course, there has been derivative poetry—but the present distance between genuine avant-garde poetry and that in the "slick" magazine gives the epigones varied areas in which to exploit not only the mannerisms of modern poetry but those of older generations.

CHAPTER THIRTEEN

# *Tradition and Regionalism*

> *Tradition may be conceived as a by-product of right living, not to be aimed at directly. It is of the blood, so to speak, rather than of the brain.*—T. S. Eliot

A MORAL code and ideals, as well as their esthetic forms, can be maintained only through a tradition, which provides the framework for stating them and for passing them on. This tradition, also, enables the individual to define his personality and to maintain his identity—because only in terms of his relationship with the values and ideals of his tradition can his character find its definition.

Yeats, Eliot, and Tate have been preoccupied with tradition because they have been keenly aware that a violently disordered world can be refracted and characterized by the poet only through contrasting it with more stable societies and because the aspects of a traditional society are usually seen as the irrational accretions of time and therefore opposed to the sheer rationality somehow associated with modernity.

The woman in Eliot's "A Game of Chess," after what Tate calls "some desperately aimless conversation," lets go of herself and says:

> What shall I do now What shall I do?
> I shall rush out as I am, and walk the street
> With my hair down, so. What shall we do tomorrow?
> What shall we ever do?

Quite understandably Tate uses this passage, or "The Game of Chess," as a text to answer, in part, his question, "What Is a Traditional Society?"[1]

On the walls of the room in which the woman and the man are talking there are scenes from a heroic past, and earlier the poet has used the smell of perfumes as an excuse for recalling the grandeur of Cleopatra's world. What, then, is Eliot's poem about? Tate answers:

> It means that in ages which suffer the decay of manners, religion, morals, codes, our indestructible vitality demands expression in violence and chaos; it means that men who have lost both the higher myth of religion and the lower myth of historical dramatization have lost the forms of human action; it means that they are no longer capable of defining a human objective. . . .

By the term "myth" Tate means simply a body of beliefs in which ideals are incorporated or dramatized. These ideals give men their direction. Without them they exercise their "intellect to no purpose."

A tradition, Tate says elsewhere, is most important to the individual because it is "a special organization of the individual sensibility that liberates the intelligence through the possession of habitual responses to life that are, moreover, relevant to the conduct of other men."[2] The tradition furnishes the individual with his convictions, his sense of propriety and decorum. It enables him to lean on the accumulated judgments of his forebears and to assume the value in certain "fixed procedures."

> No man in one lifetime can construct out of the air an adequate system of judgments about life, and not at the same time atrophy his powers of contemplation, of seeing things, in so far as we are permitted to see them, as they are.

One aspect of modernism, certainly, is the constant experimenting with convention—with marriage, with sexual freedom, with criminal codes and punishment, with private property, with methods of education, etc. In retrospect we can see that much of modern literature has dated very quickly simply because the authors were obliged to accept or adopt a mode of conduct or belief which subsequently has appeared merely as naïve gesturing or faddishness. The writer in a satisfactory traditional society will be relieved from the insuperable task of creating an entire system of "judgments about life" and therefore be free to perceive, as an artist, the unique quality of the objects, characters, and situations he is contemplating.

A tradition, of course, can be repressive, can lose its vitality through failing to adapt itself to changing needs. If it maintains attitudes that are in essential opposition to newly evolved and inevitable beliefs, its strength will be dissipated. If a tradition breaks down, however, another must be developed to serve in its place. Otherwise, there will be many forms of disequilibrium and violence. A tradition that is vital, serving the complex needs of a society, is a means of achieving necessary equilibriums.

Among the forms of disequilibrium in our society is the overemphasis on the practical. It was the belief of John Peale Bishop that the only way in which we can establish an equilibrium between the cultural and the practical is to discover, as Joseph Frank puts it, "a cultural tradition with all the force of a religion."

It is quite possible that man as a physical being lives most fully in approximating an "organic" relationship with nature. As a personality, he finds his definition in relationship with a community, a region, which has value in terms of a tradition. For a tradition arises, it would seem, to explain man's relation to nature and to keep it in proper balance, as well as to establish rules of conduct and a way of life in which the relationships of man with man may be kept at a satisfactory equilibrium.

Contemporary historians have been concerned with the phenomenon of the "dissociated man." He has also been called a "rootless and internationalized figure." It is perhaps impossible to isolate into neatly arranged strands the divergent factors which contribute to the various moods and characteristics of modern poetry. Yet man's relationship with nature must be, as Amos Wilder states it, something more than a question of overt bodily needs; it is more subtle than that. At least childhood must not be weaned too soon from an organic tie with nature. This profound relation of man is the primordial medium of his spiritual life: witness the absolutely decisive place that nature has in poetry, the myths and the religions of the race. It is out of our ancient bond and kinship with the earth that those elations and ecstasies spring that are the commonest themes of the poet, and which are the substance of natural religion. Man deprived of this is less than man.[3]

Whatever forms of thought and living—excessive dependence upon abstraction, industrialization, mechanization, and city dwelling—that serve to widen the distance between man and nature serve likewise to lessen the amount of nature reflected in his poetry. Poetry, as implied in Wilder's statement, is a celebration of nature and of man as a sentient being. Poetry can be a means of reminding man of his essential relationship with nature, but it is not a substitute for it.

"Men are attached to places," Lewis Mumford reminds us, in his *Faith for Living*, "as they are attached to families and friends. When these loyalties come together, one has the most tenacious cement possible for human society." The strength in patriotic feeling does not inhere solely in our attachment for the abstractions of law or stated ideals. A part of the strength is in the

red soil of the Shenandoah in Virginia, with the apple trees whose boughs skirt the ground; the granite hills of Vermont with their white churches, stiff against the north wind, . . . and the enveloping loneliness of the desert, from the white alkali of Utah to the red canyons of Arizona.

In John Gould Fletcher's somewhat sentimental "Magnolia" the South becomes identified with the flower-bearing and rich-scented tree:

> Spreading about your dark trunk and your deep
>   heavy shade to still draw me
> In the stifling slow midsummer days to the red-
>   brown South I know.

Edwin Arlington Robinson, also, frequently indicates the intimate relationship between the chill New England climate and the character of her people.

A body of tradition descends and is kept unified more easily in a regional society. The economic, political, social, and philosophical elements of a society in a geographically circumscribed area are more likely to maintain a homogeneous character. Religion becomes a part of the texture of the regional society and is more easily sustained because it is also a part of the social forms of the society. And the very attitudes that are most unquestioned are unquestioned because they are a kind of reflex. The deliberations of the individual will be in terms of these givens.

## 2

The New England regionalists, with the exception of Mark Van Doren, who quite possibly should not, despite his partial kinship with Frost, be classified with them, have tended to hold more closely to their region, to a nonliterary source, for their traditional materials and matter, although Emerson has obviously influenced Frost, and Robinson has drawn upon the Arthurian legends and Shakespeare. By and large, the New England regionalists have not absorbed the modernist tendencies in poetry. Some have very consciously avoided them.

Frost has remained within his New England world. He has used its climate and topography, its locally agreed-upon virtues and attitudes; he has remained as close to New Hampshire as New Hampshire has remained to the nineteenth century. Except for the adoption of a prose idiom which was an early manifestation of the modern movement and an occasional foray against the modernists, he has stayed close to home.

In "Two Tramps in Mud Time" there is the situation likely to be found in much of Frost's work. He states the theme explicitly:

> My object in life is to unite
> My avocation and my vocation.

The subject matter is concerned with a man, the poet, chopping blocks of beech on a warm day in April, which can turn into "the

Middle of March" if a "wind comes frozen off a peak." The man is chopping the blocks cleanly—he takes pride in his workmanship, even in "unimportant tasks." He is a man who lives a "life of self-control," but whose individualism does not preclude a stroke for "the common good." From his wry pleasure in the weather, one may see that he takes as much pride in his region as in his workmanship. The two strangers who come along are quickly "sized up," for they obviously are not a part of the "respectable citizenry"—

two hulking tramps
(From sleeping God knows where last night
But not long since in the lumber camps.)

Little is said, but they and the man understand the situation. As lumberjacks the job should be theirs; that is, they "need" the work. The man would like to continue his chopping because it serves his human needs—his need to do a job well because he loves to do it. But, as a good citizen, he recognizes "Theirs was the better right."

The New England tradition has made the poem easy to write, has furnished the subject matter, the point of view, and the tone. It has even furnished the theme. It may be unnecessary to point out that the strictly modernist—traditionless—poet faces a much more difficult task.

Quite possibly Frost's strength, his peculiar consistency in point of view and tone, is derivative from the strength he feels in his position, which is his New England heritage or tradition. (It may be of significance that the New England decadence which revolted Eliot was of the city, Boston; the decadence which Frost occasionally has found in rural sections seems only a half-decadence. Again, as Robert Tristram Coffin has pointed out, it is different from the decadence reflected in Robinson.) It may be, again, that the reason so many find Frost admirable as a poet is that the fragments of a nineteenth-century tradition, the sense of personal rectitude and independence of conduct and responsibility which many of us attempt to reconcile with our more "liberal" notions of moral freedom and collective action remain relatively *pure* in Frost. His modern idiom, with a minimum of conscious "poetic effects," adds to his appeal.

The New England setting is a natural dramatic medium for Frost. It furnishes him with the stories, attitudes, characters, and expressions which are appropriate to his needs. Frost does not seem at odds with his tradition. He has kept it intact. The suspicion one might have of him, perhaps, will arise in questioning how much of the modern influences he really has understood or felt. Our admiration for him might be greater if we could feel he had bested modernism in order to maintain his tradition. There must remain a suspicion that he has lived more completely than he has been aware in the nineteenth century, somewhat like those poets who used a Georgian idiom for their poetry of World War II. As a traditionalist and a regionalist, he contrasts most sharply, say, with Tate, whose traditionalism has been brought into focus against the very problems which have made modern poetry *modern*.

There seem to be at least two sides to Frost. The admirable side is that in which he is the mature voice, as Andrew Marvell was, of the end of a literary tradition. This is the shrewd Frost who catches in his poems the subtleties and ambiguities of human motives, the man who admires integrity and moral fiber. The other side of Frost is professionally folksy, the poet who knows how to imitate himself and who seems quite willing to keep well out of the focus of his poems any significant recognition that not even in rural New England have the traditional values remained unquestioned and whole.

Two aspects of modernism in poetry may shed some light on Frost's use of his medium and his relationship to the traditions of his region. The symbols of the modernists like Tate or Eliot are likely to seem strained or "difficult" because the poet is struggling for a synthesis of image and idea that will illumine some phase of modern confusion. Thus we have Eliot's ancient women gathering fuel in vacant lots or Tate's jaguar leaping into its own image in the jungle pool: the one catches the pathos of life driven by economics to struggle for mere survival; the other symbolizes the frustration of the man whose life is informed with no purpose. Frost's symbols express an acceptance, and are a kind of celebration, of the world he lives in—apples, hay, the snow, horses, and woods. He does not feel the "desperate" need for symbols that will enable him to capture his meaning. In his longer poems he frequently falls back on the abstract, almost imageless, language which the Victorians used in their long narrative poetry. Again, the modernist feels the need for a language of images, symbols, one reflective of the physical, if only to help him recapture the *feel* of the world and to avoid neat abstractions. Frost's experience of rural living seemingly precludes such a need.

The degree of modernism of the individual critic is likely to condition his final judgment of Frost. It is apparent that traditionalists like Tate or Warren object to an industrialized and mechanized world, to relativism in moral standards, and to such an economic form as finance capitalism which enables the individual to avoid personal obligations. Yet they recognize that the tradition, based in part on religious belief and sanctions, which opposed these developments, is rapidly breaking up, even in those regions which are its last strongholds. They have been able, no more than another, to reverse the process or to suggest anything more than palliatives. Only some transcendental belief, some new myth, will be able to change the directions. Their poetry, which finds its tension in the conflicts between traditionalism and modernism, is concerned with problems which in Frost's poetry remain almost unnoticed. Tradition serves poetry well and is necessary to it—but it would seem that as minds poets have some obligation to face the problems which give their time its character.

Despite a snide and self-congratulatory introduction to his *New*

*Poetry of New England*[4]—in which Eliot is seen to run away and presently to turn "into a hawk and vulture all at once," while Charles Malam, John Holmes, and Frances Frost remain in regional blessedness—R. P. T. Coffin writes very ably of the Maine tradition, its decay and disintegration, which informed the poetry of Robinson. Coffin writes, in telling of the decay of the Big House people and their code, of a variant form of the desiccant society from which Eliot withdrew. It is another society again from Frost's, the Little House, people. Robinson's purpose and success stand out more clearly against Coffin's interpretation. One can see an appropriate irony in Robinson's mildly romantic diction as there is in his use of grand names, like Theophilus and Priscilla and Llewellyn, for miserable, lonely, or frustrated people.

The part of New England that was strong in Robinson's mind was that part that has seen a swift disintegration. "People become in-bred, blood runs thin, the economic foundations crumble, people peter out and grow eccentric and queer." The old New England religion means little, and the people Robinson wrote about do not go to church any more. But part of the code remains. The people are reticent about their personal loneliness and sufferings—and they can suddenly cease talking at all to those closest to them or, like Mr. Flood, find their solace in solitary drinking. Nightmares, if frequent, can have a way of edging in upon the daylight. Too much, of course, can be made of isolated tragedies—but if they occur often enough, they can form some kind of pattern in the mind, as they did in Robinson's, and suggest the elements of a general philosophy in terms of which the subjects and themes of other times and places are understood. Robinson's people, as Coffin suggests, may be kings and queens, but they are always "New Englanders in their brains and hearts." Nor is it surprising, when thought of in this context, that Robinson's poems are so often concerned with characterizations, with strange and twisted motivations. (It is interesting to observe that our southern regionalists, poets and novelists, are concerned with the fact that character is easily definable when seen against what are accepted as absolute moral values. Warren's "Ballad of Billie Potts" is a case in point.) For character or personality is most likely to be whole and healthy in a society whose tradition furnishes the opportunity for self-definition and fulfilment.

Yvor Winters relates the primary concerns of Robinson and even his style to "The New England Background":

> It is the moralistic tradition which predominates in Robinson, however: in the choice of subject matter, this shows itself in the moral curiosity with regard to the particular case; in the realm of style, in the honesty of statement and clarity of form; in the conduct of life, in immutable adherence to a purpose.[5]

Winters sketches in the early religious attitudes of New England and the subsequent concern with morality, despite a rather general indifference to theology. Robinson seems "to have inherited the traditional moral sense and moral curiosity, which are the sources of his better poems, and to have broken easily with the few remnants of theology which Unitarianism retained." (If Winters is implying, as other comments in his study suggest, that the moderns, like Eliot or Stevens, cannot write a poetry of direct statement because of their confused moral views, he is giving his prejudices in the matter another airing and writing nonsense. Robinson employs a more abstract diction because the idiom he inherited was from the nineteenth century.) The integrity of Robinson's characters, despite their weaknesses and isolation, is, of course, a part of the moral fiber that was in Robinson himself. However shabby their way of life or however frustrated some of his characters are, they maintain a margin of dignity and self-respect. It is with the margin itself that Robinson was preoccupied. He was able in the face of a great deal of evidence to the contrary to justify something very close to a tragic vision.

## 3

A tradition is related to a region because it is "local in origin," but it is quite possible for a writer to use his tradition without mentioning his region. His tradition furnishes him with his judgments, attitudes, and evaluations—with certain basic assumptions. Tradition enables the writer to perceive the "meaning" of his subject matter. When, however, the writer wishes to treat his region, he is able to inform his material with a significance or meaning because he understands its tradition. To rely mostly on local color for interest is merely to exploit a region; this exploitation implies small sense of its tradition, its essential values, or the significance of events or characters portrayed.

Local-color regionalism, a danger more palpably that of the novelist than the poet for the simple reason that the sensationalism—where there is nothing more than this—of parading inbred degenerates, of building up abnormal sex situations, and of exaggerating community ignorance and violence goes, like the polemics of sectionalism, more easily in prose. These problems of regionalism and sectionalism may be brought into focus by using the critical, or classroom, technique of separating theme from subject matter. The region furnishes an abundance of subject matter of use in plot construction or in arranging the substance or particulars of the poem: local types, scenery, and the local mores. It is in the ability of the poet to illumine his theme, not in reverence for local pieties, that the case for his merit must rest.

We are not surprised, then, to find many poems by regionalists which have no imagistic or specific reference to their region. The reference is oblique, or by implication—for, by understanding their relation to the past, they will understand their place in the present and their relation to their region. More specifically, they find that the scientific world picture, which includes industrialization and modern capitalism, is destroying the tradition that once gave dignity and fulness to the life of their region. Thus they are concerned with questions—religion, evil, self-definition, and the value of esthetic forms—which the beliefs and attitudes attendant upon the scientific view, technology, and industrialization, as well as the forms of positivism, have raised in different guises. For ultimately the problems of tradition are problems of regionalism.

Tate's theme is the forms of dehumanization which develop in a society denying its tradition.[6] The poetry of John Crowe Ransom, which arises from a position similar to Tate's, is concerned mostly with the modern's inability to unite the esthetic with the practical, to attend to the poetic as readily as he attends to the abstract.[7] Ransom relies only slightly more than Tate, which is very little indeed, on his regional setting for images and symbols. Donald Davidson and Warren rely a good deal on it, Davidson being the more nostalgic by far of the two and using specific themes from Tennessee history to contrast the old South with the newly industrialized South. Warren, particularly in his earlier work, manages an intimate relationship of landscape with theme, which is frequently a concern with the forms of evil operating subtly under a civilized veneer. A less subtle, but effective, instance is found in "Pondy Woods," where the horror suffered by the pursued Negro is identified with the "ominous grotesqueries of the swamp." And the poetry of John Peale Bishop often has its particularity of detail from a southern setting.[8] None of the southern regionalists of any significance, with the exception of Davidson, has attempted to draw only on the antebellum South. Like Eliot and Joyce, they draw on the older, richer, and more complex tradition of classical and English literature. Tate, Warren, and Bishop, to a far greater extent than Davidson or Ransom, use the Latin classics and the Elizabethans.

## *4*

The twentieth century also has seen two developments which put modern poetry at a far remove from the regional interests of the

New Englanders or of the southerners. These are an international and a national poetry. It may well be that the internationalist poet will largely be frustrated in so far as he attempts to write *within* or in terms of his ideology. (This is not, certainly, to question the values of an international brotherhood.) We may be startled to see how frequently the internationalists seem like Shelley in modern dress. Kenneth Patchen, for example, cries:

> Let us have madness openly, O men
> Of my generation. Let us follow
> The footsteps of this slaughtered age. . . .

The proletarian poet cannot use, as Eliot for example can, a literary tradition because it is now associated with a privileged minority. Nor can he use the Christian tradition. He must work within the abstractions which compose his belief. Without a tradition to draw upon, the emotional strength of his poetry will depend mostly upon rhetoric. The alternative, which some have used, is that part of the Christian myth which teaches the brotherhood of man. Even this, however, must be abstracted, isolated from those stories and symbols which give it its traditional strength.

Not only the poets but all who wish to promote an international as opposed to, or to supersede, a national order must win their adherents despite the almost total absence of a body of symbols which are held in common by traditional forms of society. A national state has its legends, stories, heroes, songs, flag, and history—all of which give focus and emotional force to its commonly held attitudes and ideals. The national myth is supported unquestioningly by citizens because it provides them with an orientation, gives purpose and direction to their lives. Until the internationalist poets have a body of legends and heroes to mythologize, their poetry will be thin and their audience slight.

The nationalist poet, under some circumstances, has a much easier time of it. The resistance poetry of Louis Aragon had to be suppressed by the Germans because it stirred memories and associations long identified with French liberty. An appeal to the "Crusaders" was not a denotative reference to a series of historical events alone—it set up reverberations that widened until France itself, and that meant the problems of the moment, was the issue of the poem. The parts of the myth are interfused with the same life, that is, with the national ideals, of which the myth is the body or the symbolic form. Some myths, to be sure, are more vital than others, and there are, as well, synthetic myths. It remains that a myth in some form is necessary for the poet, furnishing some measure of his idealism and giving him metaphors and symbols for his poetry.

America as a cultural "unity" will seem homogeneous when viewed in contrast to a European or oriental way of life. Within the United States, regional differences remain strong. And we cannot assume, as some critics have, that a national framework is the very smallest within which the artist can work without falling into a narrow parochialism. Critics who tend to think of literature in terms of economics, sociology, and ideologies—who see it, that is, in the *abstract* and not in its irreducible materiality in its settings, its action, its people, its symbols and concrete images—dismiss regionalism as, in Granville Hicks's words, an "escape" or a "sentimental expression of sectional pride." The regionalist, Hicks adds, does not contemplate "the fundamental unity of the nation."

Yet consideration of what this "fundamental unity" might be is hardly to be rewarded by a formulation satisfactory to a majority. A glance at the poets associated with the "fundamental unity" theme tells us, better than theorizing can, what the difference between nationalism and regionalism in the United States amounts to. Whitman, despite his grandiose attempt to create an American myth, has his chief success in the treatment of his own area.

> [I]n every passage where he wishes to be quite clearly national, slighting no special interests and neglecting no peculiarity, he resorts to the catalogue, and gives us a list of all species and subspecies of Americana. The

important aesthetic feature of the Whitman catalogue is its formlessness: the heterogeneous materials do not fuse into a splendid unity; they remain heterogeneous. They may be accepted intellectually, but they do not always persuade emotionally. The really persuasive parts of Whitman are those poems, like "Crossing Brooklyn Ferry," that touch Whitman's own special locale; and these, too, have as much form as Whitman ever achieves.[9]

The poets in Whitman's tradition, in so far as they have emulated his glorification of the geography of America, his ill-focused emotionalism, and his loosely defined democracy, have given us the same catalogues and the same formlessness. Whitman is the poet of the ideological and sociological critics—his essentially vague and abstract notions apparently do not trouble them. It should be underscored that it is not Whitman's personal inadequacies alone that make his poetry formless.

The form of a poem may be thought of as the appropriate organization of its parts—the images, symbols, meter, tone, etc. Only thus can the significance of the object or situation that is to be transmuted into art be made perceivable. This implies that the poet must grasp the object or situation in its complexity and wholeness; otherwise he cannot discover, in contemplating it, those symbols which refract its peculiar character or essence. He must, that is, be able to understand his material in its wholeness. America in its complexity can hardly be so understood. At least the poetry thus far written does not indicate that it can be. Therefore, any attempt to treat America broadly will result in a cataloguing of its parts and aspects.

Those critics who see literature through the abstractions of ideologies and economics, however, can talk loosely about "fundamental unity." They would find it difficult, as the God-bless-America poets should have learned by now, to discover symbols that catch the fundamental significance of America. There undoubtedly are characteristics which Americans, south, east, north, or west, have in common. But these cannot easily be isolated, because they exist in persons who have regional characteristics which in turn give a distinct quality to their "national" characteristics. Thus we speak of Babbitt as a national type—but when we think of Sinclair Lewis' Babbitt, we have in mind a middle westerner, who is quite distinct from a New England or a southern Babbitt. And if Lewis were to caricature one of the latter two, he would have to work with a different set of requirements in order to capture the type. An author, that is, who wants to create the specific character of a type must do it in terms of a setting, a locality, and a way of life—since it is only in terms of the standards inherent in these that a personality becomes defined. What remain in him as national charateristics, over and above the regional characteristics, are merely residue and insufficient to create a valid national type. If we think of *Ethan Frome*, *Sanctuary*, *Studs Lonigan*, or *Huckleberry Finn*, we think in terms of a region. We assume their national character in their regional character. "The great classics of American Fiction," Warren has written, "the best works of Hawthorne or of Mark Twain or of Melville are, for instance, of New England; then, almost by political or geographical definition only, or by some mystical hocus-pocus of definition, are they American." We have already seen to what advantage Frost and Robinson have put their regional knowledge in the creation of character.

It remains that the scientific emphasis has been the chief determining factor of the modern society in that it has partially disrupted the tradition. Science requires a constant reappraisal, with no preconceptions allowable, of each isolated phenomenon. A strictly scientific appraisal of all one's experience is obviously impossible. Yet even a general dependence upon the scientific viewpoint leads to a fairly constant re-evaluation of convention and belief. It leads to a constant reordering of conduct. We do not, of course, adjust ourselves to each new bit of scientific knowledge—we continue to live with habitual attitudes, taking our cues from the mores. Occasionally, as in the first flush of our old talk about genes and chromosomes and environment, we were ready to accept any acts as predetermined. Therefore, the criminal was not to be punished but redirected, etc. There is much, naturally, to be said for using such knowledge. But it became apparent soon that abolishing the traditional codes would lead to chaos. The needs of the society demand that we hold to the ideal of personal responsibility. The point is that tradition should be seen not as sacrosanct, static, and unchangeable. It should grow by accretion and be subject to adjustment. It should not be dismissed in any trust that society will somehow be infinitely improved if we have no preconceptions. Quite apparently, the individual is incapable of making isolated judgments which require consideration of numerous factors if, at the same time, he cannot draw on the society's accumulated experience.

CHAPTER FOURTEEN

# *Forms of Dehumanization*

*All that is greatest in modern literature is soliloquy.*—
W. B. YEATS

A DEFINITION of the term "dehumanization," or even the term "human," that would satisfy adherents of various faiths, opposed philosophies, or conflicting ideologies can hardly be made. It is apparent, however, that what we know as personality is dependent upon forms of belief (the head-hunter is "inhuman"), upon community (a man is hardly a personality if he has no association with other men), and upon the balanced development of human faculties (one who literally pursues only a single line of development is in a sense monstrous). It is easier, after first noting the confusion of modern belief, therefore, to interpret aspects of the problem of dehumanization in the light of an older definition of man, as one made in the image of God and possessing an eternal destiny.

Once the immortality, or the existence, of the soul was questioned, some degree of dehumanization was inevitable in literature. The identity of the person is implicit in the doctrine of the immortal soul. Whatever the experiences of flux, either in the mind, in nature, or in the history of societies, this identity would be fixed, immutable, and eternal. Implicit, too, in this doctrine is the dignity of man. Even those doctrines through which man's identity is seen as absorbed into the divine allow man his dignity—he is somehow worthy of divine consideration, of communing with or becoming identified with divinity. And during this life selfhood remains stable.

Houston Peterson in *The Melody of Chaos*[1] recalls that Socrates argued in the *Phaedo* that the soul is "immortal because a perfectly simple, unified substance is indivisible and therefore indestructible." Peterson continues:

> And probably that is the view that most western people implicitly hold. However much they may change, however subject they may be to the vicissitudes of age and disease, deep down within each one of them there is a central unchanging point which is the essential soul or self.

The Christian centuries strengthened this view. It quite probably is true that self-identity is unquestioned by most people. We are individual as physical beings. We have personal histories. And we have individual names. However, the sense of absolute identity has undergone many qualifications and changes. The consequent effects upon post-Renaissance and particularly modern literature have been considerable and important.

The first glimmerings of change, of course, were in the Renaissance. "We are such stuff/As dreams are made on,/and our little life/Is rounded with a sleep." There is nothing here to give assurance of personal immortality. On the other hand, there are lines, like those of Hamlet, on the nobility of man—and nobility of character implies a strong awareness of personal identity. However inconsistent or irrational the mind of man might be seen to be, his identity was somehow pure, single. It is one thing to view the identity, the soul, of the person as being subject to whim, to the pulls of irrationality and evil—it is something again to see the "identity" merely as the total mass of changing perceptions, with stability only momentary and memories shifting through a series of constantly dissolving scenes. Peterson attributes the first clear-cut statement of this change to David Hume:

> Aside from a few metaphysicians, "I may venture to affirm of the rest of mankind," said Hume, "that they are nothing but a bundle or collection of different perceptions, which succeed each other with an inconceivable rapidity, and are in perpetual flux and movement. . . . The mind is a kind

of theatre where several perceptions successively make their appearance; pass, repass, glide away, and mingle in an infinite variety of postures and situation."

Man became a natural object in a natural world. The notion of the immortal soul would not thereafter predispose everyone to believe in the stability and clear rationality of the mind. Peterson quotes from *Tristram Shandy* to instance Sterne's awareness of the shifting turns of mind. Propositions, Sterne said, swim "quietly in the middle of the thin juice of a man's understanding, without being carried backwards or forwards, till some little gusts of passion or interest drive them to one side."

More recently and on the heels of Darwin, the whole psychology framed by and deriving from Freud has affected our way of looking at ourselves. Our superficial notion of self is concerned with our physical being and with whatever "constants" in our behavior, attitudes, etc., make us identifiable. The Freudians have made us aware of the extent to which the conscious man is a "prey to his unconscious wishes." A definition of the self which included this awareness would necessarily cause a "reinterpretation of the total self."[2] However, "the restless search for identity is self-defeating, for it requires a denial of the superficial rational and sensory agencies which ordinarily assure identity." Even though it may be self-defeating, as Professor Hoffman suggests, many modern poets have explored their now strong awareness that identity flows beyond the outlines of consciousness.

Moderns like Bertrand Russell can now state that there is no such thing ultimately as the ego, no such indivisible and therefore indestructible entity as that conceived by Socrates. The "unity of personality," according to Russell, is simply a "causal nexus among a series of events." Apparently Russell means that man is a physical vessel through which forces flow, are deflected, dammed up, or redirected. Examination of such a problem as the nature of the self is, of course, a field for the metaphysician, psychologist, or philosopher. One need not have arrived at a final or authoritative statement regarding it to note that the view the poet takes of the self will condition the way he views and evaluates experience. The poet's own sense of depersonalization, like that of everyone else, must be in ratio with the degree of his awareness of all experience as flux. And his sense of identity must be in ratio with his beliefs, values, and attitudes.

The author in whose work the theme of flux, with the subthemes of time, death, and personality has been brought into clearest focus is, probably, Virginia Woolf. She objected to the presentation of fact and object and the employment of a strict chronology as though these were the real world. She called Joyce "spiritual" and Bennett, Wells, and Galsworthy "materialists." What she meant is that Joyce tried, as she did, to "record the atoms as they fall upon the mind . . . and to trace the pattern, however disconnected and incoherent in appearance, which each sight or incident scores upon the consciousness." In her essay, "Modern Fiction," she caught the distinction brilliantly in characteristic images: "Life is not a series of gig lamps symmetrically arranged; life is a luminous halo, a semi-transparent envelope surrounding us from the beginning of consciousness to the end."

One might attribute Mrs. Woolf's vision of reality to her specialized sensibility, adding that the technique of the novelists she repudiated implied that they, on the other hand, lacking her sensitivity, saw life merely as a series of defined events and chronological situations, "a series of gig lamps." It seems more likely that the older novelists were personally aware of the "luminous envelope" though possibly not so intensely as she. In the older tradition—Mrs. Woolf exhibits its disintegration—personal identity was unquestioned because the person acted out his life against sets of stable values and attitudes. There was little reason to break human consciousness down into its atomistic elements, because identity, which included or was larger than the elements, was itself unquestioned.

Or at least the implications of questioning it were not examined closely. The important consideration was the relation of the self to Providence. All actions had meaning in relation to the backdrop of belief. However dark the glass through which consciousness peered, the ultimate answers could be stated clearly. The mystery of the shifting consciousness was of only relative importance.

Literary techniques, which developed in terms of these beliefs, were constructed on the assumption that the hard outlines of personal identity did exist. Even though Bennett, Galsworthy, and Wells were not orthodox believers, they inherited the stable values and attitudes and the techniques, all of which continued like reflexes on into the twentieth century. But Darwinism, followed by Freudianism, was finally forcing an issue with the older assumptions. Mrs. Woolf was among the first artists to face the problem. It became apparent to her that there was little point in interpreting man's actions in terms of the events he participated in if he himself could not be clearly defined. There was no understanding his relation to situations unless one knew what flows through his mind, what makes him what he is. Many modern artists are concerned, like Mrs. Woolf, with showing how experience works through the mysterious sensibility of the human being.

As a consequence, modern poetry to a large extent has taken on a "submarine" aspect. Ruth Herschberger has suggested that to future centuries the "entire realm of modern poetry will possibly be known as the dream period." One senses the change first in Eliot's "Unreal City." There is a Freudian kind of awareness on the part of the poet that the past is shimmering in changing scenes just outside our consciousness. The entire past floats unseen over the very edge of the present so that it is somehow in our minds and bodies. In one of Warren's poems about the persistence of evil he says:

> Oh, nothing is lost, ever lost! at last you understood.

Whatever loveliness the poet may see is never pure. Always lurking in the shadow of the event or in the past which the mind knows, consciously or unconsciously, is either an aimless terror or a fear that is seen as ready to invest a physical form. The poetry is richer for its double vision. But even solid objects begin to seem haunted in their ironic contrast to the isolation of the shifting mind and sensibility that knows them and envies their permanence and stability. Man is seen by W. J. Turner as a shadowy part of the history of the universe:

All these like stars in Time are set,
They vanish but can never pass;
The Sun that with them fades is yet
Fast-fixed as they in Time like glass.

Yeats made much of flux as a theme in modern poetry, calling particular attention to the *Cantos* of Ezra Pound. Pound, he said, believes that "plot, characterization, logical discourse" are unsuitable to a poet in our time. In moving forward and backward from Greece to medieval China, from modern England to Provence or Renaissance Italy, there is no indication of a passage of time—all is "timeless, flux eternal and therefore without movement." Yeats feared that such a conception would cause Pound to deny his poem form. There will be style, because Pound is a brilliant improviser, but there will be no center to the *Cantos*. It may be noted that Eliot, equally aware of disparate facts, because of his extensive knowledge of past societies, took care to find a focus for his insights into modern society. He was able to give *The Waste Land* a center once he recognized that the myth of the wasteland, regeneration and rebirth, had an ancient origin and recurred in various ages. Pound, ignoring a framework in which men are seen sharply as individuals, can conceive men as shadows through which nature redreams itself.

You, sometimes, will lament a lost friend
  For it is a custom:
This care for past men. . . .

The indifference to the unique individual to be noted in the *Cantos* seems to have some relationship to the loosely stated and vaguely conceived ideas which Pound and Wyndham Lewis issued in *Blast: Review of the Great English Vortex:*

> The human form still runs, like a wave, through the texture or body of existence, and therefore of art.
>
> But just as the old form of egotism is no longer fit for such conditions as now Prevail, so the isolated Figure of most ancient Art is an Anachronism.
>
> Dehumanization is the chief diagnostic of the Modern World.

Overlooking the conscious artiness and posing behind such statements, one might infer that Lewis and Pound believed that the disintegration of belief in the significance of individual man caused flux to be *the* modern theme. There is also the ominous suggestion that human worth or human dignity is of no import. (In his later statements Lewis has reversed this position, so that he now emphasizes the great worth and dignity of the human being.)

We have suggested elsewhere that a tradition which supports a religion, a strong moral code, and a strict scale of values enables the individual to experience a sense of identity and a sense of belonging, both of which are necessary to personality. The sureness with which one believes in the rightness of his own insights and his general point of view or philosophy further strengthens his sense of identity. (This may be what Hume meant in excluding metaphysicians from the "rest of mankind" who live in a "perpetual flux.") The life of a person in a traditional society is circumscribed, framed as it were by ideals, attitudes, and modes of conduct. He is given a focus within the society. Thereby he achieves a greater sense of identity and thus offsets the sense of flux. In our all but traditionless society the sense of identity must come from whatever focus the individual is able to establish for himself.

Both Auden and Eliot have been concerned with the hollowness of the personality of many moderns. In his pre-war poetry Auden centered his attention on those whose lives of self-indulgence and lack of purpose and direction were empty and fruitless.

In his depersonalized characters Eliot has symbolized the effects of what Lewis Mumford has called the "materialist creed by which a large part of humanity has sought to live during the past few centuries." There has been, in Mumford's terms, a confusion of "the needs of survival" with "the needs of fulfillment." The former needs are obvious enough—food, drink, shelter, parental care, etc. "The most important needs from the standpoint of life-fulfillment are those that foster spiritual activity and promote spiritual growth: the needs for order, continuity, meaning, value, purpose and design—needs out of which language and poesy and music and science and art and religion have grown." The primary and almost exclusive emphasis in the last three centuries has been on techniques and practicality. Mumford lists Blake, Ruskin, Morris, Arnold, Melville, Dickens, Howells, Tolstoi, and Ibsen among those who protested the ill-considered effects of mechanization of industry and the profit motive. They protested the neglect of the human personality.

Henry James should be given his place among those who protested. He was fully aware of the forces making for "the awful doom of general dishumanization." In order to illustrate what he meant, he uses, in the Preface to *The Altar of the Dead*, an anecdote concerned with the refusal of an editor to publish a brief article about "a very eminent woman" who, however, was merely a "private" character. A person whose life had been of value and distinction was dead. Normal respect for human worth and dignity, it seemed to James, demanded some commemoration. The editor, however, was concerned with journalistic rather than human values. (In a later generation James could multiply instances of long "human interest" columns given over to stories about cats refusing to come down from roofs or to "male" parrots laying eggs, at the same time that space in these columns is denied the eminent dead.) James conceived the role of the artist to be a concern with discrimination, with ideals, with morals, with the cultivation and care of "the tradition of sensibility." Many of James's stories, as Blackmur notes, are treatments of characters who are saved "from the damnation and waste of a disorderly life." James detested "loose ends" in life as much as in literature. Many of the characters in *The Waste Land*—Lil, Lou, Mrs. Porter, Sweeney, the typist, and others—symbolize the "general . . . dishumanization." Their chief values are sensuality and vulgarity. They are aimless and unhappy, or, like Burbank and Bleistein, they are obtuse and crass. Together they symbolize the fag-end of the post-Renaissance society.

Two other aspects of depersonalization appear relevant. Indifference to the good, or to the worth, of the individual as individual hastens the acceptance of collectivism, and emphasis upon the abstract in preference to the concrete lessens one's awareness of one's self as a person. Both are important contemporary problems. In much of his poetry E. E. Cummings has opposed the individual to the state and to the mass or group. Allen Tate and John Crowe Ransom, in their criticism as well as in their poetry, have striven to show how incomplete or how depersonalized experience is that has only a very limited relation to the concrete.

Cummings believes that the individual loses his identity when he becomes absorbed in the state. He passionately hates those theorizers and rationalizers who interfere with individuals in order to bring about their imagined utopias. Too many individuals are hurt in the process of making everyone conform. The gods for Cummings are individuals. He believes in the individual conscience and in the freedom to act spontaneously. Yet Cummings is not attempting to rationalize individual license. He believes also in a "strict and conscientious discipline in the formation of personality." Allied to his attacks, for the sake of the individual, on collectivism is his dislike of terms like "everyone" or "mostpeople" and "they." Lloyd Frankenberg, in "Nothing as Something as One," writes:

> Such an abstraction as mostpeople, the State or Mankind is for Cummings the modern archetype of the mythological dragon. Like the dragon, its danger is the danger we put into it. We impute personality to it. In time it usurps ourselves.[3]

Cummings fears that myths like "they" and "mostpeople," when universally believed, can be manipulated and used against individuals.

Our era is given to abstraction, to the multiplication of theories in every area of activity. It is given consequently to making individuals, as Cummings objects, fit into the structure theoretically worked out. The abstractionist ignores the irrational, the irrational being unpredictable and therefore not subject to control. And to the extent that we overemphasize practicality at the expense of qualitative and contemplative experience we may be said to depersonalize ourselves. This theme may have its most explicit expressions in Tate's "The Last Days of Alice" and in Ransom's *The World's Body*.

## *2*

John Crowe Ransom has spoken of the "horror which has shaken the moderns in their accelerating progress; the sense of psychical disintegration, that is, of having a personality which has been casually acquired and still subject to alteration, therefore, hollow and insincere." This observation can be related to the sense that some have of "walking among a score of selves." And it can be related to the problem of "multiple style" in poetry. Auden has alluded to the confusion in the character of modern man, and more recently Karl Shapiro, in his *Essay on Rime*, has asked whether the

> quest
> For the lost Eurydice of character

is not, in many instances, behind the easy shifting from model to model or from style to style practiced, other than in apprenticeship, by some poets.

It remains, however, that most people, certainly the best poets, usually have a strong sense of personality. And it would seem that homogeneous beliefs and well-defined personality mutually sustain each other. Yeats and others, however, have noted a "passivity" about much modern poetry. One cause of this may be the inherited notion of the world and man as flux and the consequent sense of futility in making personal judgments. Parts of the poetry of Aiken and MacLeish would seem to fall into this category. A more basic cause of the passivity—or of relative disinterest in man as hero or as a dominating force—may lie in the fact that science turned man's interest outside himself. In a world under strict controls man has to be made to conform. He is denied personal dominion. The need modern man has to know generic man runs counter to the more basic need we have to know the individual. The sociologists and state planners are concerned with generic man, as are the psychologists with their placement tests and grouping, with their interest in similarities rather than in dissimilarities. Sensibility in all its amorphous life is far too subtle for such testing. That unique personal sensibilities do evolve is apparent enough. Mass living, on the other hand, demands a functional knowledge of similarities. The advertiser, the politician, and the teacher need such grouping. There remains, however, the individual. And within limited personal relationships nothing is more important than a knowledge of, and a respect for, individuality, for the private man. It is the individual we love, despise, tolerate, or are indifferent to. On a profoundly human level we are interested in what a person is and even in what he *looks like*. We are fascinated by the combination of traits and factors and appearances that compose the individual. We have a deeply rooted need for recognizing, understanding, and appreciating individual personality.

Poetry, or any form of literature, that is indifferent to personality, for whatever cause, ignores an opportunity to appeal to our basic interests. Significant artists in any period so experience their material that they can refract it in some form of symbolism. The poetry which is "passive," produced as though by a "mirror dawdling down a lane," is the kind of art which arises from a preoccupation with the facts of the external world. Yeats objected that it sometimes seemed as though a naturalistic poet would "write a poem by recording a fortuitous scene or thought, perhaps it might be enough to put down into some fashionable rhythm—'I am sitting in a chair, there are three dead flies on the corner of the ceiling.' " Such poetry is dehumanized in the perhaps narrow sense that it has never gestated in the poet's mind. The American poetry which seems little more than reportage, like the following early lines from Alfred Hayes, is of this sort.

> Well, we get him here and here he dies.
> And that's where we buried him out there,
> In the goldenrod beyond them pines.
> It's a Potter's Field and nobody'd care.

Poetry is peculiarly of the mind that bodies it forth. Unless the poem arises from the lived experience of the poet, it too easily becomes a vehicle for glibness, for borrowing. The true poem, as Peter de Vries once put it, is "distilled out of [the poet's] own guts and heart, which is the true matter of art, for which the verbal celebration of something apprehended rather than lived is only a reasonably accurate facsimile." However extra-personal our interests may become, there is always the private self. And although the universe may be envisioned as flux, and the self as a part of the flux or even as nothing, it is only that "nothing" which matters in the creation of art. The shedding of one "personality" and the adoption of another seems, if not peculiarly a modern phenomenon, at least one which is more common to our era than to those in which self-definition was more easily achieved. Quite possibly the phenomenon has a part in the fashions in economics, politics, and art. The writer who never discovers his real self, who perennially is in search of a new image to symbolize his current self, will write from the outside of his subject. The poet who has beliefs in terms of which events, situations, and characters take on meaning will hardly borrow styles or reflect the idiom of other poets except as those idioms have become a part of his own idiom. The poet's personality is the source of his style. And the changes in personality will occur gradually, if he is honest with himself, as he discriminates between, qualifies, and absorbs new beliefs and attitudes. Affectations in style, as in speech, give off their own overtone of insincerity. When style is single, when it is an instrument and expression discovered by the poet for writing as his personality demands that he write, it has the stamp of originality.

Nicolas Berdyaev sees such modern art forms as impressionism, cubism, and futurism as evidence of a "final rupture with the Renaissance tradition." All analytical tendencies pushed far enough are anti-Renaissance in spirit, he says, because they denote the disintegration of the human image. "The realities of the world lose their individual aspect. Man becomes dissolved in a welter of objects, lamps, divans, streets, which dissociate him as an entity and disintegrate both his image and inimitable countenance.'

Louis MacNeice in "An Eclogue for Christmas" protests against the same tendency to splinter personality into many parts:

> I who was the harlequin in the childhood of the century,
> Posed by Picasso beside an endless opaque sea
> Have seen myself sifted and splintered in broken facets
> Tentative pencillings, endless liabilities, no assets
> Without reference to this particular life.
> And so it has gone on; I have not been allowed to be
> Myself in flesh or face, but abstracting and dissecting me
> They have made me pure form, a symbol, a pastiche,
> Stylized profile, anything but soul and flesh,
> And that is why I turn this jaded music on
> To forswear thought and become an automaton.

Artists have moved beyond man as an integral human being to an interest in his component parts, as though they were penetrating deeper into his nature by discovering the "elementary forms of his composition."

A glance at these developments in modern painting may suggest some of the ways in which the same forces have worked in modern poetry. The distortion of the human image would indicate for one thing that man has come a long way since he saw himself as made in the image of God. Some contemporary painters claim that facility in setting down in realistic detail the physical likeness and in catching the personality of the subject is not a worthy artistic value. Joseph Frank has suggested that the beginning of this history can be seen in the work of Cézanne. Frank says:

> What characterizes his work is the tension between two conflicting but deeply rooted tendencies: on the one hand, a struggle to attain esthetic form—conceived of by Cézanne as a self-enclosed unity of form-and-color harmonies—and, on the other hand, the desire to create this form through the recognizable depiction of natural objects. Later artists, abandoning Cézanne's efforts to achieve form in terms of natural objects, took over his preoccupation with formal harmonies, omitting natural objects altogether or presenting them in some distorted manner.

We are not to conclude from the reference to the representation of natural objects that the poet is to use the "mirror dawdling down the lane" techniques. There are two extremes: either the poet gives us the mere surface, the "realistic" details, or he uses images so distorted that they seem quite dissociated from the person. The middle ground, holding to characterization through symbolic means and to the easily perceived person as a natural object, enables the poet "to get both the physical and psychological aspects of character at one stroke." Frank instances Eliot's characterization of the young man carbuncular—

> One of the low on whom assurance sits
> As a silk hat on a Bradford millionaire—

as the use of an image which analyzes without dissociating. Such images "describe character but, at the same time, hold fast to the unity of personality, without splintering it to fragments in trying to seize the secret of its integration."

Our Surrealist poets, on the other hand, tend to leave us with an impression of sensibility and imagination at loose ends. Personality as it emerges from certain poems of Oscar Williams, for example, seems all sensibility and no meaning. In "On Meeting a Stranger in a Bookshop" the relation of two men is described:

> I tell you the most intimate thing I am,
> My name, and yours floats out to me, creeps
> Into ears' trumpets, folds itself around my brain:
> Holding hands thus we sail off into the deeps. . . .

Quite possibly, of course, Williams was not trying to catch a personality. Nonetheless, this poem typifies a body of modern poetry which is, as it were, an expression of maximum sensibility sustained by a minimum of intellectuality. In it there is a tendency to emphasize strangeness or novelty for its own sake. Characterization and judgment, which imply positive values, are all but excluded. Everything, as Yeats said of some of Edith Sitwell's poems, appears before us "in a hashish-eater's dream."

## *3*

José Ortega y Gasset in *The Dehumanization of Art* states that the "highly distanced" modern art, which deliberately narrows its audience to the most select few, is wholly admirable.[4] The ordinary among mankind demand, he says, the largest possible degree of "lived" experience in art. They know no other reactions but the practical and the sentimental. Ortega takes the main illustration for his thesis from painting:

> Many Englishmen have fallen in love with the Mona Lisa. With things represented in the new pictures, it is impossible to live. . . . [The artist] leaves us locked up in an abstruse universe, he forces us to associate with objects with which there is no possible human association. Thus we have to improvise a new form of association completely different from the usual

one which allows us to live with things. . . . This new life, a life invented after the annulment of spontaneous life, is precisely what we may call artistic understanding and pleasure.

Ortega believes that nineteenth-century art, which was largely naturalistic and representational, was "a monstrosity without equal in esthetic evolution." To representational art he opposed stylized art. To stylize, he adds, is "to deform the real, to derealize. Stylization implies dehumanization."

One can understand Ortega's dissatisfaction with representational art. The intention behind the recovery of symbolic forms in modern art and literature was to enable the artist to indicate significance, insights, and values. The individual style is the sum, as it were, of the techniques and characteristic ways the artist has of objectifying his insights. One may protest the excesses to which Ortega's dissatisfaction leads him. He finds that in none of the "great epochs" has the human being been "the center of gravity." He finds that center in the "will to style." The more stylized art becomes, the more abstract it becomes—and the further it takes us from our humanity. The solution suggested by Edward Bullough for maintaining a balance between human appeal and psychical distance, which is created by style, would seem a better criterion for the modern artist.[5] His rule, which he calls "the antinomy of distance," can be applied in examination of much modern poetry.

Just as the stage and lighting and a heightened language remove the action of a drama from one's everyday experience, so too does the heightened language, the use of new metaphors and indirections, as well as a metrical scheme, remove poetry from the commonplace sphere. The "psychical distance" thereby established is necessary to all art. The question thereafter is the *mean* that is to be established between personal appeal (the interest an object or situation has because it stirs our ordinary human curiosity) and "psychical distance" (achieved by stylized presentation). Bullough, unlike Ortega, believes the mean should consist of the "utmost decrease of distance without its disappearance." He believes that an art of great distance is characteristic of periods of a low cultural level. Ortega, of course, welcomes distanced art as a sign of an intellectual aristocracy. Regardless of the relative truth of either of their positions, it remains that modern poetry is more highly distanced than any other body of poetry in English literature. It follows as a corollary that its interest will arise not so much from the elements of personal appeal it may have as from the success of the techniques whereby its psychical distance is achieved. It will, of course, be an exiled poetry.

Randall Jarrell, writing the Preface to his "The Rage for the Lost Penny" in *Five Young American Poets* (1940), catalogued the characteristics of modern poetry. Few of them are designed to appeal to the personal interest of the lay reader. They are means to increase "distance":

> very interesting language, a great emphasis on connotation, texture; extreme intensity, forced emotion—violence; a good deal of obscurity; emphasis on sensation, perceptual nuances; emphasis on details, on the part rather than on the whole; experimental or novel qualities of some sort; a tendency toward external formlessness and internal disorganization—these are justified, generally, as the disorganization required to express a disorganized age, or alternatively, as newly-discovered and more complex types of organization; and extremely personal style—*refine your singularities;* lack of restraint—all tendencies are forced to their limits; there is a good deal of emphasis on the unconscious, dream-structure, the thoroughly subjective. . . .

We need not agree entirely with Bullough that "distance" must be decreased to the utmost. Much of the splendor of our best poetry would be unnecessarily diminished. In fact, his emphasis might be reversed; that is, the poet should employ the utmost distance *compatible* with a clearly perceivable subject. If a poem is about a journey or a subway or a rainy Sunday, it should be *about* a journey or a subway or a rainy Sunday—none of these should be the point in the actual world from which the subjective tangent of the poet goes off. The reader of the poem, pursuing the line of the tangent, may never be able to relate it to a "lived" experience. At best, he will be able to piece together only odd fragments. It is observable that in reading some of the best modern poems, *The Waste Land*, "Sunday Morning," "Sailing to Byzantium," or "Voyages II," one has little difficulty in grasping the essential theme. The elements of the poet's technique—however "difficult" they may be—serve to enlarge and qualify a unique presentation and understanding of the subject. There is no effort to dehumanize such poetry by divorcing it from the interests of the general run of humanity.

The techniques of modernism, as described by Jarrell, are, as Berdyaev might say, anti-Renaissance in spirit. (In Jarrell's own later work there is much less emphasis on "external formlessness and internal disorganization.") In so far as modern poets have wilfully obscured their meaning and been studiedly indifferent to poetry as communication, they have encouraged the dehumanization of art so applauded by Ortega.

CHAPTER FIFTEEN

# *Forms of Obscurity*

> *We can only say that it appears likely that poets in our civilization, as it exists at present, must be* difficult. *Our civilization comprehends great variety and complexity, and this variety and complexity, playing upon a refined sensibility, must produce various and complex results.*—T. S. Eliot

The opponents of modern poetry usually attack it on the grounds that it is obscure. Quite possibly it is, as a body of poetry, more obscure than any other in English literature. In condemning it, however, some critics use only eighteenth- or nineteenth-century poetry as the norm, forgetting that Elizabethan and Jacobean poetry tend to be obscure and forgetting, further, that the nature of poetic language invites obscurity. It may be necessary, therefore, to examine these related points before investigating obscurity as a modern phenomenon.

The relationship between the concept and the texture of the poem is a common source of obscurity. It does not follow, of course, that all obscure poems are obscure for the same reason. It does follow that the specific reasons stem from a failure or inability of the poet to make the sensuous and rational elements correlates of each other. If the rational or conceptual meaning is essentially clear, then the textural elements, which serve to qualify or enlarge the statement of the concept, as well as to give it emotional force, are, conceivably at least, explicable. If the textural elements are presented individually or in the mass for their own sake only, the poem is protoplasmic and formless, and the obscurity, except for chance personal associations, is inexplicable. In this event the poem is vague rather than obscure; quite literally, it approaches meaninglessness. A similar distinction should be made between ambiguity, or isolable layers of meaning, and vagueness, in which no clear perception inheres and which is therefore without real significance. No amount of exegesis can make the vague poem more understandable. Any effort to reduce the obscurity of a legitimately obscure poem will lessen its quality and make its meaning less precise. (Precision should not be confused with the simplicity which is possible only in uncomplex statements. The most complicated machinery can be—indeed, must be—precise. Inherent simplicity which is wilfully roughened and complicated approaches, to some degree, vagueness.) The texture of the poem is a part of the poet's statement, and the reader's understanding of it enables him to understand the precise nature of the poet's perception. This is merely another way of saying that the meaning of a poem is in the interrelationship of all its parts, not its paraphrasable content; the meaning of the poem, as John Berryman has put it, is "an accretion of knowledge, of which only the flimsiest portion can be translated into bromide."

In trying to perceive these interrelationships, the poet runs counter to the dominant spirit of his time. With the scientific world picture before them, the societies of the post-Renaissance world turned reverently toward the isolated fact, as though, by reducing knowledge to its smallest components, they would necessarily achieve understanding. Acceptance of the fact *as fact* is one of the modern forms of idolatry. (It does not follow that all scientists *et al.* are the unaware victims of this development.) The isolation of facts is the necessary prerequisite to rebuilding forms of knowledge and understanding. Yet, holding tightly to facts as facts, denying them symbolic value, has become an ideal of our world, an ideal that functions in opposition to the development of values, belief, and myth. But this is a tangential, even though significant, consideration. The point here is that we are used to contemplating facts, isolated or added up. We are far less used to contemplating facts that have a paradoxical relationship, facts that must be mutually qualified when brought into relationship with an idea or attitude, or facts that take on variedly refracted meanings when the imagination plays upon them in a structure of words, images, sounds, and meaning—that is, as in a poem.

Lloyd Frankenberg has shown how Marianne Moore has created a concentrated and complex set of relationships in her "What Are Years?"[1]

> . . . He
> sees deep and is glad, who
> accedes to mortality
> and in his imprisonment, rises
> upon himself as
> the sea in a chasm. . . .
>
> . . . The very bird,
> grown taller as he sings, steels
> his form straight up. Though he is
> captive,
> his mighty singing
> says, satisfaction is a lowly
> thing, how pure a thing is joy.

"The word 'steels' is the crux of the poem. In its literal and figurative meanings the ideas of imprisonment and liberation meet. The bird, in his mighty singing, triumphs over captivity; he becomes the bars that confined him.

"The symbols of imprisoned bird and enchasmed sea are integrally related to the form of the poem. Its rhythms rove with vine-like freedom from line to line in a profusion that is made possible by their underlying metric." With our usual single-minded way of examining a situation or event, we find it either this or that. We have a traditional association with imprisonment—that it is a painful and unhappy state. Yet the images and situation the poet has presented are indications that this need not be so, that, in accepting the limitations of the flesh, we may transcend them. (It is upon such paradoxes that Christianity depends.)

We are used to a kind of one-to-one relationship between a situation and meaning (prison equals unpleasantness). In Miss Moore's poem the meaning goes in at least two ways from the situation (prison equals physical restriction; prison equals opportunity for the development of spiritual resiliency). This is an oversimplification, but it suggests an important difference. Prose usually proceeds unilaterally, from fact to fact, slurring over associational and subsidiary meanings. Poetry (modern poetry to a far greater extent than eighteenth- or nineteenth-century poetry) functions tensionally, building its meanings internally, suggesting by metaphor, irony, paradox, etc., the varied ways in which the facts relate to one another. Eighteenth- and nineteenth-century poetry sacrificed the paradoxical, associative, and qualifying meanings to the denotative meaning. The faith in denotation has been a part of the scientific world picture. It is against such a limited vision that modern poetry is in part a revolt. Again, as several critics have pointed out, modern poetry is an effort to renew an older tradition of English poetry.

E. E. Cummings' use of a term like "angry candy" is not more far-fetched than Shakespeare's use of "whey face" or "Taffeta phrases." Each depends upon wit, a union of disparate elements, and is centered in an image. Each figurative expression that carries illumination is of necessity somewhat incongruous. The depth of insight depends upon the appropriateness of the incongruity. It is quite possible that we are more willing to accept Shakespeare's "multitudinous seas incarnadine" than Hart Crane's "this great wink of eternity."

Used to simplicities of a nonfigurative prose, we must move slowly through a passage like the following from Donne:

Doth not man die even in his birth? The breaking of prison is death, and what is our birth, but a breaking of prison? As soon as we were clothed by God, our very apparell was an Embleme of death. In the skins of dead beasts, he covered the sins of dying men. As soon as God set us on work, our very occupation was an Embleme of death; It was to digge the earth; not to digge pitfals for other men, but graves for our selves.

We read more quickly if the meaning is not carried by figurative language. We must assume, however, that Donne's congregation could follow him readily enough. A part of our hesitancy to accept such language may not rest so much in our being baffled by the obscurity of it as in our inherited fear of metaphors and our lack of practice in perceiving their implications. A good deal of modern poetry that was once held obscure is now easily read by those who are practiced in such reading.

Many of our poets, nonetheless, feeling their isolation from society keenly, exploit the advantages of their positions as members of the intelligentsia. Their minds are filled with tags of learning, arcana, and quaint bits of knowledge, and they are sophisticated. If one did not know, for example, that the cuttlefish envelops itself in a black, inky fluid, then finding it as a symbol, as in one of Tate's poems, would cause confusion. Undoubtedly the proportion of obscure poetry is greater in modern literature than in Renaissance literature. It is true, as F. W. Dupee has pointed out, that a "high degree of difficulty" is a characteristic of modern poetry "just as a peculiarly brilliant and aggressive clarity was a stylistic feature of the School of Pope."

Yet it should not be forgotten that the difficulty in reading modern poetry is partially, as Tate has observed, a matter of practice. The readers of much eighteenth- and nineteenth-century poetry are unpracticed in reading poetry in which all the "complications can be returned . . . to a definite, literal, coherent field of imagery." Much of the poetry between the Jacobeans and the moderns begins with an initially stated abstraction so that the imagery is unnecessary or merely decorative. In much Jacobean and modern poetry, the poet qualifies and deepens his meaning without moving beyond his coherent and consistent field of metaphor. Despite the scientific world picture, which makes for a prose-minded world, many modern poets have attempted to recover the older techniques—to lessen the prose element in their poetry. Thus modern poems can hardly be read as prose is read, by starting at the beginning and proceeding through the middle to the end. In poetry we have, in effect, to "start from somewhere in the middle and work both ways."

## 2

Because of the frustrations suffered in his isolation, in addition, the modern poet to some extent has been tempted to emphasize his separation from the society by exaggerating the obscure elements in his poetry, by, in effect, indulging himself in the public-be-damned attitude. He has, in addition, suffered the thinly veiled, sometimes outspoken, distrust of the poet by those intellectuals who have had visions of a society under scientific control. Some among the intelligentsia, with their emphasis upon a scientific approach and "debunking feudal values," have been undermining the position of the poet. The most forthright attack in recent years, indicative of a general attitude, appeared in Max Eastman's *The Literary Mind.* But the antecedents of this attack could be traced in steady progression from the seventeenth century.

One perceives the character of the resultant tensions in the poet most distinctly perhaps in figures like Edith Sitwell or Marianne Moore. They are characteristic enough of modern writers. We can find similar tensions in Henry James, Marcel Proust, James Joyce, and Virginia Woolf. The ordinary heightening that is usual in art is intensified in modern literature. There is a kind of preciousness in modern poetry that could hardly be maintained if the subject matter of most poetry were found in the interests and problems of the bulk of the society. If the poet's sensibilities cannot be related to large and public matters, they can be related to small and private matters. In order that highly personal observations and interest may be brought alive through language, it is sometimes necessary to point up through idiosyncratic metaphors or similes the unique pattern perceived. Thus Marianne Moore sees waves "as formal as the scales on a fish," or a

> medieval decorated
> hat-box
> in which there are hounds with waists diminishing like the
> waist of the hour glass.

Richard Eberhart has referred to Miss Moore, albeit admiringly, as "an annotator by 'desperate neatness,' . . . constructing an odd world from odd facts oddly considered, made into a substance of delighting peculiarity." Wallace Stevens, too, is capable of this fastidious yet wholly admirable artistry. His discrimination causes him to distinguish among sea surfaces which suggest rosy chocolate and gilt umbrellas, chophouse chocolate and sham umbrellas, porcelain chocolate and pied umbrellas, and Chinese chocolate and large umbrellas. One learns, too, that there are thirteen ways of looking at a blackbird. Their artistry is impeccable, and we are grateful to the intellects and sensibilities so refined that such subtly distinguished aspects of the world can be re-created. Preciousness in art, however, implies isolated concerns, perhaps even a mild form of neuroticism.

There is a danger in emphasizing this neurosis—if we may call it that—of the artist, not only because the philistine may find therein justification for dismissing modern art forms as distortions of reality and therefore untrue but because individual artists sometimes seem well adjusted in their personal lives at the same time that they create the kinds of distortions we associate with neuroticism.[2] Most of all, it will not do to think of all artists or all modern artists as neurotic. It may be possible to think of members of a group as specialists, as having neurotic characteristics as a group, without the individual members being neurotic. Jargon, for example, develops, for one reason, as the compensation the group offers itself and the world for withdrawing from the larger to the smaller orientation. In this instance, "neuroticism" may be the wrong word. Or it may be that the poet, for example, will be neurotic only in so far as he thinks of himself and writes as a part of the modern movement. In the other aspects of his life, and the poet is not a poet all the time, he may be quite as satisfactorily adjusted as members of any profession or group. These observations simply suggest that our poetry, in its character as modern, has, like other pursuits, become *specialized*.

## *3*

This poetry, John Crowe Ransom says in his "Poets without Laurels," is "modern because the age is modern."[3] He means by this mainly that our period differs from other periods in its craving "to perfect the parts of experience separately." This, of course, is to point to the atomistic nature of the modern society. As a poet and critic, Ransom notes the aspects which concern him personally and professionally. Among the fields of experience which have become specialized, or, as he says, "purified," are religion, morality, politics, language, and business. Two illustrations, with which we have been concerned elsewhere, may suffice.

Religion was separated from its esthetic properties in order that it might be made "purer." These properties, which were associated with medieval Christianity, were myth, symbols, and ceremonial.

> Under the progressive zeal of the Reformation the being of God has become rarefied in the degree that it has been purified, until we find difficulty in grasping it, and there are people who tell me, just as there are people who tell the reader, that religion as a living force here in the Western world is spent.

The desire to isolate experience and to separate it from its esthetic elements also effected changes in language. "In the earlier days poetry kept close to science, and it did not seem strange if Lucretius wanted to set forth the body of accepted science in verse." But, as we know, science employs an abstract method of statement and poetry a figurative and associative one. The esthetic elements are kept out of science in order that scientific ends may be achieved more readily.

These illustrations suggest their relevance to the history we have been sketching. Specializations are a part of the scientific world picture. An area is isolated from neighboring areas. No longer do we consider politics, science, art, and business subsumed under religion. We see each separately. Most significantly, too, esthetic considerations are largely limited to art. Antecedent to these developments was the separation of thought from feeling. Only thus could the specializations, kept free from esthetic considerations, hold to their special purposes and develop so intensively and quickly.

In Ransom's view the modern poets write what he calls "pure" poetry, which is quite unconcerned with morality or science; or they write "obscure" poetry, which is involved with important predications of a moral or theoretical sort but which stops short of "conclusions." We can hardly go all the way with Professor Ransom on the latter point because it is fairly obvious that many moderns are greatly concerned to state their conclusions or theories. They are shy of a moral discussion only when this is not so fused with the poetic structure that there is no separating the two. We can agree when he says the poets "are moved by a universal tendency into their own appropriate kind of specialization, which can be, as they have been at pains to show, as formidable as any other." An effort at compensation may be behind the close and careful lines; it is as though the poets were suggesting that their specialty, through its cultivation of delicate beauties and the evocation of subtle feelings, is, possibly, more important than any other specialty. Ransom's thesis, then, more or less explicitly brings us back to our original recognition that the poet's frustration is caused by a society whose values are in accordance with attitudes derived from the scientific emphasis.

## 4

Eliot has gone so far as to say that the only way the modern writer has of "giving shape and significance to the immense panorama of futility and anarchy which is contemporary history" is by indicating or "manipulating a continuous parallel between contemporaneity and antiquity." The negative qualities of our world, that is, can be sensed only through their contrast to the positive qualities of an older world. Eliot's own method, in part, is to rely on echoes from past literatures. Thus, for example, in three lines—

> But at my back from time to time I hear
> The sound of horns and motors, which shall bring
> Sweeney to Mrs Porter in the spring—

he works in echoes, as his notes indicate, from John Day and Andrew Marvell. Yet Eliot is not merely contrasting a sordid present with the splendor of the past.

The educated and sensitive man today, for whom the past has been examined segment by segment and as a vast panorama, has a feeling, Eliot says, "that the whole of the literature of Europe from Homer . . . has a simultaneous existence." "Such a realization," Matthiessen adds, "can lead either to chaos or to a sense of the potential unity of life." The variety of details can bewilder or oppress the artist until he finds some pattern running through the variety.

> Such understanding and resultant stress form the heart of Eliot's reason for introducing so many reminiscences of other poets into the texture of his own verse. In this way he can at once suggest the extensive consciousness of the past that is inevitably possessed by any cultivated reader of to-day, and, more importantly, can greatly increase the implications of his

lines by this tacit revelation of the sameness (as well as the contrasts) between the life of the present and that of other ages.

Anthropology, too, has profoundly deepened and even changed the modern forms of belief. In Jessie Weston's *From Ritual to Romance*, Eliot read of the recurring "pattern of similarity in various myths." From her book he obtained not only a way of suggesting the haunting presence of all wastelands of the past but a legend, with images and symbols and a dramatic action. There was no such living myth in his own society, which has distrusted symbols and myths because they smack of "feudal values." Yet, as a poet, Eliot needed some body of iconographic knowledge. Otherwise he had no way of giving order and informing significance to the disparate elements of his world. To the degree that he was unable to incorporate the entire myth(s) in understandable terms into the body of his poem (to the degree, that is, that he had to rely on notes) obscurity may be said to have been forced upon him by the society. If no adequate myth exists whereby the isolated facts can be given a pattern with radical significance, then the poet is obliged to borrow what he can from the myths of the past.

Some of the passages in Eliot's poetry are obscure because we miss the historical allusions. In much of Yeats's work the obscurity is of a different character. In addition, there is the obscurity resulting from the latter's employment of a private system of symbols and meanings. Yeats in *A Vision* has created his own myth, organizing history into cyclical periods which he interprets as having special characteristics and values. These characteristics and values he describes in terms of metaphors and symbols.[4] By allowing his poetry to find its source in his myth, Yeats achieved two ends. The individual poem has a meaning in relation to a coherent body of beliefs, a world view, and the symbols he employs have layers of meaning which in qualifying one another increase the intensity of the poetic effect. Yeats, in other words, felt obliged to give an order to his beliefs in the face of the "anarchy which is contemporary history," and, for his purposes as a poet, to hold these beliefs in focus within a body of iconographic knowledge.

In his very perceptive essay, "Poetry and the Common Store," Marc Friedlander has explained the obscurity of modern poetry in terms of the "disintegration of our iconological knowledge."[5] His emphasis is upon the need for a body of knowledge commonly held by educated men.

> Since the eighteenth century, artists have not been able to employ a set of images which any *educated* man would be able to identify, much less understand in its nuances and implications. This has happened because with the disappearance of the subject core of the liberal arts curriculum there are no literary sources with which all *educated* men may with reason be presumed to be familiar. . . . One has only to read Mann's account, in his essay on Freud, of the implications, the symbolism of the Joseph story to see how unprepared we are to comprehend the *meaning* of one of the few stories from a literary source that remains generally familiar. . . .
>
> The disintegration of group culture that followed upon the Renaissance and the Reformation and that expressed itself in the disparateness of curricula, left the artist . . . with a fairly private set of myths which tended to become more and more esoteric, to show the marks of pedantry.

The loss of the "common store," then, is more than a curriculum problem. If the society were secure in its belief and values, the stories, symbols, and myth in which these found embodiment would be not only central in formal education but vital in the entire texture of the culture. Certainly it was not the schools alone that kept the Greek, Roman, and medieval stories and myths alive for the Elizabethans. Their more subtle implications no doubt were left for the schools—but the materials lived because they had meaning for the society. The poet awaits a "common store of reference," but it will have to be composed of symbols which we have found to express our commonly held beliefs and values. The poetry of exile, pedantry, and private meanings, that is, will disappear following a reintegration of culture which is in accordance with the needs of the whole society and the whole man.

This is not to excuse all the modern poets from all charges of perverse and wilful obscurities. In those poets, like Pound, who do not always trouble to give us their sources, the use of specific detail is sometimes meaningless. Louis MacNeice objects, in one instance, to what seems to be Pound's reference to a money problem in Renaissance Italy:

> 1622 January assigned on the Paschi
> Off de Paschi
> March 1622 Donna Orsola of wherever removed from the
> book of
> the Sienese public women (motion approved by the
> Bailey). . . .

Pedantry of this sort in poetry has even less value perhaps than its equivalent in scholarship. The use, too, of associations which cannot be understood unless one is aware of odd tags in Catalan or Provençal seems sheer wilfulness and serves only to emphasize the exile of the poet.

CHAPTER SIXTEEN

# *The Political Emphasis*

*To say that the proletariat is better than any other class, that the proletarian revolution is the historic future of the world, is to blind myself as an artist. It is the business of the artists to insist on human values. If there is need for a revolution, it is these human values that will make the revolution.*—STEPHEN SPENDER

THE contemporary preoccupation with politics and the tendency to subordinate other forms of knowledge to it furnishes perhaps the chief example of the cultural inversion in our society.[1] A society, like that of pre-war Germany, may have developed highly efficient techniques and skills and be at the same time a "highly inverted and barbarous state." The inversion is the result of subordinating higher ends to lower ends or of allowing a means to dominate an end.

Means and ends are confused when technological and practical knowledge are emphasized to the exclusion of those more fundamental and permanently valuable pursuits we sometimes refer to as cultural subjects. And means and ends are confused when poetry is made to serve politics. The poet's ends are larger than those of the politician, even when the latter's are conceived in generous and broadly human terms; or, if the poet's ends are not larger, they are, at least, different. The poet may include the political element—he should not be subsumed under it. The poet who in treating a theme and subject subordinates his insights to a political purpose inverts the function of poetry. He denies himself complexity and fulness of expression.

The phenomenon is a part of the same historical process in which antiquarianism supersedes philosophy or criticism, education is seen not as a means of individual growth but as a means of "social success," and the "economic man" replaces the whole human being. In a traditional society, possessing a vital religion and a philosophy to which all insights and specific considerations could be referred, possessing a clearly stable and functional body of values, politics could hardly be forced into a foremost position. Some source of order or control is necessary, and in times of crisis the political factor, which should ordinarily be subordinate, becomes dominant. The terrible danger is that the inverted order may be conceived as the inevitable and best order.

That many contemporaries have been obsessed with the political is evident in much of the literature of the thirties.[2] If they are less so at the moment, it remains necessary to review such an interpretation as Joseph Freeman's in order to recall how large the political factor loomed in the thirties and to what extent it affected the writing of poetry.

The economic crisis, according to this interpretation, caused America to give up the "illusion" that it was "classless." "Once they were compelled to face the basic facts of class society, [American] writers of necessity faced the problem of poetry and class. It was impossible to share the experiences of the unemployed worker and continue to create the poetry of the secure bourgeois." Their closeness to the leftist movement blinded critics like Freeman to the fact that the great majority of Americans never gave up the notion of a classless society. It does not follow that they did not have strong political allegiances. The point is that political differences were not viewed in terms of a clearly defined class war. Freeman, too, failed to note that the "bourgeois society" had not conspicuously supported modernist poetry. For the most part, it opposed it. Because the modernist poet had long been a member of the intelligentsia, which found itself involved in the political ferment, he was in the center of the political activity. Not all poets, by any means, felt that all important considerations and all the arts had meaning only in relation to political themes. Many, with Eliot and Yeats, were concerned with the breakup of a tradition which could cause politics to seem so important.

Within four or five years after 1929, Freeman said, poets were facing the dilemma of supporting "the working class" as *men*, and holding to their bourgeois culture as *poets*. Those who could not straddle the chasm between the two classes either "accepted the fact that art has a class basis" or proclaimed their "independence," thereby becoming partisans of the opposing class. Some who chose, as men and as poets, the proletarian side could believe, with Edwin Seaver, that the time was fast approaching "when we will no longer classify authors as proletarian writers and fellow travellers, but as Party writers and non-Party writers." The obvious comment is that the pressure of political events had become so intense that some poets could willingly sacrifice their individual judgment and insights to those of a political party.

The thirties in England saw the rise of C. Day Lewis, W. H. Auden, Stephen Spender, and Louis MacNeice. If there is a clear-cut distinction between these poets and the bulk of American leftist poets, though not all, it is their concern to relate the past and the present. They have tried, David Daiches said, "to find a way of carrying the past into the future, of combining tradition with revolution." In "The Funeral" Spender caught the overtones of a society in which the individual has been cut off from inherited ideals:

> Death is another milestone on their way.
> With laughter on their lips and with winds blowing
> round them
> They record simply
> How this one excelled all others in making driving
> belts.

These poets did not break with Eliot and the tradition he represented because they recognized, eventually at least, that the values therein were enskeined within the weaknesses, errors, and evils the tradition had also produced. In fact, they belonged to the "other side" or "the old gang" themselves, to the extent that they were able to utilize the past in their poetry and in the formulation of their ideals. They were not ready to sacrifice the individual to an abstract future that was to be foaled from an ideology. They were not willing to cut themselves from the past.

Increasingly it became clear, as Philip Rahv remarked after his break with the Communist party, that proletarian literature was the literature of a party rather than of a class. Ridiculously narrow statements were made by certain Marxist critics, men with standing in their respective professions from whom more considered judgments were to be expected. Edwin Berry Burgum, for example, objected to Spender's envisioning the revolution in these lines:

> Through torn-down portions of old fabric let their eyes
> Watch the admiring dawn explode like a shell
> Around us, dazing us with its light like snow.

"The passive position," Burgum wrote, "of watching the dawn is hardly fitting to the revolutionary; nor should the dawn daze like snow those who under self-discipline have known what to expect and are ready for the next move." But two other points in Burgum's critique were more ominous. He was suspicious of using a word like "honor" in a Communist poem because "it will remain a term of dangerous connotation"—it will suggest some virtue in the opposing class and recall the long tradition with which the new order was attempting a violent break. Further, Communists could not depend on Spender, he said, because the "vital forces he feels in the present are all individual." Burgum was quite right to suspect Spender. Any poet, particularly a young poet, who attempted to observe closely the "line" Burgum suggests would be writing in a present that had, for him, no past. Further, a rigid effort to see the individual only impersonally, as a part of the movement, to write of the movement and not of the individual, eventually would have precluded the need for poetry. Certainly the more mature leftist poets, like Malcolm Cowley and Horace Gregory, who pointed out the absurdity of questioning Spender's use of "honor," were not taken in by this sort of criticism. The danger it presented for those less secure is evidenced by much that remains of leftist poetry.

One of the most frequently quoted proletarian poems, Muriel Rukeyser's "Citation for Horace Gregory," is more patently naive when seen against most of Spender, Auden, or MacNeice. Eliot is seen as having

> led us to the precipice
> subtly and perfectly; there striking an attitude
> rigid and aging on the penultimate step.

MacLeish is "the thoughtful man" writing about the dead, and Jeffers is preoccupied with a "nightmare world." But "to the left" are the poets who dare to follow the "machines of change." Spender's "The Funeral" is a poem of particulars. One can feel and understand the values he was concerned with—but Miss Rukeyser's ends vaguely, with mention of loosely conceived gifts which the new ideology wills the future:

> Deep into time extend the impersonal stairs
> established barricades will stand
> before they die the brave have set their hand
> on rich particular beauty for their heirs.

Because the ideological poets could not use the past, except negatively, their values had to be "realized" in a future no one could understand. Frequently, therefore, the poetry is abstract at the same time that it is loosely romantic.

In reading through the work of the leftist poets—Maxwell Bodenheim, Robert Gessner, Alfred Hayes, Joseph Kalar, Alfred Kreymborg, Norman McLeod, Kenneth Patchen, Richard Wright, Arturo Giovannitti, S. Funaroff, *et al.*—one finds that *abstraction* is central to their method. Only one point of view ever emerges. People are not people; they are workers and revolutionaries, or managers and exploiters. The present order is insufferable, but the future, under the new order, will be the end of injustice and suffering. It is a poetry of black and white, of all innocence and all evil. Thus Bodenheim's "To a Revolutionary Girl":

> you are a girl,
> A revolutionist, a worker
> Sworn to give the last, undaunted jerk
> Of your mind and heart
> To every other worker
> In the slow, hard fight
> That leads to the barricade, to victory
> Against the ruling swine.

This refusal of the Marxist poets, with a few exceptions, to qualify the "rightness" of their beliefs in any way, as well as their monstrous way of relating every human impulse and interest to the movement, caused their work to appear, and to be, naïve and sentimental.

Kenneth Burke, one of the most resourceful of the Marxist critics, explained in "Art under Capitalism"[3] that forensic, hortatory, or propagandistic art was necessary to counterbalance a "pure" or "acquiescent" art—the "pure" art was not, however, to be abandoned or ignored—which promoted acceptance of the immoralities inherent in the capitalistic order. Such a statement suggests implications which demand examination at several points. Does all "pure" art imply approval of the society? In what way does the practical drive, in which the propagandists are interested, conflict with the esthetic drive, with which the "pure" poets are concerned?

Burke believed that acceptance of "pure" art usually implies an acceptance of the society which produced it. This is true of some poetry, to be sure. That it is not true of all poetry is readily evidenced in moderns like Cummings, Tate, or Eliot, none of whom was held in reverence by the leftist poets who put their politics before their poetry. One understands the world a little more fully after reading them. In so far as they imply a point of view, they are propagandistic. Yet they are not writing their poems as an impetus to action. That is not their function as poets. They are not attempting to reorder history, eliminate evil, or change the nature of man. Their task as poets is to refract the world they see and experience, whether as citizens or men of action they want to change anything that is changeable or whether they want to "acquiesce" in what they see. Unlike them, the leftist poets and critics, or most of them, saw in poetry an instrument for arousing impulsive action.

Most estheticians agree with Benedetto Croce that a primary characteristic of the work of art is that it is produced and valued for itself. We do not ordinarily hurry through the reading of a poem in order to attain some further end. Croce compares a love poem with a declaration of love. The poem is valued for the experience it gives the reader, but the declaration is valued for the end it may enable the suitor to achieve. If the declaration were made in the form of a poem, it would tend to drain interest away from the poem. If, moreover, the poet is so concerned with a practical purpose that he is willing to subordinate his poem to it, he will incline to force statements from situation and images that would not, as it were, deliver themselves of such meanings. Thus Michael Gold's juxtaposition of capitalism, the American Legion, dogs, and toads.

> I am resigning from the American Legion
> It reminds me of a dog I used to have
> That picked up toads in her mouth
> And was sick of the yellow acid in their glands
> But did it again and again, the dumb fool
> And the more misery and famine and bunk
> The more the Legion seems to like it.
> But I am not a dog and can understand
> That now is the time to end capitalism.

In one sense all successful art, as Burke suggests, "tends to promote a state of acceptance." We see a problem objectified and are therefore free to reflect upon it in lieu of taking to impetuous action. We even find pleasure in contemplating the problem because of the way it has been caught in the medium of the artist. "It enables us to 'resign' ourselves by resolving in aesthetic fusions trends or yearnings not resolvable in the practical sphere." Ironically, then, the most successful poems, as many by Kenneth Fearing, served to "solve" in art problems that were not solved in the "practical sphere." More especially, the humor, biting or warmly sympathetic, that Fearing found where others saw only drabness and stupidity served even more completely to qualify and lessen the humorless intensity that went with carrying on the class war.

The shortcomings of the leftist position, however, were quickly noted. Allen Tate emphasized the preposterousness of a narrowly propagandistic art.

> The task of poetry is the constant rediscovery of the permanent nature of man. Propagandistic art exhibits that side of his nature in which he is most interested at the moment; it is a temporary over-simplification of the human predicament unexplored.[4]

Edmund Wilson, who was far more sympathetic with the leftist position, warned the proletarian poets, as did several others, that they were at a far remove from the theory of art and literature held by Marx, Engels, Lenin, and Trotsky. These men were not prepared, Wilson said, to bury all the art produced by the bourgeoisie. What they wanted was "to make it possible for more people to get the benefit" of it. Wilson quoted such statements as "all art is useful if it shows talent," and the "more important questions of style" should be "solved on the basis of merit rather than political pressure."[5] But the heat generated by those talking and writing leftist and economic theory in the early thirties was not conducive to reflection in tranquillity—so that at that time Clifton Fadiman, although somewhat sadly, was prepared in the interests of Marxism to deliver Goethe into the limbo of unread authors, and so that Hicks could say that the primary function of Marxist literature was to "lead the proletarian reader to recognize his role in the class struggle." Generally the criticism can be leveled at the leftist poets that was leveled at Bernard Smith for his interpretation of American criticism. He, like them, revealed himself as victimized by a "crudity of sympathy that keeps him in petty fear of admitting 'beauty' . . . as the proper concern of any serious artist; of sensibility as a critical instrument of infinitely greater importance . . . than popular or political passions."

## 2

The proletarian poet faces an "index." If he is restricted by it, the uniqueness of his insights as an individual will, to a considerable measure, be precluded. The very fact of his worth as a poet implies that he is not entirely of the group—their clichés, their patterned way of viewing and explaining, are not his or not completely his. "The artist," as Babette Deutsch said, "who sacrifices his identity to his church or his class or nation is lost as an artist, though church or class or nation may be the main root of his art."

Cummings was the first American poet to attack the ideal of political control as *the* control. His *Eimi* (1933) was the evaluation he, after a trip to Russia, put on the Marxian claim that economics is the determining factor in man's history, that the world is a struggle between the "possessing and the proletarian," and that the coming historical phase would see the individual brought under control. Cummings' book is a record of his objection, as Paul Rosenfeld put it, to a "desire of a part—an individual, a class, a nation—to be the creative basis, the 'whole thing,' to rival God himself; the Titanic egotism which rationalizes itself by claiming that all things are predestined to fulfill its wishes." Cummings chose to have no part in the general denial of selfhood. But 1933 was too early for the general reaction and the reappraisal.

Toward the close of the thirties the proletarian element in literature began to decline. Whatever the contributing causes—the

Soviet-Nazi pact, the easing of the depression, and the danger of class conflict in the face of impending war—American poetry was returned, as it were, to the individual poets. Randall Jarrell, in fact, has taken as a fairly recurrent theme the danger he suggests in "The Death of the Ball Turret Gunner"—

> From my mother's sleep I fell into the State
> And I hunched in its belly till my wet fur froze.
> Six miles from earth, loosed from its dream of life,
> I woke to black flak and the nightmare fighters.
> When I died they washed me out of the turret with a hose.

Indeed, one notes a progressive lessening of political considerations, except as incidental to other considerations in the poetry of most of those whose work matured in the early forties—Karl Shapiro, Robert Lowell, George Marion O'Donnell, John Berryman, and Delmore Schwartz. Some of the proletarian poets seem to have stopped writing entirely. Others, like Patchen, Hayes, MacLeod, and Gregory, have enlarged their scope so that the political is no longer the all-embracing. Critical interests have broadened and matured. If the bulk of the leftist poetry has left little for anthologists of the future, the emphasis will have reminded all poets that the political is not an aspect of experience to be left entirely to those who profess no esthetic or intellectual interests.

But if the leftists misunderstood the nature and function of poetry and attempted to make it largely a vehicle for class warfare, the poets, indeed artists generally, since at least the middle of the nineteenth century have failed to understand that their indifference to politics cuts them off from a large area of human experience. It was Joel Spingarn, among modern critics, who first perceived the importance of restoring this area of experience to the poet.[6] Spingarn believed that the notion that "politics are rotten," and petty and mean clouded an important truth. The gift for governing men, he said, is a rare and noble one. The politician can be as successful and as noble as the poet or philosopher.

I know that politics are out of fashion today among the intelligentsia of the world. We are told that politics no longer count, that the important thing today is economics. But the truth is that poetry and philosophy and religion and politics are the four noblest occupations of men, and all of us who have not some profound realization of the meaning of each one of them misses something from the life of the spirit.

Spingarn intended the word "politics" to be understood in a broad sense. He had no intention of narrowing it to mean leftist poetry. When poets as a group regain a "sense of *civitas*, of a whole," they will celebrate heroes, and they will necessarily capture a sense of the real and the universal. "The man who deeply loves his country begins with work, play, the daily task, the family; but eventually he embraces a higher country, which is the world." Spingarn warned against identifying love of country with "nationalism, an abstraction which leads to separateness from everything else and finally to hate for every rival abstraction." Spingarn is really to be associated with the traditionalists, with those who see the need for common ideals, held by men who are attached to their people, community, and country. He meant that poets should recover the sense of politics held by Virgil, or Shakespeare, or Milton. They viewed themselves as a part of the community, not as exiles. And in their participation they restored "direct contact with the practical, and through that with the whole of life." It should be noted most strongly, however, that Spingarn was "far from saying that every poet should take political material." He did not believe that the subjects of poems could be predetermined. He did believe that the mental health of the poet required that he should have the interests of whole men and that a part of these would be political.

Isolation theories of art were widely current in the nineteenth century. By the end of that century Whistler could believe, as we have noted, that the artist "stands in no relation to the moment in which he occurs" and has "no part in the progress of his fellow men." Many poets agreed with him. Once the separation of artist and society was relatively complete, the poet could believe that isolation was his natural status; and, if not natural, at least satisfactory, since it allowed him to go his own way, experimenting and exploring subject matter and themes far removed from vulgar or commonplace interests. The economic and political crisis brought many artists and poets back to an interest in public matters.

Unfortunately, no American poet has yet published a volume that could be considered political in any large sense. Stephen Vincent Benét in *John Brown's Body* and *Western Star* approached it—but one feels uneasy with their unabashed idealism and sentimentality. The poetry with a political cast has come unfortunately from the proletarian poets and from the "professional" Americans, the latter using a formula which is employed with merely slight differences from poet to poet. The result is a kind of children's guide to the grandeur of one's homeland. There is far too much contriving and self-consciousness, after the debunking tradition, in our present making of American heroes. The only young poet, apparently, who has attempted the political theme at a mature level is John Malcolm Brinnin. But his *The Garden Is Political*, despite its title, does not indicate that he is *inside* his subject, or even primarily concerned with it. We have no American poet, except for MacLeish, whose personal history indicates his need for reconciling his tradition of isolation as an artist with his need for coming to terms with the factors which determine his very existence as an artist.

The development of Thomas Mann must, in lieu, serve our purpose, more especially since he has recorded the history of his changing attitudes and suggested the manner in which the political finds its way into a work of art.

The artist who considers himself an artist and *only* an artist is hastening the drying-up of the sources of his art. His art depends upon his wholeness of being. The whole man is religious, esthetic, social, and political. Perhaps the history of no artist in our time illustrates this truth so readily as that of Mann. Having perceived the peril he so narrowly escaped before reaching this understanding, he addressed pleas to his countrymen, then to Europe and the world, using meanwhile his personal history as a focal point of analysis that other artists might have an *exemplum* to guide them. Mann's political self-searchings go back nearly a generation, to the year 1914, when he wrote "Reflections of a Non-political." In the years between the wars, Mann's position, subject to his almost "clairvoyant perception of the time and the future," changed from a belief in the divisibility of the intellectual and the political to a firm faith in their inseparableness. The history of his early beliefs can be seen as a homogeneous part of German national development, but in the history of his later beliefs the artist can be seen fusing the constituent elements of the mind into human wholes and drawing the only reasonable political deduction from them. (That the early position of Mann is held by some to be indefensible and that his later polemics are sometimes seen as confused and sentimental are subjects hardly relevant to this context.)

Mann admits, in "Culture and Politics," that his personal allegiance to democracy was individually earned: it was not a part of his "bourgeois intellectual origins and upbringing." The society he knew did not recognize that indifference to the "political" and the "social" leaves a "dangerous gap in our cultural life." To him at that time culture "meant music, metaphysics, psychology; meant a pessimistic ethic and an individualistic idealism." Artists in all Western countries lived with one form or another of this cultural isolation. An aspect of it, of course, was the attempt of many temporary exiles from America to cut themselves off from their origins, nationally and culturally.

Self-examination, carefully pursued, proved to Mann that any concern with the problem of humanity could not long remain indifferent to the political. The history of contemporary Germany—"which in the end has not been saved by all its music and all its intellectualism from a worship of power, nor from barbarism"—has been conclusive. Those who ignore political developments, who are "superior" to them, may find themselves suddenly the victims of those obsessively concerned with politics. Yet Mann points to the distinction between writing things in general terms—direct expository analysis and controversy—and imaginative writing. He has written hundreds of articles and essays, and he has labored, given "patient devotion to the weaving of epic music." The two forms are not to be confused. The political, in no narrow sense of the term, is infused in a number of his stories, particularly in several of his short stories and in *The Magic Mountain*. One might condemn the emphasis on the political in certain artists simply because a too narrow conception of the political warps their vision and forces them to be the servant of a limited theory of the state or even of economics. The examination of one of Mann's stories indicates that his artistry is in no way compromised by his belief in democracy.

"Mario and the Magician" studied by itself would be proof enough of the ability of the artist to treat the political. In a time less violently concerned with threats of enslavement, this story might be read as the work of a philosopher-artist, "an examination into the freedom of the will, a reflection of human tyranny." But we live in a period in which study of a local situation and an academic problem in philosophy ineluctably leads one to related political problems in which the entire world is involved.

It is not strange that Mann is concerned with the image or symbol that reflexively gathers to itself innumerable significations which a lesser artist would be satisfied to leave in what are held to be their respective spheres. Politics, philosophy, and morals are fused artistically into a human understanding. In Cavaliere Cipolla, the magician, inhere the frustrations, the cynicism, the feverish energy, the soulessness, the warped mentality, that characterize the Fascist mind. In Mario, the ingenuous boy waiter, inhere the dregs of a once rich and noble theological, artistic, and intellectual culture. As an individual he is, if judged according to contemporary secular standards, a nonentity. Within him, however, there is gentleness and an unquestioned faith in human dignity. He is an appropriate symbol of a world that nearly succumbed to a more general hypnosis cynically designed to enslave it. The sudden and violent destruction of Cipolla is appropriately the function of Mario.

"While there is no word of politics in the tale," says Clifton Fadiman, "and not a sentence that endeavors to change our ideas about anything, it is nevertheless the most searching indictment of current domination-ideals penned in our time." There is no avoiding the political implications. If we were to doubt this, there are many signs to convince us that the magician is the symbol not only of tyrants generally but of those we have known: Cipolla reverences the "Fatherland," boasts that "the brother of the Duce honored me by his presence at one of my evenings," refers to illiterates as humiliating the government, and occasionally thrusts his arm forward in what is obviously the Fascist salute. There are other less direct signs: Cipolla's physical deformities are shown to be a cause of his sadistic love of humiliating those with healthy bodies; he delights in exaggerated sartorial effects which set him apart, in showing off his power despite the distress this causes; he snaps a whip to control those he has hypnotized, and as a backdrop to his continual "triumphs" of the will are the automaton figures, no longer with wills of their own, whom he keeps dancing. Mann as an artist has used a minimum of exposition but has patiently caught up all the images and indirections which, "in an instant of time," explain themselves to the reader. If there were any doubt that the artist looks upon Mario's killing of the magician as the end of a symbol of tyranny, there are the final sentences of the story: "An end of horror, a fatal end. And yet a liberation—for I could not, and I cannot, but find it so."

Not Germany alone but the Western world has come through a

period of skepticism, of a specious and hollow kind of irony. Intellect divorced itself from the elementary facts of existence. The basic distinctions between good and evil were easily lost because the religious epoch in terms of which we had learned moral distinctions was itself waning. Rationalizations of the kind that hastened the end of scholastic philosophy—but theories with a far more fatal import—became a part of the sophisticate intellectual life. Intellect served *intellection*. Only in the face of a barbarous indifference to the elementary moral distinctions were we able to free ourselves. "Spirit today," says Mann, "unmistakably, is about to enter upon a *moral* epoch of religious and moral distinctions between good and evil. That means a certain simplification and condensation of the intellect in opposition to everything savouring of a weary skeptical refinement—the mind's way of 'rebarbarizing' itself."

The religious and the philosophical and the artistic are integrally related to the political. The intellectual world at large drew a knowledgeable and fallacious distinction between the religious and the moral. The educated upper classes in Western countries drew a sharp line between culture and politics. Art itself, as Mann explains in "What I Believe," serves a religious function in relating man's nature, attitudes, and actions to universal ideals. In terms of it, man arrives at a better understanding of himself in relation to the universe and to other men. Ultimately, the problem of emphasis is neither religious, artistic, nor political—but human. "The true totality," Mann says, "is that of the human being." Mann's history has obvious implications for the poet. And it may be read as further proof of the wisdom of the position which Spingarn attempted to make clear to American poets early in the 1930's.

The sharp line, if we may repeat, which the Western world drew between politics and the arts was easily rationalized in a culture given to specializations. Intensive preoccupation with isolated interests in a world of multiple specializations has worked a hardship on the poet because his specialty has not been among those having the most immediately "practical" value. His new awareness of the political problem as a specialization he cannot afford to ignore should suggest, however, that, as a man and as a poet, he cannot afford to be a narrow specialist either.

In looking back at the not too remote as well as the more recent attempts to write pure poetry—further attempts at specialization—he can see that poetry written in accordance with school manifestoes is poetry from which certain elements, morality, politics, the earthy, the abstract, etc., have been consciously excluded. Poetry cannot feed itself.

Further, in employing his medium in the twentieth century, the poet has had to accommodate himself to a world that has no unifying spirit. And he has been obliged to recover for himself the right to employ his medium in ways other than those that best served objective forms of knowledge and to recover it, as well, from the misty emotionalism of poets who retreated from the sheerly rationalistic.

In employing his medium, the modern poet is now aware, to some extent, of the cultural pattern of which he is a part, the longstanding emphasis on the objective, the rational, the strictly factual, and the inevitable reactions. In terms of the more recent history of his medium he can see that the break with verism is an attempt to reinstate a more subjective, personalized idiom; at the same time he is aware that he cannot afford to retreat from the commonplace world, from what Wallace Stevens calls "things-as-they-are." He is quite willing to acknowledge, also, that from the Symbolists, the Metaphysicals, and the first of the moderns he has learned techniques enabling him to move easily within both objective and subjective realms.

No single poet, nonetheless, can bring the disparate parts of his world together. The personal myths of the poet, for the greater part, remain personal. And in a world possessing no coherent, universal body of belief he must maintain a constant ironic consciousness. In the very facing of his problems as a poet, he has forced us to examine and clarify the factors in our cultural history. Neither he nor the critics who sympathize with him in his problems are attempting to ridicule or to suggest that we dismiss the scientific emphasis; he and they, on the other hand, are quite justified in pointing out that attempts to view the arts in the focus we now label "scientific" have imposed unnecessary limitations on the poet. "The main element of the modern spirit's life," Matthew Arnold wrote, "is neither the senses, nor the heart and imagination; it is the imaginative reason." More positively, however, a considerable number of poets, in employing a language in which sensibility is a correlate of intelligence, have satisfied the human need for experiencing knowledge.

# Notes

## CHAPTER ONE

1. For useful accounts of the effects of a too rigid dependence upon what were believed to be scientific attitudes see A. N. Whitehead, *Science and the Modern World* (Macmillan Co., 1925); Michael Roberts, *The Modern Mind* (Faber & Faber, 1935); Melvin Rader, "New Wine and Old Bottles," *Antioch Review*, I, No. 2 (summer, 1941), 156–74; and Lewis Mumford, *The Condition of Man* (Harcourt, Brace & Co., 1944).

2. See Herbert Muller, *Science and Criticism* (Yale University Press, 1943), pp. 90–95, and Mumford, *op. cit.*, pp. 241–49.

3. Walter J. Ong, "The Meaning of the 'New Criticism,' " *Twentieth Century English* (Philosophical Library, 1946), pp. 344–70, and Basil Willey, *The Seventeenth Century Background* (Chatto & Windus, 1934), *passim.*

4. M. W. Bundy, "Bacon's True Opinion of Poetry," *Studies in Philology*, XIX, No. 4 (April, 1930), 362–403, and L. C. Knights, "Bacon and the Seventeenth Century Dissociation of Sensibility," *Explorations* (G. W. Stewart, Publisher, Inc., 1947).

5. J. C. Ransom, "Poetry: A Note in Ontology," in *The World's Body* (Charles Scribner's Sons, 1938), and Cleanth Brooks, *Modern Poetry and the Tradition* (University of North Carolina Press, 1939), *passim.*

6. See Edmund Wilson, *Axel's Castle* (Charles Scribner's Sons, 1931).

7. See Alan Swallow, "Subjectivism as Poetic Method," *New Mexico Quarterly*, XIII, No. 1 (spring, 1943), 10–20; S. H. Monk, "From Jacobean to Augustan," *Southern Review*, VII, No. 2 (autumn, 1941), 366–84; and "Dryden Studies: A Survey, 1920–1945," *ELH*, XIV, No. 1 (March, 1947), 46–63.

8. See Martin Lebowitz, "Thought and Sensibility," *Kenyon Review*, V, No. 2 (spring, 1943), 219–27.

9. See Yvor Winters, *Primitivism and Decadence* (Arrow Editions, 1937).

10. See Brooks, *op. cit.*

11. For opposing views see Wallace Stevens, "The Noble Rider and the Sound of Words," in *The Language of Poetry*, ed. Allen Tate (Princeton University Press, 1942), and Max Eastman, *The Literary Mind: Its Place in an Age of Science* (Charles Scribner's Sons, 1931).

12. See "The Metaphysical Poets" and "Andrew Marvell" (1921).

13. See R. P. Warren, "Pure and Impure Poetry," *Kenyon Review*, V, No. 2 (spring, 1943), 228–54, and F. R. Leavis, " 'Thought' and Emotional Quality," *Scrutiny*, XIII, No. 1 (spring, 1945), 53–71.

14. See Susanne Langer, *Philosophy in a New Key* (Harvard University Press, 1942).

15. See George Santayana, "Penitent Art," *Obiter Scripta dicta* (Charles Scribner's Sons, 1936); Melvin Rader (ed.), Introduction, in *A Modern Book of*

*Esthetics* (Henry Holt & Co., 1935); and Ernst Cassirer, *Language and Myth* (Harper & Bros., 1946).

16. W. Y. Tindall, "Exile," in *Forces in Modern British Literature, 1885–1946* (Alfred A. Knopf, 1947), and Delmore Schwartz, "The Isolation of Modern Poetry," *Kenyon Review*, III, No. 2 (spring, 1941), 209–20.

## CHAPTER TWO

1. See, e.g., David Daiches, "T. E. Hulme and T. S. Eliot," in *Poetry and the Modern World* (University of Chicago Press, 1940), pp. 90–105; Louise Bogan, "The Secular Hell," *Chimera*, IV, No. 3 (spring, 1943), 12–20; F. O. Matthiessen, *American Renaissance* (Oxford University Press, 1941), *passim;* Ruth Herschberger, " 'Poised between the two alarums,' " *Accent*, IV, No. 4 (summer, 1944), 240–46. These commentaries are listed at random, merely to suggest the extent of the awareness of evil in modern poetry.

2. For Pound's concern with usury, however, see H. H. Watts, "Pound's Cantos: Means to an End," *Yale Poetry Review*, No. 6, 1947, pp. 9–26.

3. See Yvor Winters, *Primitivism and Decadence*, pp. 30–32; Allen Tate, "Hart Crane," in *Reactionary Essays* (Charles Scribner's Sons, 1936), pp. 26–42; and Howard Moss, "Disorder as Myth," *Poetry*, LXII, No. 1 (April, 1943), 32–45.

4. See Malcolm Cowley, "Walt Whitman: Poet of America?" *New York Times Book Review*, February 24, 1946, pp. 1 and 36.

## CHAPTER THREE

1. " 'Nature' as Aesthetic Norm," *Modern Language Notes*, XLII, No. 7 (November, 1927), 444–50.

2. *English Poetry and the English Language* (Clarendon Press, 1934).

3. See, e.g., Ernst Cassirer, *Language and Myth*, Preface and translation by Susanne Langer.

4. See Mark Schorer, *William Blake* (Henry Holt & Co., 1946), pp. 27–30.

5. See, e.g., William Empson, *Seven Types of Ambiguity* (Chatto & Windus, 1930), and T. S. Eliot, "Hamlet," in *Selected Essays* (Harcourt, Brace & Co., 1932).

6. "The 'Difference' of Literature," *New Republic*, XXXIII, No. 417 (November 29, 1922), 18–19.

## CHAPTER FOUR

1. "Is Verse a Dying Technique?" in *The Triple Thinkers* (Harcourt, Brace & Co., 1938), p. 38.

2. See Helen M. Lynd, *England in the Eighteen-eighties* (Oxford University Press, 1945), pp. 62–64.

3. See F. R. Leavis, *New Bearings in English Poetry* (Chatto & Windus, 1932), pp. 5–74.

## CHAPTER FIVE

1. René Taupin has documented the relationship for a decade in *L'Influence du symbolisme français sur la poésie américaine (1910–1920)* (Librairie Ancienne Honoré Champion, 1929).

2. *From Cubism to Surrealism in French Literature* (Harvard University Press, 1941).

3. See Hi Simons, "Wallace Stevens and Mallarmé," *Modern Philology*, XLIII, No. 4 (May, 1946), 235–59.

## CHAPTER SIX

1. See D. S. Savage, "Poetry and Nature," *Poetry*, LXI (December, 1942), 496–504; Allen Tate, "A Reading of Keats," *American Scholar*, XV, No. 1 (winter, 1945–46), 55–63; Cleanth Brooks, "The Case of Miss Arabella Fermor," *Sewanee Review*, LI, No. 4 (autumn, 1943), 505–25; and William Van O'Connor, "Nature and the Anti-Poetic," *Journal of Aesthetics and Art Criticism*, V, No. 1 (September, 1946), 35–44.

## CHAPTER SEVEN

1. "The Poetics of Henry James," *Poetry*, XLV (February, 1935), 270–76.

2. See Willard Thorp (ed.), *Herman Melville* (American Book Co., 1938), pp. cxix–cxxix.

3. *Roadside Meetings* (Macmillan Co., 1930), pp. 193–94.

## CHAPTER EIGHT

1. "Three Types of Poetry," *Reactionary Essays*, pp. 83–112. Tate, of course, does not mean to imply that there are only three kinds of poetry.

2. See, however, Eliot's use of color in "Ash Wednesday."

3. See F. O. Matthiessen, *The Achievement of T. S. Eliot* (Houghton Mifflin Co., 1935), and T. S. Eliot, "Hamlet," in *Selected Essays*.

4. For an opinion opposite to the one presented in this chapter see Yvor Winters, *The Anatomy of Nonsense* (New Directions, 1943).

## CHAPTER NINE

1. "Irony: A French Approach," *Sewanee Review*, XLVII, No. 2 (April–June, 1935), 175–84.

2. *The Art of Satire* (Harvard University Press, 1940), p. 142.

3. See, e.g., *Modern Poetry and the Tradition*, pp.151–57.

## CHAPTER TEN

1. "Tension in Poetry," *Reason in Madness* (G. P. Putnam & Sons, 1941); see also Robert Penn Warren, "Pure and Impure Poetry," *Kenyon Review*, V, No. 2 (spring, 1943), 228–54.

## CHAPTER ELEVEN

1. "The Isolation of Modern Poetry," *Kenyon Review*, III, No. 2 (spring, 1941), 209–20.

2. "Exiles: Rimbaud to Joyce," *American Scholar*, XIV, No. 3 (summer, 1945), 351–54.

3. See Margaret Mead, "The European in Our Midst," in *And Keep Your Powder Dry* (William Morrow & Co., 1943); and R. P. Blackmur, "The American Literary Expatriate," in *Foreign Influences in American Life* (Princeton University Press, 1944), pp. 126–45.

4. *Saturday Evening Post*, CIC, No. 11 (November, 1926), 12–13.

5. See Conrad Aiken, "Why Poets Leave Home," *Scribner's Magazine*, LXXXIX, No. 1 (January, 1931), 84–86.

## CHAPTER TWELVE

1. "Yeats and the Centaur," *Southern Review*, VII, No. 3 (spring, 1942), 510–16.

2. *Partisan Review*, VI, No. 5 (fall, 1939), 34–49.

3. *Politics*, I, No. 1 (February, 1944), 20–23.

4. "The New York Wits," *Kenyon Review*, VII, No. 1 (winter, 1945), 12–28.

5. "Some Notes on Popular and Unpopular Art," *Partisan Review*, X, No. 5 (September–October, 1943), 391–401.

6. Arthur Hawley Scouten in his "Thoughts on Listening to Burl Ives," *Sewanee Review*, LIII, No. 2 (spring, 1945), 279–87, tells a story which dramatizes the way in which the popular urbanized song has worked into the groups which are the last stronghold of those English, Irish, and Scotch ballads that were kept intact or transformed in becoming a part of regional culture in America.

7. "The Poet on Capitol Hill," *Partisan Review*, VIII, No. 1 (January, 1941), 2–9.

## CHAPTER THIRTEEN

1. *Reason in Madness*, pp. 217–30.

2. "Regionalism and Sectionalism," *New Republic*, LXIX, No. 890 (December 23, 1931), 158–61.

3. "A World without Roots," in *The Spiritual Aspects of the New Poetry* (Harper & Bros., 1940), pp. 89–95.

4. Johns Hopkins Press, 1938.

5. *Edwin Arlington Robinson* (New Directions, 1946).

6. See Cleanth Brooks, *Modern Poetry and the Tradition*, pp. 95–109, and Delmore Schwartz, "The Poetry of Allen Tate," *Southern Review*, V, No. 3 (winter, 1939), 419–38.

7. See Brooks, *op. cit.*, pp. 88–95, and Robert Penn Warren, "John Crowe Ransom: A Study in Irony," *Virginia Quarterly*, XI, No. 1 (January, 1935), 93–112.

8. See Joseph Frank, "Force and Form: A Study of John Peale Bishop," *Sewanee Review*, LV, No. 1 (January, 1947), 71–107.

9. Donald Davidson, "Regionalism and Nationalism in American Literature," in *The Attack on Leviathan* (University of North Carolina Press, 1938), pp. 228–39.

## CHAPTER FOURTEEN

1. Longmans, Green & Co., 1931. Mr. Peterson's study affords a brief and clear discussion of the problem here sketched, relating it not only to his chief subject, Conrad Aiken, but to dominant figures in literature since the Renaissance.

2. See Frederick Hoffman, *Freudianism and the Literary Mind* (Louisiana State University Press, 1945), pp. 289–90 *et passim*. Professor Hoffman gives particular attention to Aiken and to Dylan Thomas.

3. *Harvard Wake*, V (spring, 1946), 46–54.

4. See translation by C. Garcia-Prada and M. M. Rader reprinted in *A Modern Book of Esthetics*, pp. 343–56.

5. "Psychical Distance," in *A Modern Book of Esthetics*, pp. 315–42.

## CHAPTER FIFTEEN

1. "Meaning in Modern Poetry," *Saturday Review of Literature*, XXXIX, No. 12 (March 23, 1946), 5–6 and 56–57.

2. The place of neurosis in art has been clearly discussed by Lionel Trilling in "Art and Neurosis," *Partisan Review*, XII, No. 1 (winter, 1945), 41–48.

3. *The World's Body*, pp. 55–75.

4. For an illustration of this see Cleanth Brooks and Robert Penn Warren, *Understanding Poetry* (Henry Holt & Co., 1938), pp. 614–21.

5. *American Scholar*, XIV, No. 3 (summer, 1945), 362–65.

## CHAPTER SIXTEEN

1. See John Wild, "The Inversion of Culture and the World Revolution," *Sewanee Review*, LI, No. 4 (October–December, 1943), 449–66.

2. See *Proletarian Literature in the United States* (International Publishers, 1935), Introduction.

3. *The Philosophy of Literary Form* (Louisiana State UniversityPress, 1942), pp. 314–22. The essay was originally published in the *Nation*.

4. "Poetry and Politics," *New Republic*, LXXV, No. 974 (August 2, 1933), 308–11.

5. "Art, the Proletariat and Marx," *New Republic*, LXXVI, No. 977 (August, 1933), 41–45.

6. See "Politics and the Poet," with introduction by Lewis Mumford, *Atlantic Monthly*, CLXX (November, 1942), 73–78. The lecture was originally given in the spring of 1931.

# *Bibliography*

In "I. General References and Bibliography" the reader will find a guide to fairly extensive bibliographies, although there is as yet no really adequate bibliography in which the serious student of modern poetry can find a large number of listings.

The items listed under "II. Books" and "III. Periodicals" are, for the most part, strictly relevant to the theme and subthemes developed in this book. Not all the items listed in footnotes are repeated here.

## I. GENERAL REFERENCES AND BIBLIOGRAPHIES


EDITORS *et al.* OF *Accent*. "American Poetry: 1930–1940: A Bibliography . . . ," *Accent*, I, No. 4 (summer, 1941), 213–28.

GREGORY, HORACE, and ZATURENSKA, MARYA. *A History of American Poetry, 1900–1940*. New York: Harcourt, Brace & Co., 1946. (Bibliography.)

HOFFMAN, F. J., *et al. The Little Magazines*. Princeton: Princeton University Press, 1946.

KUNITZ, S. J., and HAYCRAFT, H. *Twentieth Century Authors*. New York: H. W. Wilson Co., 1942.

MILLETT, F. B. *Contemporary British Authors*. New York: Harcourt, Brace & Co., 1935.

———. *Contemporary American Authors*. New York: Harcourt, Brace & Co., 1943.

RADER, MELVIN (ed.). *A Modern Book of Esthetics*. New York: Henry Holt & Co., 1935. (Bibliography.)

SHIPLEY, JOSEPH (ed.). *Dictionary of World Literature*. New York: Philosophical Library, 1943.

STALLMAN, ROBERT. "A Selective Bibliography on the Criticism of Poetry, 1920–1942," *University Review*, X, No. 1 (autumn, 1943), 65–71.

ZABEL, M. D. (ed.). *Literary Opinion in America*. New York: Harper & Bros., 1937. (Bibliography.)


## II. BOOKS


BATESON, F. W. *English Poetry and the English Language*. London: Clarendon Press, 1934.

## BIBLIOGRAPHY


BLACKMUR, R. P. (ed.). *The Art of the Novel*, Introduction. New York: Charles Scribner's Sons, 1934.

———. *The Double Agent*. New York: Arrow Editions, 1935.

———. *The Expense of Greatness*. New York: Arrow Editions, 1940.

BROOKS, CLEANTH. *Modern Poetry and the Tradition*. Chapel Hill: University of North Carolina Press, 1939.

———. *The Well Wrought Urn*. New York: Reynal & Hitchcock, 1947.

BURKE, KENNETH. *Counter Statement*. New York: Harcourt, Brace & Co., 1931.

———. *Permanence and Change*. New York: New Republic, 1935.

———. *The Philosophy of Literary Form*. Baton Rouge: Louisiana State University Press, 1941.

———. *A Grammar of Motives*. New York: Prentice-Hall, Inc., 1945.

CARGILL, OSCAR. *Intellectual America: Ideas on the March*. New York: Macmillan Co., 1941.

DAICHES, DAVID. *The Place of Meaning in Poetry*. Edinburgh: Oliver & Boyd, 1935.

———. *Poetry and the Modern World*. Chicago: University of Chicago Press, 1940.

DAVIDSON, DONALD. *The Attack on Leviathan*. Chapel Hill: University of North Carolina Press, 1938.

EASTMAN, MAX. *The Literary Mind: Its Place in an Age of Science*. New York: Charles Scribner's Sons, 1931.

ELIOT, T. S. *Ezra Pound, His Metric and Poetry*. New York: Alfred A. Knopf, 1917.

———. *The Sacred Wood*. New York: Alfred A. Knopf, 1921.

———. *Homage to John Dryden*. London: Hogarth Press, 1924.

———. *Selected Essays, 1917–1932*. New York: Harcourt, Brace & Co., 1932.

———. *Essays Ancient and Modern*. London: Faber & Faber, 1936.

———. *The Use of Poetry and the Use of Criticism*. Cambridge: Harvard University Press, 1938.

———. *The Music of Poetry*. Glasgow: Jackson, Son & Co., 1942.

EMPSON, WILLIAM. *Seven Types of Ambiguity*. London: Chatto & Windus, 1930.

———. *English Pastoral Poetry*. London: Norton's, 1938.

HULME, T. E. *Speculations*. New York: Harcourt, Brace & Co., 1924.

———. *Notes on Language and Style*. Seattle: University of Washington Bookstore, 1932.

KNIGHTS, L. C. *Explorations*. New York: G. W. Stewart, Publisher, Inc., 1947.

LEAVIS, F. R. *New Bearings in English Poetry*. London: Chatto & Windus, 1932.

——— (ed.). *Determinations*. London: Chatto & Windus, 1934.

MATTHIESSEN, F. O. *The Achievement of T. S. Eliot*. London: Oxford University Press, 1935.

———. *The American Renaissance*. London: Oxford University Press, 1941.

POTTLE, FREDERICK. *The Idiom of Poetry*. Ithaca, N.Y.: Cornell University Press, 1941.

RANSOM, JOHN CROWE. *Gods without Thunder*. New York: Harcourt, Brace & Co., 1930.

———. *The World's Body*. New York: Charles Scribner's Sons, 1938.

———. *The New Criticism*. New York: New Directions, 1941.

RICHARDS, I. A. *Science and Poetry*. London: Norton's, 1926.

———. *Practical Criticism*. London: Kegan Paul, Trench, Trubner & Co., 1929.

———. *Coleridge on Imagination*. New York: Harcourt, Brace & Co., 1935.

———. *The Philosophy of Rhetoric*. London: Oxford University Press, 1936.

———. *Principles of Literary Criticism*. London: Kegan Paul, Trench, Trubner & Co., 1938.

ROBERTS, MICHAEL. *The Modern Mind*. London: Faber & Faber, 1935.

———. *T. E. Hulme*. London: Faber & Faber, 1938.

SANTAYANA, GEORGE. *Interpretations of Poetry and Religion*. New York: Charles Scribner's Sons, 1900.

SCHORER, MARK. *William Blake*. New York: Henry Holt & Co., 1946.

SHAPIRO, KARL. *Essay on Rime*. New York: Reynal & Hitchcock, 1945.

SPENDER, STEPHEN. *The Destructive Element*. London: Jonathan Cape, 1935.

TATE, ALLEN. *Reactionary Essays*. New York: Charles Scribner's Sons 1936.

———. *Reason in Madness*. New York: G. P. Putnam & Co., 1941.

TATE, ALLEN (ed.). *The Language of Poetry*. Princeton: Princeton University Press, 1942.

WELLS, HENRY. *New Poets from Old*. New York: Columbia University Press, 1940.

WILLIAMSON, GEORGE. *The Talent of T. S. Eliot*. Seattle: University of Washington Bookstore, 1929.

———. *The Donne Tradition*. Cambridge: Harvard University Press, 1930.

WILSON, EDMUND. *Axel's Castle*. New York: Charles Scribner's Sons, 1931.
———. *The Triple Thinkers*. New York: Harcourt, Brace & Co., 1938.
———. *The Wound and the Bow*. Boston: Houghton Mifflin Co., 1941.
——— (ed.). *The Shock of Recognition*. New York: Doubleday-Doran & Co., 1943.
WINTERS, YVOR. *Primitivism and Decadence*. New York: Arrow Editions, 1937.
———. *The Anatomy of Nonsense*. New York: New Directions, 1943.
———. *Edwin Arlington Robinson*. New York: New Directions, 1946.
YEATS, W. B. *Ideas of Good and Evil*. London: A. H. Bullen, 1914.
———. *Autobiographies*. London: Macmillan & Co., 1938.
———. *A Vision*. London: Macmillan & Co., 1938.

## III. PERIODICALS

AUDEN, W. H. "Against Romanticism," *New Republic*, CII (January–June, 1940), 187.
———. "Tradition and Value," *ibid.*, p. 9.
BOGAN, LOUISE. "The Secular Hell," *Chimera*, IV, No. 3 (spring, 1943), 12–20.
———. "Some Notes on Popular and Unpopular Art," *Partisan Review*, X, No. 5 (September–October, 1943), 391–401.
CAZAMIAN, LOUIS. "Symbolism and Poetry," *University of Toronto Quarterly*, V, No. 4 (July, 1936), 520–43.
COWLEY, MALCOLM. "Walt Whitman: Poet of America?" *New York Times Book Review*, February 24, 1948, pp. 1 and 36.
FRANK, JOSEPH. "Spatial Form in Modern Literature," *Sewanee Review*, LIII (spring, 1945), 221–40. (And in the following issue.)
———. "Force and Form: A Study of John Peale Bishop," *ibid.*, LV, No. 1 (January, 1947), 71–107.
FRANKENBERG, LLOYD. "Meaning in Modern Poetry," *Saturday Review of Literature*, XXXIX, No. 12 (March 23, 1946), 5–6 and 56–57.
FRIEDLANDER, MARC. "Poetry and the Common Store," *American Scholar*, XIV, No. 3 (summer, 1945), 362–65.
GOLFFING, FRANCIS. "Stéphane Mallarmé: A Reconsideration," *New Mexico Quarterly*, XVI, No. 1 (spring, 1946), 63–73.
GREENBERG, CLEMENT. "Avant-Garde and Kitsch," *Partisan Review*, VI, No. 5 (fall, 1939), 34–49.
HEILMAN, R. B. "Artist and Patria," *Sewanee Review*, LI, No. 3 (summer, 1943), 382–89.

HERSCHBERGER, RUTH. " 'Poised between two alarms,' " *Accent*, IV, No. 4 (summer, 1944), 240–46.

LEBOWITZ, MARTIN. "Thought and Sensibility," *Kenyon Review*, V, No. 2 (spring, 1943), 219–27.

LINDSAY, VACHEL. "What It Means To Be a Poet in America," *Saturday Evening Post*, CIC, No. 11 (November, 1926), 12–13 ff.

MACDONALD, DWIGHT. "A Theory of Popular Culture," *Politics*, I, No. 1 (February, 1944), 20–23.

MARITAIN, JACQUES. "Poetry's Dark Night," *Kenyon Review*, IV, No. 2 (spring, 1942), 149–59.

MATTHIESSEN, F. O. "American Poetry, 1920–1940," *Sewanee Review*, LV, No. 1 (winter, 1947), 24–55.

MIZENER, ARTHUR. "Some Notes on the Nature of English Poetry," *Sewanee Review*, LI, No. 1 (winter, 1943), 27–51.

MOORE, MARIANNE. "Feeling and Precision," *Sewanee Review*, LII, No. 4 (fall, 1944), 499–507.

SCHWARTZ, DELMORE. "The Isolation of Modern Poetry," *Kenyon Review*, III, No. 2 (spring, 1941), 209–20.

SPINGARN, JOEL. "Politics and the Poet," *Atlantic Monthly*, CLXX (November, 1942), 73–78.

STEVENS, WALLACE. "The Figure of the Youth as Virile Poet," *Sewanee Review*, LII, No. 4 (fall, 1944), 508–29.

SWALLOW, ALAN. "Subjectivism as Poetic Method," *New Mexico Quarterly Review*, XIII, No. 1 (spring, 1943), 10–20.

TINDALL, W. Y. "Exiles: Rimbaud to Joyce," *American Scholar*, XIV, No. 3 (summer, 1945), 351–54.

TRILLING, LIONEL. "Art and Neurosis," *Partisan Review*, XII, No. 1 (winter, 1945), 41–48.

WARREN, R. P. "Pure and Impure Poetry," *Kenyon Review*, V, No. 2 (spring, 1943), 228–54.

WHEELWRIGHT, PHILIP E. "Poetry and Logic," *Symposium*, I, No. 4 (October, 1930), 440–57.

———. "On the Semantics of Poetry," *Kenyon Review*, II, No. 3 (summer, 1940), 263–83.

ZABEL, M. D. "The Poetics of Henry James," *Poetry*, XLV, No. 5 (February, 1935), 270–76.

# Index